Real World
Mac OS X Fonts

Sharon Zardetto Aker

Peachpit Press   Take Control Books

Real World Mac OS X Fonts

Sharon Zardetto Aker

Peachpit Press
1249 Eighth Street
Berkeley, CA 94710
510/524-2178, 800/283-9444, 510/524-2221 (fax)

Find us on the Web at: www.peachpit.com
To report errors, please send a note to errata@peachpit.com

Peachpit Press is a division of Pearson Education

Real World Mac OS X Fonts is published in association with Take Control Books and was originally published by Take Control Books as *Take Control of Fonts in Mac OS X, Tiger Edition* (ISBN 1-933671-13-0) and *Take Control of Font Problems in Mac OS X, Tiger Edition* (ISBN 1-933671-14-9), both by Sharon Zardetto Aker and copyright © 2006 by Sharon Zardetto Aker. Learn more about Take Control at www.takecontrolbooks.com.

Copyright © 2007 by TidBITS Electronic Publishing and Sharon Zardetto Aker

Editor: Tonya Engst
Production Editor: Susan Rimerman
Copyeditor: Lea Galanter
Tech Editor: Take Control authors and TidBITS Irregulars
Proofreader: Clark Humphrey
Compositor: Sharon Zardetto Aker
Indexer: Rebecca Plunkett
Cover design: Aren Howell
Cover illustration: Alicia Buelow

ISBN 0-321-47401-5
9 8 7 6 5 4 3 2 1
Printed and bound in the United States of America

Dedication

With love and appreciation, to

Dr. Lori Steinberg Zucker

for her expertise, generosity, and friendship.

Thank You

First, I'd like to blame—no, no, I mean *thank*—Tonya and Adam Engst, who convinced me to write about fonts when what I really wanted to do at the time was write about FileMaker.

Thanks to: my first-round readers, Marilyn Rose, Jerry Szubin (extra thanks to him for layout help, too), and Rich Wolfson; all the Control Freaks and TidBITS Irregulars for their time and efforts, with extra thanks to Joe Kissell and especially to Tom Gewecke for his above-and-beyond correspondence; Lea Galanter for her professional nitpickiness on the initial ebook version; Natasha Koltko, who, while visiting from Ukraine, was somehow roped into helping with all the page references; Clark Humphrey for copy-editing skills; Rebecca Plunkett for indexing; at Peachpit Press, Nancy Davis and Susan Rimerman; and, as usual and always, Rich.

Colophon

Fonts: The body text is Utopia (from Adobe); titles and subheads are in Optima (also from Adobe); the monospaced font for pathnames and URLs has the strange name TheSansMonoCondensed (from the also strangely named Luc(as) De Groot).

Software: This book was written and edited in Microsoft Word, versions X and 2004 (depending on who was writing or editing), and laid out in Adobe InDesign from Creative Suite 2. Graphics were created and/or manipulated in Photoshop CS2; screenshots were captured with Ambrosia Software's Snapz Pro X. Additional, indispensable utilities: QuicKeys X (CE Software) and SpellCatcher (RainMaker Research).

Overview

Contents

Tables

Introduction

It's utterly astonishing that a computer platform whose initial claim to fame was not just its interface but also its use of different fonts could celebrate its almost-20th anniversary with a new operating system that totally ignored the importance of fonts, pretending that the difficulty—or total inability—to install and manage fonts didn't matter.

As a Mac fanatic from way back (1984, to be precise), I hate to admit that it took Mac OS X *years* to get its act together concerning fonts, and that I also totally ignored the issue as long as I could. I know I felt frustrated; I think I also felt insulted.

But Mac OS X has its act together now, even if it's not entirely polished. With the release of Tiger (the 10.4 version of the operating system), fonts became manageable (literally, with Font Book 2.0), and their Unicode-inspired wealth of characters and advanced typographical features became more accessible. The situation continues to improve with system updates, with tiny, usually unannounced, changes to Font Book and general font-handling issues. So now we can quit whining about how bad it *was* and look at how good it *is*.

You'll find all the basics of font management in this book: what font types are supported in Mac OS X, installation, removal, verification of font file integrity, and the Font Book how-to (and why). You'll get the background details you need about Unicode and its ripple effect on almost every font-related thing you do, why document exchanges cause font problems, and how to access foreign language characters and keyboards. You'll also find information you didn't know you needed, such as how to find a font in a menu, where to find elusive characters hiding in so many fonts, and how to pack a suitcase (of fonts, that is).

While I touch upon font problems in PDFs and on Web pages, you won't find enough information to, say, start creating trouble-free, perfectly encoded Web pages; that's a topic for some other author. I don't review font management software (because software changes so quickly and printed books... well, printed books take longer to change) or round up the dozens of font-related shareware utilities; instead, I discuss what to look for in font management beyond Font Book, and I highlight a few especially good shareware utilities in context of related topics.

As for serious troubleshooting, I've included two chapters for that: one explains how to perform basic and special troubleshooting procedures (such as safe booting, repairing permissions, and setting up a separate user account for test purposes), and the other describes specific problems (such as your font icons going wonky or Font Book repeatedly quitting) and their solutions.

The main mission of the this book is self-evident, but there are two minor ones I'd also like to accomplish: to pique your interest regarding characters buried in many common fonts, and to help you achieve a certain comfort level in dealing with Unicode and glyph IDs for characters. To kill both those birds with one stone (and use an awkward metaphor at the same time), where parts of figures need emphasis, I've used red-colored characters from different fonts to point, circle, label, or otherwise command your attention. In red text in the margin, I identify the character by its font and Unicode or glyph ID (or both). It looks something like the figure on the next page, though much more sensible and sedate.

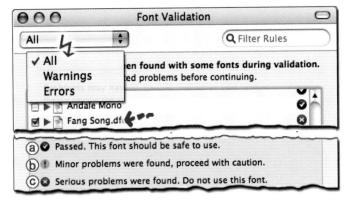

Jagged arrow:
Apple Symbols
U+2189

Dashed arrow:
Sand U+2198,
GID 350

Circled letters:
MS PGothic
starting at
U+24D0
GID 17543

This combination of arrows and letters is just for fun.

Assumptions

Yes, I know what they say about "assume" but I'm going to anyway. As long as you know what the assumptions are, we can prevent some misunderstandings:

◆ **You're working in Tiger at minimum:** Font management in Mac OS X changed drastically in its earliest versions; Font Book changed immensely just for Tiger (Mac OS 10.4). And, if you're in Tiger, you're in at least the 10.4.3 version, by which time Font Book had been enhanced to the state described in this book.

◆ **You have administrative access to your Mac:** I do mention, in a few places, the difference having access (or not) might mean to a font situation, but the general assumption is that you're in charge. (If you're uncomfortable with, or confused by, the very idea of "administrative access," Appendix F can ease your mind.)

◆ **You're not using third-party font management software:** Wherever I discuss Font Book and its use, I proceed with the assumption that Font Book *is* your font management software. You shouldn't have more than one of these utilities running at a time, so if you're working with a third-party solution but want to try (or go back to) Font Book, disable the third-party manager.

♦ **You have Microsoft Office 2004 and/or Adobe Creative Suite:** (CS1 or 2, or a standalone InDesign). That's not to say that you need any of these programs to use the information in this book or that if you use QuarkXPress this book won't help you. It is merely that I generally use Adobe InDesign and Microsoft Word as the non-Apple standards of how fonts are handled in Mac OS X; they work very well as the extremes of the sublime-to-ridiculous range. And, because they are so popular, font problems specific to those application suites are included in the troubleshooting chapter. When it comes to the "Organize Your Fonts" segment, I take into account that you may have Apple's iLife or iWork and the fonts that they donate to your system.

Basics

When reading this book, you may get stuck if you don't know certain basic terms or procedures or don't understand my syntax for things like working with menus or finding items in the Finder. Please note:

♦ **Tiger:** The name Tiger refers to any version of Mac OS X that begins with 10.4 (which is sometimes written as 10.4.x, to indicate that it could be 10.4.1, 10.4.2, and so on). You can check what version you're using by choosing About This Mac from the Apple menu.

♦ **Path names:** The route you take to a file on your hard drive, whether by looking through columns in a window or by double-clicking your way through folders, is the file's *path*.

The syntax for paths conforms to Unix standards, because that's what underlies Mac OS X. The disk's name is always the first thing in an actual path; since we can assume that the disk is always there, we don't include its name in the path—but we preserve the slash that would separate it from the next item. So, `HardDrive/System/Library/Fonts` becomes `/System/Library/Fonts`.

A path to something in a user's home directory starts with the drive's name, followed by Users and then the user's name. The handy convention, however, is to replace those first three items with ~ (tilde), so `HardDrive/Users/Masha/Library/Fonts` becomes simply `~/Library/ Fonts`. (You've probably noticed by now that path text is formatted in special type.)

For something a little further down, or back up, in a path that was just described, or if the beginning of the path is unknown (because, for instance, it varies from one user to another), we use two periods to indicate the missing part of the path: "With Creative Suite, you get `/Library/Application Support/Adobe/Fonts`, and its subfolder, `../Adobe/Fonts/Reqrd/Base`."

♦ **Menus:** To describe choosing a command from a menu in the menu bar, this book uses an abbreviated description like Edit > Resolve Duplicates. When the actual command name changes based on a special situation or selection, there's a generic reference: if the command would be File > Remove "NewFlier" based on the name of the selection, the description is File > Remove *CollectionName*.

♦ **System Preferences:** Working with certain aspects of fonts means some trips to System Preferences. To get there, choose System Preferences from the Apple menu. Each icon in the Preferences window opens a *pane* of information. So, if I say "In the International pane of System Preferences" or "in the International preference pane," you'll know you have to choose Apple > System Preferences and click on the International icon. Some panes have multiple screens, accessed by clicking their tabs (titles) in the pane, so the directions might say "…in the Input Menu tab of the International pane…".

Quick Start

The material in this book is presented with the mild assumption that you'll read it linearly, but that doesn't mean that you *have* to read it that way. You could, instead, start with font installation techniques, or troubleshooting procedures, or why you can't seamlessly share documents with a PC user.

Beginning at the beginning:

♦ Whether you're a font minimalist with nary a problem or a font fanatic with nothing but, covering the basics is a good place to start. Check out the *Supported Font Types* (page 2), and the oh-so-many places you can store them, in *Where Tiger Stores Fonts* (page 10).

♦ *Explore the Unicode Universe* (page 16), discover the wealth of characters stored in fonts with *The Joy of Character-Rich Fonts* (page 10), get up to speed with the latest font buzzword (and important concepts) in *The World According to Glyphs* (page 149), and learn how to *Utilize Smart-Font Typography* (page 172).

♦ Whether your font collection is a mess or merely a nightmare waiting to happen, get things in order with *Organize Your Fonts* (page 21), and keep them that way with *Stay Organized* (page 43).

Installing and managing fonts:

♦ If you'd like just a minimum introduction to Font Book, read *Tour the Interface* (page 48); if you'd like more than a passing familiarity with this invaluable utility, read the rest of Chapter 3. For details on specific functions, check out *Validate Fonts* (page 75), *Turn Off Fonts Temporarily* (page 101), *Create and Edit Collections* (page 117), and *Use Libraries to Control Your Fonts* (page 124).

♦ To learn about installing all types of fonts, with and without Font Book, see *Install New Fonts* (page 61); later, you'll need *Remove Fonts You Don't Want* (page 85). To keep track of all the additions to your collection, use the tricks in *Font-Tracking Techniques* (page 44).

♦ Are duplicate fonts driving you crazy? If you think that duplicates are… well, *duplicates*, jump directly to *All Duplicates Are Not Created Equal* (page 105). The sections that follow, starting with *Mac OS X Duplicates* (page 107) cover both general and Font Book issues regarding duplicate fonts.

♦ Old fonts? *Update Legacy Fonts* (Chapter 8, page 129) helps you make (most of) them usable. Old applications? If you still use Classic applications, you can find special advice in *Control Your Classic Fonts* (page 80).

Working with fonts and typing special characters:

♦ Font menus, never as straightforward as they seemed, have a few added wrinkles in Mac OS X; iron them out with *Master Font Menus and Font Formatting* (page 137).

♦ As for typing any of the thousands of special characters available in some fonts, start with a survey of "input methods" in *Turn On the Tools* (page 164). If you need to type accented characters, check out *Use Keyboard Viewer to Type Accented Characters* (page 167) and *Type More Accents with the U.S. Extended Keyboard* (page 169). To learn how to enter (and find!) the zillion other characters in modern fonts, read *Find and Enter Characters with Character Palette* (page 176).

♦ If you want to type entirely in another language, or in a different "system," like the Dvorak method, read *Use Alternate Keyboards for Foreign Languages or Other Special Input* (page 188).

Going beyond your Mac:

♦ There's only one sure way to keep fonts in your documents from transmogrifying, and that's to never let them leave your Mac. But when you have to let go, you should know how to *Synchronize with the Rest of the World* (page 199), and especially how to *Minimize Document-Exchange Problems* (page 200).

Dealing with problems:

♦ If you're not in trouble right now, read *Take Preventive Measures and Plan Ahead* (page 212) (and implement its suggestions). Otherwise, come back to it as soon as you're back on track so you won't be derailed again.

♦ If you're unfamiliar with Mac troubleshooting methods, check **Table 19** (page 221) for a list of the techniques you'll need for analyzing and solving font problems; review the details in *Learn Troubleshooting Procedures* (page 220). **Table 18** (page 215) describes the software utilities you'll need for some of the solutions (most of them are provided with Tiger).

♦ If you're having a problem but don't know whether it's a font problem or a system problem, review **Table 20** (page 239). If you suspect it's font-related but you can't pinpoint it, try the steps in *Tackle General Font Problems* (page 238). When the problem seems more specific, check the topics in Chapter 14 and see if your problem, or a similar one, is described there.

Learn
Font Basics

We've come a long way from the bitmapped fonts on the original Mac, which were a miracle in the days of the blocky, one-size-fits-all text on other computers. Along that long way, new font technologies have been developed, praised, accepted as a standard, and then nudged aside by the next new thing.

I've broken the topic of learning font basics into three sections. You need to understand them all before you can really wrangle your fonts:

♦ **Supported font types:** Some fonts are new to Mac OS X, others are on their way out (next page).

♦ **Font locations:** Read *Where Tiger Stores Fonts* (page 10). Be sure to read the entire section since the last topic, *The Font Access Order*, is especially important to understand.

♦ **Unicode:** You might be tempted to skip my short treatise, *Explore the Unicode Universe* (page16), but I'm warning you: you'll have to come back to it sooner or later!

Supported Font Types

Mac OS X supports an amazingly wide variety of fonts. Here's the cast, in order of appearance on the computer scene:

- PostScript Type 1 and companion bitmapped suitcases

- TrueType (Mac)

- TrueType (Windows)

- Multiple Master instances

- OpenType

- dfont

You can find details on all the font types in this chapter, and see a roundup of all the font specifications, in Appendix A.

PostScript Type 1 and Companion Bitmapped Suitcases

Bitmapped fonts were the earliest, and at first the only, font technology for the Mac. A *bitmapped* font file describes character shapes using a matrix of dots. Because a matrix pattern becomes distorted when enlarged or shrunk, different sizes of a font (9 points, 12 points, and so on) had to be designed individually; specifying an unavailable size led to the famous, dreaded *jaggies*.

Initially, fonts were part of the "system file" and not meant to be accessed by mere mortal users. They were eventually separated from the core system file and given their own file structure, called a *suitcase*. A suitcase could be limited to a collection of bitmapped font descriptions for different sizes of the same font family, or hold descriptions for several different families in many sizes.

Bitmapped fonts, originally an independent format, are now supported only as *companions* to PostScript Type 1 printer files, which we'll get to in a moment. (There's no difference between "companion" bitmaps and regular ones; it's the presence of the printer file that defines the bitmap as a companion, and therefore supported, font.)

PostScript Type 1 fonts, with their capability to take advantage of the highest resolution available on an output device, launched the desktop publishing industry. Instead of using dot-by-dot bitmaps to describe a character's shape, they use mathematically defined outlines that easily scale up or down and remain jaggie-free.

It originally took two files to support a PostScript font: one for the printer (the *outline* or *printer* font), and a bitmapped font for the Mac to put in its menus and draw on the screen. We're still stuck with the double-file approach when it comes to PostScript Type 1 fonts: it takes both a printer font and a suitcased bitmapped version for the font to work. Because a suitcase can hold more than one font, you won't always have a one-to-one relationship between these two file types: a single suitcase might serve as the companion to several printer fonts in the same family.

Specs: Bitmapped Suitcase

- **Name/extension:** A bitmapped font suitcase is usually named after the font family it contains. Some old suitcases have extensions such as .bmap or .scr, but the suffixes are as unnecessary now as they were under previous systems.

- **Icon:** The basic font icon, stamped FFIL.

- **Finder Kind:** Font Suitcase.

- **Font Book Kind:** Although the Font Info for these fonts shows the suitcase file as the location, Font Book otherwise ignores the lowly bitmapped font and reports the Kind as PostScript Type 1. (Font Book's Info view displays a font's Kind that seldom matches the Finder's Kind label.)

- **Future:** With the companion printer file, these fonts will be supported passively for years because they're so established, but they're being supplanted by OpenType.

Specs: PostScript Type 1 Printer Font

- **Name/extension:** The naming convention for a printer font is a simple formula: the first five letters of the font family name, followed by the first three letters of every word after that. So, the printer font for Whedon has the simple name Whedo, while Whedon Script Bold Italic becomes WhedoScrBolIta.

♦ **Icon:** The basic font icon, stamped LWFN.

♦ **Finder Kind:** PostScript Type 1 outline font.

♦ **Font Book Kind:** PostScript Type 1.

♦ **Future:** With the companion bitmap suitcase, these fonts will be supported passively for years because they're so established, but they're being supplanted by OpenType.

Note: Windows Type 1 fonts are not supported. PostScript fonts made for Windows, identifiable by their .pfb extension, are not supported in Mac OS X.

Note: FFIL? LWFN? Wondering why these font icons are branded FFIL or LWFN? Files on systems prior to Mac OS X had two four-letter codes embedded in every file to identify the parent application and the type of file. These codes made file extensions (like .doc and .txt) unnecessary and gave documents an invisible umbilical cord to their creators so you could just double-click to open them. FFIL and LWFN were the file-type codes for font suitcases and printer fonts.

TrueType (Mac)

Apple's TrueType font technology provided the PostScript advantage of smooth font rendering at any resolution while overcoming its chief drawback: the need for two files. (Actually, the chief drawback from Apple's point of view was surely the royalties Apple paid to include the fonts on computers and printers—$700 *per printer* at one point!) TrueType fonts were not acceptable for graphics professionals: although the technology supported output as meticulous as PostScript, the initial TrueType fonts weren't as finely crafted as PostScript fonts were, and there weren't many available. In addition, the pros knew and trusted PostScript fonts and had invested a lot of money in them. But the rest of the Mac world was thrilled with TrueType, which used the same suitcase file format as bitmaps.

Within a year of its release with System 7, TrueType technology was licensed to Microsoft (who apparently had to choose which enemy to sleep with—Apple or Adobe). Although the core technology is the same, the platforms implemented it differently, so there are Mac-format TrueType fonts and Windows-format TrueType fonts.

Specs: TrueType (Mac)

- **Name/extension:** Usually just the font family name; no extension.

- **Icon:** The basic font icon, stamped FFIL.

- **Finder Kind:** Font Suitcase.

- **Font Book Kind:** TrueType.

- **Future:** Short; may be dropped by OS XI. Previously the alternative to PostScript Type 1, these fonts will be totally supplanted by Windows TrueType.

Suitcases Only—No Loose Fonts!

Mac OS X handles bitmapped and Mac TrueType fonts only if they're in the special file format known as a suitcase—nomenclature left over from previous systems. A suitcase can hold a single font or multiple fonts from the same or different families; it can even hold a mix of bitmapped and TrueType fonts.

This is a totally transparent matter for most users because the TrueType fonts that come with the operating system or applications, and the bitmapped fonts that accompany PostScript Type 1 files, are already in the suitcase format, neatly packed one family to a suitcase file.

But if you get fonts from other sources—your older Mac system, a CD, the Web, a friend, a client—pay close attention to suitcases and "loose"—that is,

non-suitcased—font files. You may need to reorganize existing suitcases and put loose fonts into suitcases. (That's all covered in Chapter 8.)

This is the icon for a non-suitcased, "loose" TrueType or bitmapped font. Its Kind in the Finder is *Font.mdimporter Document.*

Note: Bitmapped vs. TrueType suitcases. The icons (FFIL-stamped) and Finder Kind (Font Suitcase) are the same for bitmapped and Mac-format TrueType fonts because they're both suitcase files; a single suitcase can actually hold both font types. So how can you tell which type of font is in a suitcase file?

Well, you can't, just by looking at it. You can, however, tell the difference by how the suitcase behaves:

♦ A bitmapped font can't be installed unless its PostScript Type 1 partner is available, and, once it's installed, its Font Book Kind is identified as PostScript Type 1.

♦ A TrueType font can stand on its own. Font Book identifies an installed TrueType suitcase as TrueType.

TrueType (Windows)

Mac OS X supports the Windows format of TrueType. Let me say that again: *Mac OS X supports Windows TrueType fonts.* These font files can be used on both platforms with no conversion, and, with the same exact font available on both sides, documents that go back and forth don't go all wonky. In addition, you can use the zillions of free or inexpensive Windows TrueType fonts on your Mac too.

Most Windows TrueType fonts have the extension *.ttf;* some have a *.ttc* extension, for "TrueType Collection." A .ttc file is not related to a font collection as defined by Font Book, nor is it a Windows version of the Mac font suitcase: it's a special space-saving file format used for some foreign language fonts that share certain characters. Because Tiger provides plenty of language-specific fonts, it's unlikely you'll ever need, or even see, a .ttc file, but they are supported.

Specs: TrueType (Windows)

♦ **Name/extension:** The font or family name, with a .ttf or .ttc extension.

♦ **Icon:** The basic font icon, stamped TTF.

♦ **Finder Kind:** Windows TrueType font.

♦ **Font Book Kind:** TrueType.

♦ **Future:** Long; it will survive the eventual shakedown to two font types—this one and OpenType.

Multiple Master Instances

Adobe's Multiple Master approach to fonts was exceptionally intriguing, but it didn't last. Picture a row of letters whose weights change from the far left (very thin) to the far right (extra, extra bold). Next, imagine a column of letters extending down from the leftmost letter, with its letters increasingly italicized as you travel downward. Now, fill in this imaginary grid: the bottom right corner would be occupied by a very bold, completely italic letter. Pick any point on the grid and you get a bold italic letter whose degrees of "boldness" and "italic-ness" depend on its position in the grid. Then picture the same procedure with other style parameters, such as condensed/extended.

The Multiple Master font was, as the name implies, the font that contained all the information for the extremes of certain design axes: a PostScript Type 1 font on steroids. The custom font you created with the Master was called an *instance*. While you can't create instances in Mac OS X (or anyplace else, for that matter, since Adobe dumped the whole idea years ago), previously created ones can be used, although in a more limited way than you'd expect since they're on the list of supported font types. Multiple Master instances are, at heart, PostScript Type 1's, so you need two files (suitcase and printer font) to make them work, and they're generally treated like other PostScript fonts in Mac OS X.

Specs: Multiple Master Instances

- **Name/extension:** The printer filename uses the Type 1 naming convention (five letters for the font name, followed by three letters for each style descriptor) and adds an MM suffix; the companion suitcase usually has an MM suffix, too.

- **Icon:** The basic font icons for PostScript and bitmapped suitcases.

- **Finder Kind:** PostScript Type 1 outline font and Font Suitcase.

- **Font Book Kind:** PostScript Type 1.

- **Future:** Already past.

OpenType

OpenType isn't so much a new font technology as it is a new file format, cooked up by Adobe and Microsoft (when the fickle Microsoft decided to sleep with the other enemy). The goal was to develop a single format that could: replace the Type 1 double-file approach with a single file; use either PostScript or TrueType outline descriptions; contain additional, more advanced typographic capabilities; provide full Unicode support for extended character sets, as well as deal with other common encoding schemes; and, run on both platforms with no conversion necessary.

Specs: OpenType

♦ **Name/extension:** Typeface name with extension .otf.

♦ **Icon:** The basic font icon, stamped OTF.

♦ **Finder Kind:** OpenType font.

♦ **Font Book Kind:** OpenType PostScript.

♦ **Future:** Long and healthy; the new standard for both casual and professional users.

Note: OpenType comes in two flavors. And your Mac likes them both.

One of the goals of the OpenType standard was to let *either* a PostScript *or* a TrueType description be the core of the font design. An OpenType font (with the .otf extension) has a PostScript description at its center Some TrueType fonts with the .ttf extension are actually the other flavor: OpenTypes with a core of TrueType.

PostScript-core OpenType always have .otf extensions, but a TrueType-core OpenType could use either .ttf or .otf. The .ttf is usually used to provide backward compatibility with older PC systems or with older versions of the font.

Mac OS X Fonts Folders

Fonts

Every user has at least three Tiger Fonts folders, but Mac OS X can use up to five:

- **System:** The fonts in /System/Library/Fonts, sometimes referred to as the "system fonts," are available to every user. Some are absolutely essential to the operating system because it uses them for menus, dialogs, and other important system-level things; deleting one of the essentials can render your Mac so helpless that it won't even start up. You need administrator access to add fonts to or delete fonts from this location.

- **Library:** The fonts in /Library/Fonts are available to every user. Apple documentation often refers to this as the "local folder," but that can be confusing in terms of *local* versus *network*. We'll stick with one of the other references used for this folder: the *Library* folder—even though the word "library" is in the path name of almost every Fonts folder. You need administrator access to add fonts to or delete fonts from this location.

- **User:** The fonts in ~/Library/Fonts are available to only a specific user; Tiger starts out with the user's Fonts folder completely empty.

- **Classic:** The fonts in /System Folder/Fonts are the only ones that applications running under Classic can use. However, everything in Mac OS X can access them, so this is the folder of choice when you want fonts accessed by both Classic and Mac OS X programs.

- **Network:** If you're on a network, the server may have a Fonts folder (/Network/Library/Fonts); these fonts are accessible to everyone connected to the server.

Note: Font subfolders. Put a folder of fonts in any official Fonts folder, and your Mac automatically sees the fonts in the subfolder, too. This includes nested folders in the subfolders, and it doesn't matter what any of the subfolders are named.

The accessibility of fonts in subfolders is inherited from the parent Fonts folder. So, for instance, fonts in a subfolder of ~/Library/Fonts are available to only that user.

Speed-Reading Fonts Folder Paths

When I refer to the Fonts folders by a descriptive name, such as System or User, you'll likely have an immediate sense of which folder I mean. But their paths all look pretty much alike (because they *are* pretty much alike). Let's take a few minutes to analyze them, so it's easier for you to recognize which folder is which without having to decode the path names each time you see them. (If you're unfamiliar with the concept of users and accounts on the Mac, it would be helpful to read Appendix F at this point.)

Fonts among the many resources the operating system uses on its various levels (system, user, and the in-between shared level). Collections of such resources are generically referred to as *libraries,* so each of the Mac OS X Fonts folders is inside a Library folder. Since every Fonts folder path name ends in *Library/Fonts,* you can ignore the end of the path. You have to read only the beginning of the path name to know which folder I'm talking about, as shown in **Table 1**.

Table 1: Paths for Fonts Folders		
Path	**Description/Mnemonic**	**Name***
~/Library/Fonts	That squiggle (also known as a tilde) in front of the name is *you*. When you see that, you know we're talking about the User folder.	User
/System/Library/Fonts	The first word is *System*; it's the stuff that the operating system uses (and shares with you).	System
/Library/Fonts	The first word is *Library*. Like a public library, open to all—all users of the computer share this folder.	Library
/System Folder/Fonts	There's no *Library* in this pathname because the folder doesn't know it's an OS X Fonts folder: it's for the Classic environment. The giveaway is the phrase "System Folder," from the days when the system fit in a single folder.	Classic
* The actual name of each folder is Fonts; this column shows the informal name used throughout this book for easy reference—"put it in the User Fonts folder," for instance.		

Application Fonts Folders

I remember the thrill of discovering that, with a few tricks, you could install fonts in an application, or even in a document, so they would appear only when you used those items. I don't remember what year that was, but it was back in the black-and-white Mac world.

While it doesn't rate as a thrill—in fact, it can be downright disconcerting—Mac OS X allows an application to have its own Fonts folder. Sometimes these "private" fonts are meant for the user of the program and appear in only that program's Font menu; sometimes they're used by the program itself for things such as text in pop-ups, or palette titles and labels. Why is it disconcerting? Let me count the ways:

♦ Lack of adequate documentation leaves users baffled when font menus change from one application to the next, and formatted text copied in one program doesn't paste correctly into another.

♦ Some vendors—notably Adobe—take the give-me-an-inch-and-I'll-take-a-mile approach and use more than one "private" Fonts folder.

♦ Fonts in subfolders inside the private Fonts folders are also available to the application. This is, in general, a good thing, but confusing to the uninformed.

♦ You can't use Font Book to add fonts to or delete fonts from an application's Fonts folder.

♦ Fonts in these private Fonts folders don't show up in Font Book even when you choose the All Fonts option; not only can you not preview the fonts, you won't know if they're duplicates—and, of course, it's conceptually confounding to have an All Fonts option that doesn't show all the fonts you have.

An application's Fonts folder is a subfolder inside a Mac OS X Application Support folder. (Lest things be too easy, there are three of these!) The path is basically /Library/Application Support/ApplicationName/Fonts.

The application is in charge of its font approach: *You can't just create a Fonts folder, put it in the right place, and—presto!—get fonts in the program's menu. The application has to be one that uses the these-are-my-fonts approach and actively accesses the private Fonts folder. But if an application has a private Fonts folder, you can move fonts in and out of it manually, and even set up subfolders inside it.*

The Adobe approach

If you install Adobe products, you'll get Adobe fonts along with them—no big surprise there. But it takes a bit of looking to find them, even if you have only one Adobe application.

With Creative Suite, you get `/Library/Application Support/Adobe/Fonts`, which includes a subfolder: `../Adobe/Fonts/Reqrd/Base`. That Reqrd folder means *required*, and you'd better believe it; some of the CS applications won't even run if the fonts aren't available.

If you have Acrobat Professional, you'll have another Adobe fonts folder: `/Library/Application Support/Adobe/PDFL/7.0/Fonts`. (You might have an older version, with a 6.0 or even 5.0 folder.)

The Microsoft method

At first glance, Microsoft seems to take a reasonable approach, putting a Fonts folder in `/Applications/Microsoft Office 2004/Office/Fonts`, and it's fair to assume that all the Office applications can share them. However, the files in this folder aren't used directly; they're just held in reserve. When you run an Office application for the first time, it copies the fonts to your User Fonts folder. If there's another User account on your Mac, the first time that user runs Office, the fonts are copied into *her* User Fonts folder, and so on.

User Libraries

User-defined font libraries are Tiger's biggest secret, one that's been trickling to the surface over time. (It wasn't meant to be a hidden feature; it was a secret due to lack of documentation. The Font Book Help system used to merely say that you can create a library by using the New Library command.)

By defining a font library, you can access fonts that live *anywhere* on your hard drive, without their being copied to any Fonts folder.

The Font Access Order

With all those Fonts folders scattered across your drive, there are bound to be duplicate fonts, right? Right. When Tiger looks for a font, it goes through the Fonts folders (including their subfolders) in this order:

1. The current application's Fonts folder

2. User-defined libraries, in reverse creation order (most recent first)

3. User (`~/Library/Fonts`)

4. Library (`/Library/Fonts`)

5. Network (`/Network/Library/Fonts`)

6. System (`/System/Library/Fonts`)

7. Classic (`/System Folder/Fonts`)

When Tiger finds the font, it stops looking—which means it doesn't go crazy if you have duplicate fonts available to the system. *(You*, however, might go crazy when you don't get the font version you wanted or expected; learn how to subvert the normal font-access order in Chapter 6.)

Note: Stealth fonts. You have eight "stealth" fonts on your drive: you can see the files in Fonts folders, but they don't appear in Font Book or any Font menu. These fonts are used in the background by the system or certain applications:

- **Keyboard.dfont, LastResort.dfont, AquaKanaBold.otf, and AquaKanaRegular.otf:** System fonts that can't be removed.

- **Helvetica LT MM/HelveLTMM and Times LT MM/TimesLTMM:** New in Tiger, used by Preview to render approximations of missing fonts.

- **Adobe Sans MM/AdobeSanMM and Adobe Serif MM/AdobeSerMM:** Used by Adobe Acrobat or Reader for font rendering.

Just because you can't see them doesn't mean you can get rid of them, as described in *Trim the Excess Font Fat* (page 89).

Explore the Unicode Universe

What's a "Unicode font," and why all the fuss? Unicode isn't a font technology or format; it's an *encoding scheme*, a way of assigning each character a numeric ID. So, a "Unicode font" is more accurately a "Unicode-compliant" font, but the shorthand reference is much easier. All OpenType fonts are Unicode; most Windows TrueType fonts, and newer Mac TrueTypes, are Unicode.

As for the fuss, it's easier to understand if you know what preceded Unicode.

In the Beginning Was ASCII

Since computers think in numbers, all characters—letters, numbers, punctuation, dingbats—have always been represented internally by numbers. You probably have at least a passing familiarity with the concept of ASCII (*"ask-key"*) codes. The original ASCII standard fit all its characters, as well as some special codes, into a list of 128 numbers (which, because computers always start counting at zero, ends at 127). Luckily, there was an unused bit (a single binary digit) in the binary number pattern used to describe those first 128 characters; through the miracle of binary, using that single bit *doubled* the number of numbers, to 256 different possibilities. This second set of 128 characters was usually referred to as "high" or "upper" ASCII.

Many fonts used those extra slots for special characters—foreign letters, bullets, mathematical symbols—without regard to what everyone else was doing. So, you could never be sure, as you moved from one font to another, what might be available with Option (Alt on PCs) and Option-Shift, a situation that held an eccentric sort of charm. (Some of the original Option characters on the Mac were whimsical surprises like the ones shown here.) The second set of 128 characters settled down to some sem-

 blance of standardization based on what had already been done (that's why the bullet character is always Option-8), though few existing fonts bothered re-aligning any nonstandard characters.

Many other encoding standards, and subsets and supersets of standards—even different basic ones for Macs and PCs—have been defined and used over the years. (The differences between Mac and PC standards still haunt us, as described in *Minimize Document-Exchange Problems,* page 200.) Despite background changes, however, we've long had fonts that could easily provide 256 different items in a character set.

Asian in ASCII: *Representing the thousands of characters required for basic Japanese and Chinese required some clever gymnastics to overcome the basic 256-character ASCII limit: two successive ASCII codes were used for a single character.*

The More Things Change...

The development of the ASCII standard came about 130 years after the most famous, longest-lasting, still-in-use encoding scheme for transmitting textual data: Morse code.

It's tempting to call Morse code a binary system, since it uses dots and dashes to represent letters. But we'd be stretching the truth, since Morse actually uses three elements in its scheme, with "spaces" (pauses in transmission) of different lengths to indicate breaks between letters, words, and sentences. But other parallels between Morse and our current computer-based schemes and concerns are so intriguing as to warrant this side trip.

♦ Because letters use dot/dash patterns of different lengths, Morse assigned shorter patterns to the more frequently used

letters: E is a single dot, and T is a single dash. For a computer, every letter is exactly the same length: 8 bits. But this most-often-used-is-shortest-cipher approach is exactly the one taken in compression schemes for transmitting computer data. When you compress a text file, for instance, E and T are represented by fewer bits than are Q and Z.

♦ When telegraphing became *the* mode of swift communication, telegraph companies charged per word for a message. To save money, five-letter codes were used for common phrases, such as LIOUY for "Why do you not answer my question?" BTW, I don't know the exact relationship between those letters and the phrase, but I did LOL when I found them. In addition, there were (are!) abbreviations to save

input effort, and any IM-ing preteen would be able to translate CUZ, TNX, and UR.

♦ Hard-working "telegraphists" did a lot of "brass-pounding" on the job, which led to something called "glass arm," the nineteenth-century version of carpal-tunnel syndrome, leading to the development of more ergonomic telegraph keys.

♦ In the Saved the Best for Last and Incredibly Apropos categories: How did Morse determine the letter frequency when assigning dot/dash patterns? In a flash of inspiration (or perhaps just to avoid the tedium of counting letters on printed pages), he went to a local newspaper printer and counted the individual pieces of type in the type boxes.

Back to Unicode

Here in the 21st century, with technology so much more global than it was in, say, 1984, ASCII and its close relatives just can't cut it anymore: different encodings for various languages make multilingual computing and document exchange essentially impossible. The nonprofit Unicode Consortium spent years developing new guidelines for an encoding standard that could accommodate all the world's languages, assigning a number and name to every character. A character's Unicode ID number, or *code point*, is usually referred to by a U+ followed by a hexadecimal number: U+2FA6, for example.

Unicode, with room for a million characters, has defined over 100,000 so far, for commonly used characters in roughly a gazillion languages, including some you never knew existed (*Ogham? Lepcha? Gurmukhi??*). It also includes all sorts of interesting categories, such as Supplemental Arrows, Letterlike Symbols, and Enclosed Alphanumerics, as well as "private areas"—blocks of ID codes that anyone can use for anything.

Current font technology, however, limits a font to a mere 65,536 different characters (hereinafter referred to as the easier-to-read 65K). So, Unicode IDs are divided into groups, or *planes*, of 65K characters. Most Roman-based fonts, even when they include multiple foreign language alphabets, limit themselves to the first plane, the *Basic Multilingual Plain* (BMP, or Plane 0—there's that start-counting-at-zero thing again). But nothing limits a font to characters from only a single plane, and, in fact, some Mac OS X Asian fonts contain characters from multiple planes.

Most fonts use only a tiny percentage of the 65K "slots" available; some have no more characters than they used to, without even filling the Shift and Shift-Option key sets. On the other hand, many newer fonts include characters for several languages, all in one file; this is an initially confusing concept, since we're used to switching fonts to use foreign language characters. The important thing for a Unicode font is that the available characters are in the right slots, with the correct numeric IDs. Most older fonts have correct ID mapping by default, since the Unicode numbers match the ASCII codes for the first 128 numbers; for some, the second 128 spots also match Unicode standards, except, in many cases, for the euro symbol.

It has, perhaps, occurred to you that to take advantage of all these extra characters you need a humongous keyboard or clever software. Mac OS X offers "input keyboards" that provide foreign language and other special input, and tools like Character Palette to help you access all the available characters in a font; these are covered in Chapter 11.

When Unicode isn't enough: *As if a million characters weren't enough, many fonts provide characters outside the Unicode set; in fact, some Adobe fonts include thousands of characters that aren't defined by Unicode. (There's more about this in Chapter 10.)*

Note: "Why do I have to know all this?" Well, judging from the tone of your question, I guess "For the joy of learning!" isn't the right answer.

 Unfortunately, Mac OS X and computers in general here in the 21st century don't shield us from their underpinnings as much as we'd like (or as much as they did back in the last century). As you work with various facets of Mac OS X font-handling like Character Palette (this picture shows one of its help tags), and application-specific solutions like InDesign's Glyphs palette, you'll see characters variously identified by Unicode IDs in hexadecimal, with UTF-8 labels, and by references to glyph names and GID numbers. If you plan to use characters beyond the basic alphanumerics you can see on your keyboard, you're just going to have to learn some of this stuff. Sorry.

Is it a Unicode Font?

€ € €€ Here's a quick, simple way to tell if a font is Unicode-compliant: Select it in Font Book, set the preview area to Custom (Preview > Custom), and type Option-Shift-2. If you get a euro character like the ones shown here (top), it's 99.9 percent certain the font is Unicode compliant. If you get the graphic shown here (bottom), the font is not a Unicode font. This assumes, by the way, that you're using the U.S. input keyboard—which is a little ironic considering the euro symbol is the test character. With the U.K. input keyboard, for instance, pressing Option-2 produces the euro symbol if it's part of the font. (Input keyboards? See page 189.)

The graphic is brought to you by the LastResort font, whose sole purpose is to step in at times like this—when a character is unavailable. The words at the top and bottom of the frame describe the Unicode category of the unavailable character; in this case, it's "Currency Symbols." The numbers in the sides of the frame (20A0 and 20CF in this picture) describe, in hexadecimal, the ID range for the category.

The fact that the character in the middle of the graphic is actually a euro symbol is coincidental to this example. The middle figure is just symbolic of the category, and the euro character is used for the Currency Symbols category. If it were a missing alphabetic character, there would be an A in the middle.

This test isn't valid for fonts that aren't expected to have a euro symbol, such as dingbat (small symbols/pictures) or non-Roman fonts (Asian, Arabic, and so on); they can still be Unicode-compliant, with all their characters having correct IDs, without the inclusion of a euro symbol.

Organize Your Fonts

Are you just beginning your Mac OS X font experience and have no idea where to start? Are you drowning in extra fonts that you've installed in various places and have no idea how get out from under the mess you now have on your hands?

No matter where you fall on the font-muddle spectrum, the guidelines and step-by-step procedures in this section get you back on track—and keep you there. I'll show you how to:

♦ **Get organized:** Clean up your current Fonts folders: add missing fonts, delete duplicates, and generally sift through what might already be an out-of-control font collection with *Clean Up the Fonts Folders* (next page).

♦ **Back up the clean setup:** Just in case things go kerflooey later, in *Make Backup Archives* (page 41).

♦ **Stay organized:** Use subfolders and other methods of tracking old and new fonts, in *Stay Organized* (page 43).

Clean Up the Fonts Folders

There's more to organizing your fonts than just dragging them to the right locations—although that's an important part of it. Cleaning up your three basic Fonts folders (System, User, and Library) is a simple, but multi-step, process. Before we get started, here's a quick overview of what you'll do:

1. **Restore each folder to the way Tiger meant it to be:** We'll reinstate missing fonts and offload nonmembers. If you've removed fonts and don't want them back, that's okay, but you can get them back if you've changed your mind. We'll clean up these folders:

   ♦ **System Fonts** (/System/Library/Fonts): Tiger installs 30 font files in this folder.

   ♦ **Library Fonts** (/Library/Fonts): Tiger installs 35 font files here, and iLife and iWork add their fonts to this folder, too.

   ♦ **User Fonts** (~/Library/Fonts): Tiger doesn't install any fonts in this folder, but Microsoft Office does; Office X puts in about 15, and Office 2004 donates a generous 77 items. If you've installed any fonts with an intuitive double-click on the Desktop, they probably wound up in this folder, too.

2. **Delete duplicate fonts:** A basic installation of Tiger, Microsoft Office, and some Apple applications leaves copies of the same font in different folders. I'll show you which ones you should keep, and where they belong.

3. **Assess available fonts:** You can follow my general "keep or not" guidelines if you're in a hurry, but I'll show you an easy way to view the fonts in each folder so you can decide which ones you like enough to keep.

4. **Organize the folder contents:** We'll colorize and subfolder-ize the survivors of the steps above, so you can differentiate them from fonts you add later.

To prepare for your housekeeping chores:

♦ **Quit all your applications.**

♦ **Create four folders on your Desktop:** In the Finder, choose File > New Folder (Command-Option-N), and name each folder as I describe here. I precede the names of these font-related folders with ƒ (that's the Option-F character, not a lowercase f), so you can easily identify them later. Create:

◊ **ƒArchives:** For archived (condensed) copies of unneeded fonts, cleaned-up Fonts folders, and backups of font utilities.

◊ **ƒHolding:** For non-Tiger fonts that need to go *someplace* while we clean up the standard Fonts folders; you'll be able to put them back after all the housekeeping chores are done.

◊ **ƒOffloads:** For fonts that aren't going to stay in their Fonts folders, but should be kept in case you change your mind. We'll archive them all later so they won't take up much room.

◊ **Create the following subfolders inside this folder:** ƒLibrary, ƒSystem, and if you have iWork or iLife, ƒLifeWork.

◊ **ƒView:** For fonts that you want to view before deciding whether to keep or remove them.

The "Don't say we didn't warn you!" warning: My editor would like you to note that if you are a beginning Macintosh user, or if you are not fully confident of things like the difference between a folder and a file, and how pressing the Option key while dragging files copies them, you should be extremely *careful when working with fonts in the System Fonts folder. Further, even if you are an experienced Macintosh user, she would feel more comfortable if you had a bootable backup of your boot drive before you began.*

Organize the System Fonts folder

Treat the System Fonts folder, /System/Library/Fonts, as sacrosanct: nothing goes in it that Tiger doesn't put in itself. You can take stuff out, but the only things you can put back are the fonts that Tiger put in originally. (The instructions that follow include several references to **Table 2**, which provides a categorized listing of the System Fonts folder contents.

Appendix B provides an alphabetical listing, which you may find a helpful supplement or alternative.)

Working with the System Fonts folder is different from working with any other Fonts folder: you can't add or remove files without an administrative password. In addition, dragging something out of the folder doesn't remove it, but merely puts a copy of it in the target destination; to actually *remove* a font file, you must move it directly to the Trash, either by dragging it there or by selecting it and holding down Command-Delete. (*Remove or Replace System Fonts,* page 87, details this procedure.)

Warning! *The fonts listed in* Table 2 *under Absolutely Necessary really are. Removing them can keep your Mac from starting up and require a system reinstall to get it started again.*

To whip the System Fonts folder back into shape:

1. **In the Finder, navigate to and open** `/System/Library/Fonts`**.**

2. **Remove *non-Tiger* fonts**—anything that's not listed in **Table 2** (page 26).

    ◆ If you want to keep a font for later reinstallation (into a different folder—this one's for *only* Tiger system fonts!), drag it to the Desktop's ƒHolding folder.

    ◆ If you don't want to keep the font, drag it to the Trash.

    Reminder: *Moving fonts out of* `/System/Library/Fonts` *is a two-step process: dragging them to a folder puts copies there; the originals must then be dragged to the Trash.*

3. **Restore missing Tiger fonts to the folder if necessary or desired.** Use **Table 2** as a guide.

    ◆ Of course, if you don't want missing a font (and it's not in the table's Absolutely Necessary list), you don't have to restore it.

    ◆ If you're missing anything that you want, read *Restore or Add Tiger Fonts* (page 235), which explains how to obtain missing fonts. (If you moved fonts and then "lost" them somewhere on your drive, see *Find Misplaced Fo*nts, page 96.)

4. **Remove the Tiger fonts you don't want.** Whether they've been in the folder all along or you added them inadvertently in Step 3, the quick way to handle **them** is to **follow** the guidelines built into the categories in **Table 2**:

    ◆   **Absolutely Necessary or Recommended:** Leave it in place.

    ◆   **Suggested:** If the possibilities in *Asian Font Fun Sampler* (page 162) intrigue you, leave the Suggested fonts in place and delete them individually later through Font Book if you feel they're cluttering your Font menus. If you don't care about the special characters, move the Suggested fonts to the ƒSystem subfolder in ƒOffloads.

    ◆   **Unnecessary:** Move it to the ƒSystem subfolder of ƒOffloads.

That's it for the System Fonts folder; you can close its window and move on to the next chore.

Important! *If you stop at this point to do any work on your Mac, you should take a few minutes to delete your font caches to avoid problems:*

1. *Drag the folder* /Library/Caches/com.apple.ATS *to the Trash.*

2. *Restart your Mac.*

Stubborn system fonts: If you've "removed" a system font from /System/ Library/Fonts *through Font Book, the font file remains in the folder but won't appear in Font Book's list again unless you remove it from the folder and then put it back. Remove or Replace System Fonts, page 87, provides more details.)*

Decide Which Fonts to Keep

As you organize each of your fonts folders, you'll have to decide which fonts you want to keep. To help that process along, I've listed the basic fonts for each folder in various tables, and divided them into these categories:

Absolutely necessary: The title says it all.

Recommended: Fonts that are in common use on the Web or in cross-platform documents.

Suggested: You don't need them, but you might want them because they provide special, useful characters; they're either dingbat fonts or non-Roman fonts with a wealth of Roman-based characters. (The *Asian Font Fun Sampler*, page 162,

shows you what you'll be missing if you get rid of Mac OS X's Asian fonts).

Unnecessary: This categorization is not meant to imply that you wouldn't want the font; even the most beautiful or useful of fonts can be unnecessary.

Table 2: The System Fonts Folder		/System/Library/Fonts
Absolutely Necessary		
AquaKanaBold.otf	Helvetica LT MM	LucidaGrande.dfont
AquaKanaRegular.otf	Helvetica.dfont	Monaco.dfont
Geneva.dfont	Keyboard.dfont	Times LT MM
HelveLTMM	LastResort.dfont	TimesLTMM
Recommended		
Courier.dfont	Times.dfont	ZapfDingbats.dfont
Symbol.dfont		
Suggested		
AppleGothic.dfont	Hiragino Maru Gothic Pro W4.otf*	
Apple LiGothic Medium.dfont	Hiragino Mincho Pro W3.otf*	
Hei.dfont	Hiragino Mincho Pro W6.otf*	
Hiragino Kaku Gothic Pro W3.otf*	STHeiti Light.ttf*	
Hiragino Kaku Gothic Pro W6.otf*	STHeiti Regular.ttf*	
Hiragino Kaku Gothic Std W8.otf*		
Unnecessary		
Geeza Pro Bold.ttf	LiHei Pro.ttf*	OsakaMono.dfont
Geeza Pro.ttf	Osaka.dfont	
Purple = Dingbat font		
Green = Fonts that don't appear in Font Book or in Font menus (Figure 1)		
Small Caps = Non-Roman font		
*These are listed in the Finder in Asian characters		

Figure 1

You can see a font's internal "Full name" in its Finder Info window.

The fonts that don't appear in Font Book or font menus—in green in Table 2—are invisible because their "full names," embedded in their files, begin with a period—a signal to the operating system to keep them hidden.

Note: Keep the Foreign Language Fonts YOU Need. None of the advice about "recommended" or "unnecessary" fonts considers your possible need for a specific foreign language (or two, or three). Presumably, if you need to keep a specific language font, or set of fonts, you'll know it and consider them "absolutely necessary" when you purge your other fonts. If you're not sure which fonts are for which languages, check the tables in Appendix B, which note the language scripts for each font.

And, if you don't mind extra fonts around, you should consider keeping some of the otherwise unnecessary foreign language fonts just for the fun of seeing Web pages—or just Google listings—in their original Chinese or Arabic scripts.

Tip: Identifying Asian font names, Part I. It's amazing what an author is called upon to learn in order to impart knowledge to the reader. In my case, I spent months learning the rudiments of several Asian languages so I could translate font names for you.

This screenshot shows how some font names appear in /System/Library/ Fonts. You can probably deduce two of the names from the W4 and W8 suffixes, matching them with the Hiragino fonts listed in Table 2, but the rest aren't so easy to figure out.

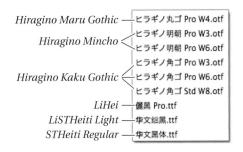

Organize the User Fonts Folder

Most fonts in ~/Library/Fonts, your User Fonts folder, come from two sources: Microsoft Office and *you*. If you don't have Microsoft Office products, all you have to do is:

1. Navigate to and open ~/Library/Fonts.

2. Select all the fonts in it and drag them to the Desktop folder
   ƒHolding.

Otherwise, you'll need to focus your efforts in organizing this folder around the Microsoft contributions, and the procedure starts in the Microsoft fonts folder:

1. **Find the folder:** In the Finder, navigate to /Applications/Microsoft
   Office 2004/Office/Fonts.

   These are not the fonts you've been using; this is the Office secret stash, copied into each user's ~/Library/Fonts folder the first time he runs an Office application.

   Using Office X, not 2004? *All the steps here are the same, except you'll have fewer fonts to shuffle around. Some of the Office X fonts are identical to the Tiger ones (where the Office 2004 versions are more advanced), but other Office X fonts are still better than the Tiger versions. You don't have to worry about which ones are which—the most that will happen by following these instructions is that you'll replace a font with an identical version of itself. The path to the Office X fonts folder is* /Applications/Microsoft Office X/Office/Fonts.

2. **Select the fonts:** Working inside the folder, choose Edit > Select All.

3. **Color the font files:** Choose a color from File > Color Label. The rest of this example refers to "purple," but you can select any color.

   All the Microsoft font files are now colorized in their "home" folder. We're going to use them to colorize the ones in your User folder simply by copying these into that folder. As a convenient side effect, all the Microsoft fonts will be where they belong (for now), in the User folder, so if you deleted some of them in a fit of "there are too many fonts in here!" pique, you'll get them back.

4. **Open a second window:** In the Finder, choose File > New Finder Window (Command-N) and, in that window, navigate to ~/Library/ Fonts.

You should have two windows open now, one for your User Fonts folder, and the other showing the marked Microsoft fonts (**Figure 2**).

Figure 2

The User Fonts folder (left) and the Microsoft Fonts folder (right), with all its fonts "purple-ized."

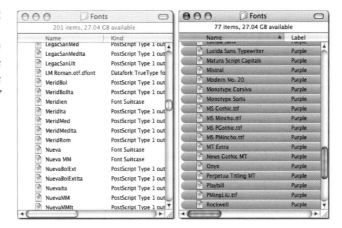

5. **Select all the fonts in the Microsoft folder.** (They might still be selected from the colorizing step.)

6. **Move the Microsoft fonts:**

   a. *Hold down the Option key* and drag all the fonts from the Microsoft folder to your User Fonts folder.

   Since Office has already installed these fonts in your User folder, the Finder alerts you to the fact that the fonts you're copying into ~/Library/Fonts are already there and asks if you want to copy over the existing files.

   Warning! *It's* very *important that you use the Option key, because this drags* copies *of the font files, leaving the originals in place. If you miss, and actually* move *all the fonts out of the Microsoft folder, Option-drag them back in, leaving copies in both the User Fonts folder and Microsoft Fonts folder.*

   b. Check Apply To All, and click Replace (**Figure 3**).

   The colorized version of your font files replaces the previous files, so now all your Microsoft-supplied fonts are tagged purple in your User Fonts folder.

   c. Close the Microsoft fonts folder.

Figure 3

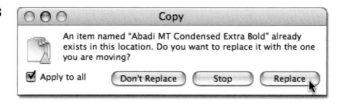

Tell the Finder to replace all the previous font files in your User folder with the newly colorized versions from the Microsoft Office Fonts folder.

Tip: Don't worry about duplicates. Although the instructions throughout this Organize section tell you how to replace one version of a font with another, Mac OS X knows how to handle duplicate versions of a font without a fuss. *The Font Access Orde*r (page 15) describes the automatic handling of duplicates; *Use Font Book to Handle Duplicates* (page 110) tells you how to subvert the default access order.

Now we'll organize and winnow all the Microsoft fonts:

1. **Sort the fonts in the window by Label.** This puts all the purple Microsoft fonts together, in alphabetical order at the bottom of the window:

   a. Choose View > As List (Command-2) or click the center View button in the window's toolbar.

   b. Click the Label column head to sort the fonts by labels.

   No View button? Click the lozenge-shaped button in the upper right of the window to display the toolbar.

   No Label column? Make sure your window is in List view. Still no label column? Choose View > Show View Options (Command-J) to open the palette for List View window options; click the This Window Only button, and check Label to add the column to your window (Figure 4).

Figure 4

Add a Label column to your window in the Show View Options window.

2. **Remove all the non-Microsoft fonts.** If it's not purple, move it to the ƒHolding folder on your Desktop.

3. **Move Arial, Times New Roman, Trebuchet MS, and Verdana out onto your Desktop.** Leave them out loose on the Desktop for now, for easy retrieval later (don't worry about the Arial variants—Black, Narrow, and Rounded Bold—for now). These commonly used fonts for Web pages and inter-platform documents are better than the versions Tiger supplies; we'll put them where they belong later, when we organize the System Fonts folder. (You might not have Trebuchet MS or Times New Roman if you're using Office X.)

Warning! Microsoft Office needs some version of Verdana in order to display definitions in its Reference Tools window, so make sure you keep either this version or the Tiger version available.

Note: Keep Tiger versions for Arabic Web pages in Safari. The Microsoft versions of Arial and Times New Roman interfere with Safari's rendering of Arabic-language Web pages. So, although the directions in this section instruct you to replace the Tiger versions of these fonts with the Microsoft versions, if you want to view Arabic-language sites, you should keep both versions. Leave the Microsoft versions in User Fonts (or, as directed in this section, in the ƒOffice2004 subfolder) and the Tiger versions in /Library/Fonts, where they were installed originally. Move between the more-characters Microsoft version and the Safari-Arabic-friendly Tiger one by disabling or enabling them as necessary (see *Disable a Font Fa*mily, page 102).

---

4. **Trash the fonts that Tiger also supplies.** Tiger installs identical versions of these fonts, so they're already available in another Fonts folder:

   ◆ Andale Mono   ◆ Arial Black   ◆ Comic Sans MS

   ◆ Georgia   ◆ Impact

5. **Create a folder inside ~/Library/Fonts.** If you're following the naming conventions I suggested earlier, this one should be: ƒOffice2004.

Since Mac OS X can see fonts in subfolders of any official Fonts folder, you can use this folder to segregate the Microsoft fonts from anything else you put in your User Fonts folder.

6. **Drag the Microsoft fonts you *know* you want to keep into the new subfolder:**

    a. Since you can't assess the Asian fonts without installing them and checking their character sets, do the same thing I recommended earlier in regard to the System Fonts folder: if you like the samples in *Asian Font Fun Sampler (page 162)*, keep the Asian fonts in the Suggested category of **Table 3**; otherwise, consider them unwanted.

    b. If you want to keep Arial Narrow, Arial Rounded Bold, or Brush Script (these versions are better than the Tiger-installed ones), drag them to the Desktop for now to keep company with the others you put aside earlier.

    c. If you use Word's Equation Editor, or want to view documents created with it, put MT Extra in the new subfolder.

    d. As for the rest of the fonts, if you're a font fanatic (of the non-professional ilk), you can just put all of them into the ƒOffice2004 subfolder. Otherwise, move just the fonts you're sure you want into this new subfolder; the next step helps you decide about the rest of them.

7. **Evaluate the Microsoft fonts that you aren't sure of:**

    a. Drag all the purple fonts that are left in the main level of your User Fonts folders into the Desktop folder ƒView.

    b. Open the ƒView folder.

    c. Select all the fonts by choosing Edit > Select All.

    d. Open all the font files by choosing File > Open.

        Font Book opens, and a Preview window opens for each font in your ƒView folder.

    e. Choose Font Book > Preferences.

    f. Choose User from the pop-up menu to set the default install location to the User folder you've been working in.

Table 3: Microsoft Office 2004 Fonts

◆ **Originals in** /Applications/Microsoft Office 2004/Office/Fonts
◆ **Automatically copied to** ~/Library/Fonts

Recommended

*Arial** Times New Roman*	Trebuchet MS *Verdana†*	*Arial Black* *Comic Sans MS*	Georgia

Suggested

Gulim.ttf *Monotype Sorts* MS Gothic.ttf	MS Mincho.ttf MS PGothic.ttf	MS PMincho.ttf *Wingdings*	Wingdings 2 Wingdings 3

Unnecessary

Abadi MT Condensed Extra Bold	*Copperplate Gothic Bold*	Lucida Fax
Abadi MT Condensed Light	Copperplate Gothic Light	*Lucida Handwriting*
Andale Mono	*Curlz MT*	Lucida Sans
Arial Narrow	Desdemona	Lucida Sans Typewriter
Arial Rounded Bold	*Edwardian Script ITC*	Matura Script Capitals
Baskerville Old Face	Engravers MT	Mistral
Batang.ttf	Eurostile	Modern No. 20
Bauhaus 93	Footlight Light	Monotype Corsiva
Bell MT	Garamond	MT Extra††
Bernard MT Condensed	Gill Sans Ultra Bold	News Gothic MT
Book Antiqua	Gloucester MT Extra Condensed	Onyx
Bookman Old Style	Goudy Old Style	Perpetua Titling MT
Braggadocio	Haettenschweiler	PMingLiU.ttf
Britannic Bold	Harrington	Playbill
Brush Script	*Impact*	Rockwell
Calisto MT	Imprint MT Shadow	Rockwell Extra Bold
Century	Kino	SimSun.ttf
Century Gothic	Lucida Blackletter	Stencil
Century Schoolbook	Lucida Bright	*Tahoma*
Colonna	Lucida Calligraphy	Wide Latin
Cooper Black		

Red = Better than the Tiger one Blue = Identical to the Tiger one Purple = Dingbat font Small Caps = Non-Roman languages *Italic* = Provided by Office X	* Tiger version is needed for viewing Arabic-language Web pages † Needed (any version) if you run Office applications †† Needed for the Equation Editor

g. Review each font Preview window in turn. If you like the font, click the Install font button; if you don't want it, click the window's Close button.

Any font you install is copied back into ~/Library/Fonts, since that's what you set as the default install location.

Validation problems: *If anything is wrong with a font you're trying to install, Font Book presents a Validation window describing the problem. See* Find your way around the Validation window *(page 77) if you encounter one during this process.*

h. Quit Font Book.

8. Delete all the fonts in the *f*View folder.

All the purple fonts you put in are still there, because Font Book put *copies* of the installed fonts back into the User Fonts folder. You can trash all of these because the originals are still in the Microsoft font folder.

That's it for the Microsoft fonts! (What else could there possibly be?) You're also finished with the User Fonts folder, so you can close its window.

Important! *If you stop at this point to do any work on your Mac, you should take a few minutes to delete your font caches to avoid problems:*

1. Drag the folder /Library/Caches/com.apple.ATS *to the Trash.*

2. Restart your Mac.

Organize the Library Fonts Folder

Even if you haven't (purposely) touched the contents of /Library/Fonts, you may find quite a few fonts beyond those Tiger installs. (The instructions that follow include many references to **Tables 4** and **5**, which provide a categorized listing of the Tiger fonts in the Library Fonts folder. Appendix B provides an alphabetical listing, which you may find a helpful supplement or alternative.) Here's where the sometimes unintended collection of fonts in the Library Fonts folder comes from:

♦ **Basic Tiger fonts:** A standard system installation puts 35 font files in the folder; they're listed in **Table 4**.

◆ **Additional Tiger fonts:** If you chose to install "Additional Fonts" during the Mac OS X installation, the non-Roman fonts listed in **Table 5** are in the Library folder.

◆ **iLife and iWork fonts:** A combined list of fonts that come with these programs is in **Table 6**.

Is your Mac shared? The fonts in the Library Fonts folder are common to all users of a Mac. The instructions that follow for bringing order to this folder refer to what you *like when it comes to "unnecessary" fonts; if you're sharing your Mac, keep other users' needs and preferences in mind.*

Navigate to the /Library/Fonts folder and open it so you can whip it into shape:

1. **Temporarily remove the iLife and iWork fonts.** Create a new folder on the Desktop named Life/Work and, using **Table 6** to identify the fonts these programs installed, move them into this folder. (Since the table identifies the fonts provided with the 2006 versions of *both* these programs, you may not have all the fonts listed if you have only one program, or earlier versions.)

2. **Bring in the Microsoft replacements.** If you have Microsoft Office 2004 and you've been following the steps so far, you have at least four font files on your Desktop:

   ◆ Arial   ◆ Times New Roman

   ◆ Trebuchet MS   ◆ Verdana

   You might also have any of these sitting there if you chose to keep them from the Unnecessary list:

   ◆ Arial Narrow   ◆ Arial Rounded Bold

   ◆ Brush Script

   Drag all of these files into your Library Fonts folder, and agree when the Finder asks if you want the existing ones replaced. They'll stand out in the crowd because they're purple—that's just to remind you where they came from. (**Table 13** describes why these are superior to the Tiger versions of the same fonts.)

3. **Create a subfolder in the Library Fonts folder for the Tiger fonts.** Name it ƒTiger; you'll use this to segregate Tiger fonts from others.

4. **Divide your basic Tiger fonts.** None of these fonts is absolutely necessary, but several are highly recommended. Using **Table 4** as your guide, decide which are staying and which are going, and move them according to your decision:

   ♦ **Fonts you want:** to the ƒTiger subfolder.

   ♦ **Fonts you don't want:** to the ƒLibrary subfolder in the ƒOffloads folder.

   ♦ **Fonts you're not sure about:** to the ƒView folder.

Missing some Tiger Library fonts? You can retrieve the basics, discussed in Step 4, and the "Additionals," in Step 5, from your Tiger install disk; see Restore System Components (page 233).

5. **Divide your Tiger "Additionals."** The extra non-Roman fonts in Tiger, from the "Additional Fonts" package at system installation, are listed in **Table 5**.

   ♦ **Suggested fonts:** If you keep these fonts for their nifty characters (as shown in *Asian Font Fun Sample*r, page 162), put them in the ƒTiger subfolder. If you don't want them installed, drag them to the ƒLibrary subfolder in the Desktop ƒOffloads folder.

   ♦ **Unnecessary fonts:** If you don't want these, drag them right to the Trash.

6. **Clear the rest of the fonts from Library Fonts.** The Tiger "keepers" are in their subfolder, and any iLife and iWork fonts are in their temporary folder, so you can move any remaining fonts to the ƒHolding folder on your Desktop. Make sure that no fonts remain in the main level of the Fonts folder before moving on to the next step.

7. **Assess the "maybe" fonts.** If you've put fonts into the ƒView folder, now's the time to review them and decide which ones can go back to the Library Fonts folder:

   a. Open the Desktop ƒView folder.

b. Select all the fonts in the window and choose File > Open.

Font Book opens, with a Preview window for every font you're inspecting.

c. Choose Font Book > Preferences and choose Computer from the pop-up menu (**Figure 5**).

This less-than-obvious choice actually sends installed fonts to the /Library/Fonts folder, as detailed in the next chapter, on page 69.

Figure 5

Choose Computer as the install location in Font Book's preferences.

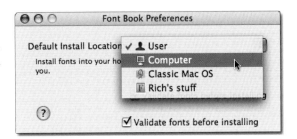

d. Review each font Preview window in turn. If you like the font, click the Install Font button; if you don't want it, click the window's Close button.

e. Quit Font Book.

f. Empty the ƒView folder: move all the fonts in it to the ƒLibrary subfolder in ƒOffloads.

Because Font Book installs copies of fonts, this group includes both the ones you installed and the ones you passed up. If you're a bit on the obsessive-compulsive side, you can pick out and trash the copies of the installed fonts, but it's not really worth the time.

8. **Move the reinstalled Tiger fonts.** Go to /Library/Fonts and move all the fonts Font Book just put back: drag them into the ƒTiger subfolder.

If you didn't install any fonts in Step 7, your ƒView folder will be empty.

9. **Finish dealing with iLife and iWork fonts.** If you have iLife or iWork and have been following all the steps so far, you have a Life/Work folder of fonts sitting on your Desktop. Here's how to handle them:

a. Open the `/Library/Fonts` folder and create a subfolder, ƒLifeWork.

b. Assess the fonts in the Life/Work folder. Follow the directions in Step 7 for reviewing fonts for installation with these changes in regard to the folders involved in the substeps:

(a) Open all the fonts in your Life/Work folder rather than the ƒView folder.

(f) Move all the fonts in the Life/Work folder to the ƒLifeWork subfolder in ƒOffloads.

Impact: I seem to be immune to the subtle charms of this particular font, but there it is, supplied by Tiger, iWork, and Microsoft Office. If you like it, and have followed previous directions about cleaning the Library folder, there should already be a copy in the ƒTiger subfolder; you can put the iLife version of it in the Trash.

c. Go to the `/Library/Fonts` folder and move the newly installed fonts into the ƒLifeWork subfolder.

d. Delete the Desktop Life/Work folder.

Important! *Don't skip the last procedure in the process of organizing your fonts,* The Last Organizational Step, *just below.*

Tip: Identifying Asian font names, Part II. Three of the Asian fonts installed with the Additional Fonts package (**Table 5**, page 40) appear in the Finder as shown at left. They are, from top to bottom, LiSong Pro, STSong, and STKaiti.

Four other Asian fonts have English names in the Finder but are sometimes identified (in Word, for instance) in Asian characters. These are, from top to bottom in the picture at left, #PCMyoungjo, #Gungseouche, #Pilgiche, and #HeadlineA.

The Last Organizational Step

You've moved so many fonts around as you cleaned up your folders that it's prudent to clear out the font caches and restart your Mac before you do anything else. The details on this procedure—including information about what a cache *is*, and why it needs deleting)—are in *Delete Caches and* plists (page 227), but here's all you have to do:

1. Drag the folder /Library/Caches/com.apple.ATS to the Trash.

2. Restart your Mac.

Table 4: The Library Fonts Folder (Basic)		/Library/Fonts
Recommended (Common on Web)	**Recommended (Common cross-platform)**	**Suggested**
Comic Sans MS Georgia Times New Roman Trebuchet MS Verdana*	Arial Arial Black	Apple Symbols.ttf Webdings
Unnecessary		
AmericanTypewriter Andale Mono Apple Chancery Arial Narrow Arial Rounded MT Bold Baskerville.dfont BigCaslon.dfont Brush Script Chalkboard.ttf	ChalkboardBold.ttf Cochin.dfont Copperplate.dfont Courier New Didot.font Futura.dfont GillSans.dfont HelveticaNeue.dfont Herculanum.dfont	Hoefler Text.dfont Kai.dfont Impact MarkerFelt.dfont Optima.dfont Papyrus.dfont Skia.dfont Zapfino.dfont
Red = Microsoft Office provides a better version of this font Blue = Microsoft Office provides an identical version of this font Purple = Dingbat font Small Caps = Non-Roman font * Needed (any version) if you run Microsoft Office applications		

Table 5: The Library Fonts Folder (Additional)		/Library/Fonts
Suggested		
#Gungseouche.dfont* #PCmyoungjo.dfont*	#Pilgiche.dfont* AlBayan.ttf	AlBayanBold.ttf AppleMyungjo.dfont
Unnecessary		
#HeadlineA.dfont* Apple LiSung Light.dfont ArialHB.ttf ArialHBBold.ttf Ayuthaya.ttf Baghdad.ttf BiauKai.dfont CharcoalCY.dfont Corsiva.ttf CorsivaBold.ttf DecoTypeNaskh.ttf DevanagariMT.ttf DevanagariMTBold.ttf EuphemiaCASBold.ttf EuphemiaCASItalic.ttf	EuphemiaCASRegular.ttf GenevaCY.dfont GujaratiMT.ttf GujaratiMTBold.ttf Gurmukhi.ttf HelveticaCY.dfont InaiMathi.ttf Krungthep.ttf KufiStandarGK.ttf LiSong Pro.ttf† MshtakanBold.ttf MshtakanBoldOblique.ttf MshtakanOblique.ttf MshtakanRegular.ttf	Nadeem.ttf NewPeninimMT.ttf NewPeninimMTBold.ttf NewPeninimMTBoldInclined.ttf NewPeninimMTInclined.ttf NISC18030.ttf PlantagenetCherokee.ttf Raanana.ttf RaananaBold.ttf Sathu.ttf Silom.ttf STKaiti.ttf† STSong.ttf† Thonburi.ttf

Small Caps = Non-Roman font

* Word lists these in Asian characters; see page 38

† The Finder lists these in Asian characters; see page 27

Table 6: iLife and iWork 2006 Fonts (Combined)		/Library/Fonts
Academy Engraved LET Fonts Algerian Condensed LET Fonts Arial Bank Gothic Blackmoor LET Fonts BlairMdITC TT-Medium Bodoni Ornaments ITC TT Bodoni SvtyTwo ITC TT Bodoni SvtyTwo OS ITC TT Bodoni SvtyTwo SC ITC TT Bordeaux Roman Bold LET Fonts Bradley Hand ITC TT-Bold	Cracked Gadget Handwriting – Dakota Humana Serif ITC TT Impact Jazz LET Fonts Machine ITC TT Mona Lisa Solid ITC TT Palatino Party LET Fonts PortagoITC TT	Princetown LET Fonts Santa Fe LET Fonts Savoye LET Fonts SchoolHouse Cursive B SchoolHouse Printed A Snell Roundhand Stone Sans ITC TT Synchro LET Fonts Textile Type Embellishment One LET Wanted LET Fonts

Red = Microsoft Office provides a better version of this font

Blue = Microsoft Office provides an identical version of this font

Note: Microsoft Office fonts are installed in ~/Library/Fonts

Make Backup Archives

Now that you have organized your fonts, you should back up the two categories of fonts you've established: the organized Fonts folders, and the offloaded fonts that you're not using but might want to restore later. (If you haven't organized your fonts according to the directions so far in this chapter, but are reading this section because you want make backups of your Fonts folders while they're still well-behaved, just ignore the references to the offloaded fonts and the desktop folders holding them.)

1. **Archive the Fonts folders:** In the Finder, select each of these folders in turn, and choose File > Create Archive of "Fonts" (**Figure 6**):

    ◆ `/System/Library/Fonts`

    ◆ `/Library/Fonts`

    ◆ `~/Library/Fonts`

    The archive that's created in each case defaults to the name Fonts.zip, since that's the name of each folder. As soon as the archive's created, select it and rename it so you know which Fonts folder it represents.

    Depending on what window view you're using in the Finder, the archive may be created in the same folder with the Fonts folder, or on the Desktop.

Figure 6

Create a backup archive of the /Library/Fonts folder with the Finder's Create Archive command.

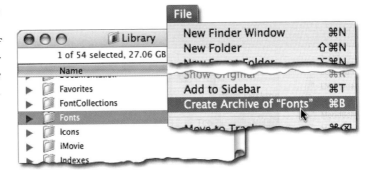

2. **Gather the archives:** Drag each archival file into the Desktop ƒArchives folder that you created way back in the beginning of this section.

3. **Archive the offloads:** Select each of these ƒOffloads subfolders in turn and make archives:

   ♦ **ƒSystem:** This holds the "rejects" from /System/Library/Fonts.

   ♦ **ƒLibrary:** This holds the "rejects" from /Library/Fonts, from both the Basic and Additional Tiger fonts.

   ♦ **ƒLifeWork:** This holds the "rejects" from the iWork and iLife font collection.

4. **Gather the archives:** Move the archival files from the previous step into ƒArchives.

5. **Put away the ƒArchives folder:** Pick a good, out-of-the-way spot on your drive.

Clean Up from the Cleanup

To help with all this font-shuffling, here's the fate of each of the four Desktop folders you made:

♦ **ƒArchives:** You moved this someplace on your drive for long-term storage.

♦ **ƒView:** This should be empty of all fonts. Trash it.

♦ **ƒOffloads:** You archived all the fonts and subfolders inside, so this can go to the Trash.

♦ **ƒHolding:** This holds all the non-Tiger, non-Microsoft, non-iLife/iWork fonts you had in your Fonts folders. You can reinstall them, of course, but not until you:

   ◊ Learn at least a little more about Font Book (Chapter 3).

   ◊ Know where the fonts should be installed (**Table 8,** page 65).

   ◊ Decide on an installation method (Table 9, page 69).

   ◊ Review the option of user-defined libraries instead of Fonts folders (Use Libraries to Control Your Fonts, page 124).

Warning! The fonts in ƒHolding at this point are not essential to your Mac, Microsoft Office, or iLife or iWork. But those are the only applications I specifically considered here. You may have specialized fonts that are essential for the operation of some of your other applications. Don't throw out any fonts in ƒHolding *until you are absolutely sure you don't need them. A touch of paranoia wouldn't hurt: instead of trashing all the fonts that you think you don't need, archive them and let the archive sit around for a while—a few months would not be too long!*

Stay Organized

Your font collection is shipshape now, but it won't stay that way—unless you never install another font or application on your Mac. If you don't expect to be quite that parochial, you can avoid another pull-it-all-apart and put-it-back-together session by practicing some simple font-management techniques:

◆ **Keep track of old and new fonts:** As you add fonts to your system, mark them or organize them with one or more of the font-tracking techniques described ahead. When you know where your fonts came from, and which are the newest additions, it's easier to pinpoint font problems.

◆ **Check if applications install fonts:** Always look in Library Fonts (/Library/Fonts) and User Fonts (~/Library/Fonts) after installing software. If you've kept up with font-tracking techniques each time you have new fonts in your folders, the "bare" new ones will stand out. Tag them to differentiate them from the next batch of newcomers.

   Application Fonts folders: Applications that install fonts in their own folders (Application Fonts Folders, page 12) don't mess up your Mac OS X Fonts folders, but they can cause duplication of some fonts. This is seldom a problem because the application in question is the only *one that can access those fonts, and it gives them priority over any other copies on your Mac.*

◆ **Make occasional backups:** Make archives of /Library/Fonts and ~/Library/Fonts at intervals so that if you have a font problem and need a quick fix, you can try returning to an earlier version of your collection.

Font-Tracking Techniques

Font problems, whose likelihood increases by some esoteric mathematical relationship as you add fonts, are easier to pinpoint if you keep track of where your fonts came from using any of the three basic techniques described here. They each have their pros and cons (which are rounded up in **Table 7**), and your best bet is to use different ones in different situations. (If you've followed the previous directions for cleaning up your folders, you've already seen how using color labels and subfolders can help font organization.)

Table 7: File-Tracking Methods Pros and Cons		
Method	**Pros**	**Cons**
Color label	◆ At-a-glance convenience ◆ Easy to sort in window ◆ Color travels with font file if you move it	◆ Hard to relate color to category
Subfolder	◆ Keeps main folder neat ◆ Most obvious of the "segregation" techniques	◆ Easy to miss font duplication ◆ Font Book can't install to the subfolder
Rename	◆ Convenient for searches ◆ Good for sorting if a prefix is added to font name ◆ Name travels with font file if you move it	◆ More complicated to set up ◆ Can't rename PostScript printer files ◆ No at-a-glance convenience

Use color labels

Labeling groups of fonts with color is a great, though limited way of categorizing them. The colors pop out—and uncolored files stick out like the proverbial sore thumb. You can sort by Label in a window to group the fonts you've colorized.

On the other hand, the colors have no intrinsic meaning, and it's hard to remember which color means what if you use too many different ones.

Use subfolders

Take advantage of the fact that Mac OS X automatically accesses sub-folders of fonts in any Fonts folder. You can set up subfolders for any grouping of fonts—by characteristics, project, client, and so on. Keep these points in mind:

◆ You can't use subfolders in /System Folder/Fonts because Classic won't see them, and you shouldn't put them in /System/Library/Fonts because you shouldn't put *anything* there.

◆ In the font access order, fonts in a subfolder are accessed immediately after those in the parent folder.

◆ In Font Book, the subfolder fonts appear in the same library (in the Collection list) as those in the parent folder; the only way you'll know they're in a subfolder is if you check the location in the Info view.

◆ You can't install a font into a subfolder through Font Book; you must manually move fonts into subfolders. Or, as we did in several places earlier in this chapter, you can install the fonts into the main level of a Fonts folder with Font Book, and then move them into their subfolder; if you make sure there are no other loose fonts in the Fonts folder, it's easy to gather the newly installed ones into a subfolder.

◆ Subfolder fonts can be removed from within Font Book, since they appear in the Font list like all other installed fonts.

◆ Using multiple subfolders increases the likelihood of your installing duplicate fonts; you can wind up with copies of the same font in the main Fonts folder and in one or more of its subfolders. Keep track of the duplicates, and which copy is being used, through Font Book (*Use Font Book to Handle Duplicates*, page 110).

Batch-change font names

Since you can change the name of a font file (except for a PostScript printer file) without affecting its performance or how its name appears in Font menus, appending a font name with its "origin" is another way to keep things identified in your Fonts folders. So, for instance, a font that comes with Microsoft Office 2004 could be named *ColonnaMS04*.

Luckily, Mac OS X has a built-in way—through AppleScript—to change the names of selected files all at once. Here's how:

1. Turn on the Script menu if it's not in the menu bar, as described in *Print Font Samples* (page 82).

2. In the Finder, select the fonts you want renamed. Don't rename PostScript printer files.

   If you have PostScript files in the folder you're working with, sorting the files by Kind makes it easier to either not select them to start with, or to deselect them after a Select All.

3. From the Script menu, choose Finder Scripts > Add to File Names.

4. In the dialog that appears, type what you want appended to the font name and click the Suffix button (**Figure 7**).

To reverse this at any time, use the Script > Finder Scripts > Trim File Names command.

Figure 7

Use the Add to File Names command to append a descriptive suffix to font names to keep track of their origins.

3 Get Acquainted with Font Book

Font Book is Tiger's font-management utility. Its obvious *raison d'être* is to install and remove fonts without your having to run around to all the Fonts folders. But it does more than just installation chores: it checks fonts for corruption, indicates and resolves duplicates, displays a font's complete character set, copies designated fonts into a separate folder to accompany your document to a printer, and generally helps you wade through the hundreds of fonts you'll have just by installing a Microsoft or Adobe application or two.

To do anything beyond blindly installing a font, you need to know at least the basics of Font Book, covered in Tour the Interface. To really take control of your fonts, and to make the most of Font Book's features, you'll eventually need to learn more about its general capabilities, described in the rest of this chapter; they're aren't immediately necessary, but they'll help you work more efficiently. I cover other Font Book capabilities, such as disabling fonts, handling duplicates, and creating collections and libraries, in related topics in Chapters 4 through 7.

Tour the Interface

It's easy to get started in Font Book, because its surface behavior and interface are predictable. But that friendly surface belies both its versatility and its—let's be kind and call it *quirkiness*—in some behaviors and interface elements.

Font Book is in your Applications folder, and opens automatically when you double-click on (the right kind of) font file (**Figure 8**); if you do a lot of font wrangling, keep it in your Dock for easy access.

Figure 8

Font Book's basic-looking interface belies both its versatility and power. The numbers and letters are keyed to descriptions in the text.

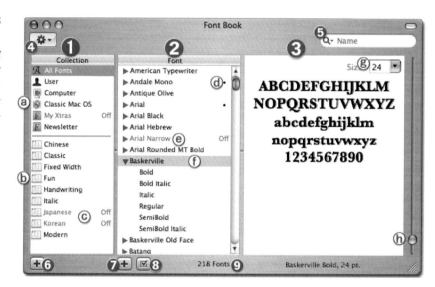

Circled numbers: MS PGothic
starting at U+278A, GID 18037
Circled letters: MS PGothic
starting at GID 20059

1. **The Collection list:** Shows standard and user libraries above the line (a) and actual collections below it (b); click an item to display its fonts in the Font list. Disabled items (c) are dimmed.

2. **The Font list:** Click a font name to see a sample in the preview area. Duplicate fonts are marked with a dot (d); disabled fonts are dimmed (e). Click on the triangle to expand and collapse a list of a font's typefaces (f). Double-click on a font name to open a separate Preview window for it.

   Warning! *The typefaces listed under a family name are ganged together even if they're from different files in the same or different Fonts folders. So, in **Figure 8**, the Baskerville typefaces could be from two separate files: one in the User Fonts folder that has the four basic faces (Bold, Bold Italic, Italic, and Regular) and another one in the Library Fonts folder that includes only SemiBold and SemiBold Italic.*

3. **The preview area:** Provides three types of samples, and an Info view, available through the Preview menu. The sample views are *Sample*, the alphanumeric set shown in the figure; *Repertoire*, the entire character set; and *Custom,* a type-it-yourself option. In Sample and Custom views, there's both a Size menu (g) and slider (h). You'll love the slider: in some views, moving it up decreases the font's point size, while in others you move it *down* to make the text smaller!

   Show or hide the preview: *You can lop off this entire section of the window with Preview > Hide Preview (Command-Option-I).*

4. **The Action menu:** The commands are context-sensitive; all are also in the regular menus, where their keyboard equivalents are noted.

5. **Search:** The search is relatively well behaved (compared to the Finder's Spotlight searches); details are a little later in *Learn Font Book's Search Function.*

6. **The Collection list ⊕ button:** Creates new *collections*—the items below the line.

7. **The Font list ⊕ button:** The equivalent of File > Add Fonts.

8. **The ☑ button:** This Disable button toggles to the ▣ Enable button; they act on the font(s) selected in the list.

9. **Font count:** This is the number of fonts currently showing in the Font list, *including* disabled ones. Since the list reflects the currently selected library or collection, it's a quick way of seeing how many fonts you have in any category.

Note: All in the family. What is it that makes "related" fonts a family? Why are Arial and Arial Black separate families (with separate listings in Font Book and in font menus), while Hoefler Text has Black listed as just one of its typefaces?

It all depends on the font's internal information as to its family name, one of the many things a font designer defines besides the shape of characters. (Font Book's Info view lists Family names.)

Decode the Collection list

Font Book's interface is not always a thing of beauty, and the Collection list is one of its more obvious flaws (**Figure 9**). Despite the title, it lists actual collections only in the lower area, below the line. Above the line, it lists two kinds of *libraries*: default and user-defined, the latter a concept new in the 2.0 version of Font Book that shipped with Tiger.

Figure 9

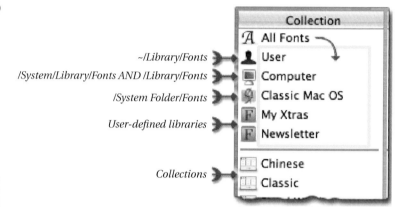

Arrows: #PCMyungjo
Straight: U+F84B GID 2288
Curved: U+2935

The Collection list can be confusing, as the items above the line do not all stand for the same type of library, and the default libraries don't always correspond directly to a single Fonts folder.

These are the components of a typical Collection list:

♦ **All Fonts:** Lists the fonts *available through Font Book*—those included in the other items above the line in the Collection list. This does *not* include fonts in application Fonts folders, like /Library/Application Support/Adobe/Fonts.

♦ **User:** Shows the fonts in ~/Library/Fonts.

♦ **Computer:** Includes the fonts from /System/Library/Fonts *and* /Library/Fonts. If you find this confusing, it's not you. It *is* confusing, since the system fonts have several restrictions that don't apply to the other fonts, and no matter your administrator status, you can't install into /System/Library/Fonts from within Font Book. In addition, the library doesn't parallel a specific single folder, as do the items immediately above and below it.

The important thing to remember is that if you put a font into the "Computer" library, whether by dragging it there or by making it the default installation location, the fonts are sent to /Library/Fonts.

♦ **Classic Mac OS and Network:** Appear in the list if you have a Mac OS 9 System Folder installed or you're on a network; they refer to the folders /System Folder/Fonts and /Network/Library/Fonts, respectively.

♦ **User-defined libraries:** Listed alphabetically, reordered as new ones are created. Note that this list doesn't reflect the order in which the libraries are accessed in case of duplicate fonts; they're accessed in reverse order of creation.

♦ **Collections:** Finally—the eponymous items, listed alphabetically. Font Book starts with a half-dozen default collections, but you can add as many as you want.

Set Font Book's Preferences

Font Book has only two preferences to set—the default install location and whether or not it should validate fonts (check them for corruption) before they're installed—but these are two very important items. Here's all you have to do:

1. In Font Book, choose Font Book > Preferences.

2. Choose a default location from the pop-up menu.

   The pop-up menu, shown in **Figure 10**, varies based on the libraries (standard and user-defined) available in Font Book. See **Table** 8, page 65, for help in deciding what you should set as the default.

3. Check Validate Fonts Before Installing so a font's health is always verified before it's installed.

Figure 10

The choices in the Default menu depend on what's available in Font Book. The last item in the menu here is a user-defined library.

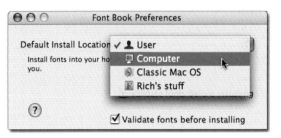

Font Book Replacements

Why do you need something else?

For the majority of general users, Font Book is flexible and powerful enough to take care of most font-management chores. But for professionals, it falls short in several areas:

No automatic activation of fonts as a document opens: This is by far the most needed professional feature; the alternative is to open a document, see what fonts are missing, and then find and enable those fonts.

Poor handling of overlapping collections/libraries: In Font Book, turning off a collection turns off all its fonts even if they also belong to another collection that is active.

Unable to handle thousands of fonts at a time: It's not that Font Book can't handle the volume—I put in well over 2000 fonts and it didn't choke. But its interface isn't conducive to handling extra-large font collections, and its launch time slows considerably with larger lists.

No automatic cataloging of fonts: Font Book can put fonts only in the main level of a Mac OS X Fonts folder. When you want another level of organization, you have to manually drag fonts in and out of subfolders, or put them in logical places for user-defined libraries. Other programs can use special folders and subfolders for storing your fonts.

Losing track of disabled fonts: Professionals enable and disable more fonts more often than the rest of us, making it necessary to trash font caches more frequently. This leads to the frustration of constantly having to re-disable things in Font Book; trying to keep special collections for re-disabling groups of fonts is a tedious workaround at best.

What are your options?

This book isn't the venue for reviewing the "big three" font-management software packages. You should check current reviews (in print and online) and the latest feature sets (in those reviews or at the vendors' Web sites) for these programs:

Suitcase Fusion: Extensis, $99.95. The fusion is that of the venerable Suitcase program and DiamondSoft's Font Reserve (www.extensis.com/en/products/product_information.jsp?id=1060).

Font Agent Pro: Insider Software, $99.95. Save 10% with the coupon at the back of the book (www.insidersoftware.com/FA_pro_osx.php).

Linotype FontExplorer X: Linotype, free. It's hard to believe this full-featured program is free; presumably after enough users consider it a necessity, the for-a-price version will be released (www.linotype.com/fontexplorerX).

Learn Font Book's Search Function

Font Book's Search function isn't perfect, but it can be handy when you have lots of fonts and don't want to look through them one at a time when you need something special. (Search for font *files* on your drive with Finder's Spotlight; see *Find Misplaced Fonts*, page 96.)

The search, confined to items selected in the Collection list, can be done in any of seven categories available through its pop-up menu (**Figure 11**). Unfortunately, *really* useful categories, such as "Disabled" and "Duplicate," aren't there.

Figure 11

Font Book's Search menu and its two submenus.

Chapter 6 includes examples that show how you can use searches to find fonts you want to disable or enable.

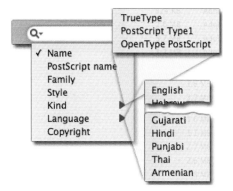

To get you started with Font Book searches, here are two examples of how it works.

Example 1—Find fonts with semibold faces. Say you're working in a document with fairly small type; some words need to be emphasized, but you feel that bold will be too overwhelming at that size. You'd like a list of fonts with semibold faces. This is a cinch with the Search function:

1. Select All Fonts in the Collection list.

2. Choose Style from the Search menu.

3. Type semibold in the Search field and hit Return.

   The "hits" show in the Font list (**Figure 12**), which displays the family names with the semibold faces listed beneath them (*only* the semibold faces, which can sometimes be confusing—*Didn't that font have a regular bold face, too?*).

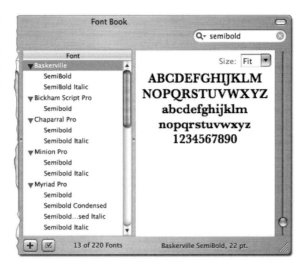

Figure 12

Searching for semibold *with* Style *as the category finds fonts with semibold styles, and lists only those faces for each font.*

To Return or not: *As with the Finder's Spotlight searches, Font Book's search function starts looking as soon as you start typing; pressing Return isn't strictly necessary, since merely typing starts the search.*

Pressing Return, however, deactivates the Search field so the next key pressed won't be appended to what you've already typed there.

Example 2—Find font faces with Hebrew characters. Now, what if you want to type the word *shalom* in its native Hebrew—שולם—but you don't know what you have in the way of Hebrew fonts? This is another easy one:

1. Select All Fonts in the Collection list.

2. Choose Language > Hebrew in the Search menu.

The results may include what seem to be unusual "Hebrew" fonts, like Lucida Grande, but that's because many Unicode fonts that are primarily Roman also include foreign language character sets.

The available search categories make some searches simple, like the two just described, but they're not always as focused as you'd expect:

♦ **Name:** If you know the beginning of your font's name, it's easier to type a few letters of it when the Font list is active. But if you only know a partial name (*hmm… Schoolbook something? Something Schoolbook?*), this is a great way to get to the font you want to preview. Unfortunately, "Name" also looks at the copyright information, not just the name of the font, so typing Apple selects not only Apple Chancery and Apple Symbols, but also every font that came with Tiger.

Note that this searches *typeface* names, so typing Bold will get you just about every font you have; the Family search category, described below, gets around that problem.

♦ **PostScript name:** This is of limited value, since the PostScript names of most PostScript fonts are simply the font name without spaces (sometimes with hyphens instead); you can just as easily search using the Name category.

♦ **Family:** If you're looking for fonts that are, say, bold in their regular face, using Bold as the search in Family finds things like *Arial Rounded MT Bold* and *Copperplate Gothic Bold* because it looks at the family name instead of the typeface names. (Using the Name category for the same search would find those as well as almost every other font in the list because it looks at typeface names.)

♦ **Style:** This option is handiest when you're building collections of fonts with particular typefaces, as in the example a few pages ago.

♦ **Kind:** The TrueType selection finds both Mac and Windows TrueType fonts. You can get a list of both types of PostScript fonts (Type 1 and OpenType) by choosing Kind from the menu, and then typing PostScript in the Search field.

♦ **Language:** The submenu is probably longer than you'll ever need; but, hey, it's probably the only way you'll ever know that *Mshtakan* is an Armenian font.

♦ **Copyright:** The copyright date can sometimes give you useful information as to the age of the font (when you're comparing duplicates). But it can also be misleading, since there are often multiple dates, and the copyrights are often renewed with no changes to the font itself. In addition, it's up to the designer to incorporate this information into the font, and sometimes that's a step that's skipped.

The Finer Points of Using Font Book

Knowing a little more about Font Book's capabilities and interface can help you work more efficiently, even if you don't want to be an expert.

Take advantage of interface features:

♦ **Get information from help tags:** You don't always have to open lists or select collections or fonts to get information about them; instead, let help tags give you the details (**Figure 13**).

Figure 13

Hover over a name in either the Collection or Font list and you'll see a help tag that provides useful information, such as the number of fonts in a Collection list or faces in a font.

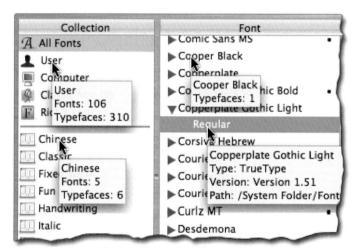

♦ **Select multiple items quickly:** You can select more than one font in the list with the usual Mac approach: Shift-click for contiguous selections, Command-click for noncontiguous ones. This makes it easy to operate on more than one font at a time, whether you're dragging them into a collection or library, expanding them to see their typefaces, removing them, disabling them, or… you get the idea.

Less obvious is the fact that you can select multiple items in the Collection list. So, if you want to see all your fonts *except* the ones in Classic Mac OS, you can select both User and Computer. Or, if you want to view or search through all the fonts in your user-defined libraries, you can select as many of them as necessary.

♦ **Use multiple Preview windows:** You can double-click on a font to open a Preview window that shows a basic alphanumeric sample; this doesn't seem any better than looking at it in the preview area, until you realize that you can open more than one at a time. So, if you want to check out the differences between certain fonts (I have a collection of handwriting fonts with names like ChelsiesHand, HanksHand, and so on, and darned if I can remember which is which) before using or activating them, you can open a Preview window for each one.

You can also open separate Preview windows for different typefaces in the same family by double-clicking on the typefaces in the Font list instead of on the family name. It's an easy way to compare different weights like bold and semibold, or other attributes, such as condensed, semicondensed, ultracondensed, and so on.

♦ **Get in the habit of using contextual menus:** Using contextual menus (Control-click to get them, or right-click if you have a two-button mouse) is faster than going to the regular menus if you're working on a big screen. The preview area's contextual menu shows up only when it is set to Custom or Info view, and you often have to click in several spots before the menu shows up.

  Just for fun: *Leave the Custom view to the default alphabet and numbers, and choose Speech > Start Speaking from the contextual menu.*

♦ **Don't expect much from custom typing:** Copying selected text from the preview area in Custom view doesn't work the way you'd expect: the font doesn't come with the information when you paste it elsewhere. You have to format the text to the font and typeface in your document.

Learn the relationship between fonts in Font Book and font files in the Finder:

♦ **Copy fonts without finding them in the Finder:** You can use Font Book's Export command to make copies of fonts used in a project so you can send them along with your documents—you don't have to go digging around your Fonts folders.

You can export a collection, a library, or individually selected fonts: just select the items you want and choose File > Export Fonts. The name you type in the Save dialog is used for the folder that will hold the copies; you'll get a subfolder inside it for each exported font. Use Font Info: the Info view (Preview > Font Info or Command-I) shows lots of handy information, like the selected font's type. But the two most convenient items are the Version and Location of the selected font. When you have duplicate fonts, you can compare version numbers before you decide which to disable or remove. The location helps you decide, too; in **Figure 14**, the location is `/Library/Fonts`.

The location also gives you the actual filename; in the figure, the typeface name is Times New Roman Bold, but the location ends with the filename, which is simply Times New Roman.

Figure 14

Font Book's preview area in Info view.

```
                Times New Roman Bold
                Times New Roman Bold, 18 pt.

PostScript name  TimesNewRomanPS-BoldMT
     Full name  Times New Roman Bold
        Family  Times New Roman
         Style  Bold
          Kind  TrueType
      Language  English, Arabic
       Version  Version 3.05
      Location  /Library/Fonts/Times New Roman
   Unique name  Monotype:Times New Roman Bold:Version
                3.05 (Microsoft)
  Manufacturer  Monotype Typography
      Designer  Monotype Type Drawing Office - Stanley
                Morison, Victor Lardent 1932
     Copyright  Typeface © The Monotype Corporation plc.
                Data © The Monotype Corporation plc/Type
                Solutions Inc. 1990-1992. All Rights Reserved
     Trademark  Times New Roman® Trademark of The
                Monotype Corporation plc registered in the US
                Pat & TM Off. and elsewhere.
   Description  This remarkable typeface first appeared in
                1932 in The Times of London newspaper, for
                which it was designed. It has subsequently
```

Arrows: Sand
U+2198 GID 350
and U+2192 GID 343

The Info view shows not just important information, such as the version and font file location, but also interesting info, like this description of the development of the Times font. Old Mac hands may remember that the New York bitmapped font was misnamed because someone thought "Times" referred to the New York Times, *and not* The Times *(of London).*

♦   **Find a font file in the Finder:** Select a font, use File > Show Font File (Command-R), and you jump right to the file in the Finder. This is a clever and hard-working command: choose a PostScript Type 1 font, and both its files are selected; select a family name and all the separate typeface files for a family are selected. If you start with several different fonts selected in the Font list, they'll all be selected in the Finder, even if that requires multiple windows to open.

Use keyboard shortcuts:

♦ **Right and Left arrow keys:** Expand and collapse the typeface list of selected fonts when the Font list is active. (I listed this first because it's the biggest time-saver.)

♦ **Tab and Shift-Tab:** Use these keys to move from one element to another in the Font Book window. The basic tab order (**Figure 15**) includes the Collection list, the Font list, and the Search field; if the Size menu is showing, it's included. When the Custom preview is in use, you can tab into it to type—but you can't tab out again, because pressing Tab types a tab in the preview area.

♦ **Extended tab control:** When the Mac OS X Full Keyboard Access feature is activated, it adds Font Book's Action menu and the ⊞, ☑, and ▣ buttons to the tab order (**Figure 15**). (Toggle this system-wide feature with Control-F7 and learn all about it in Appendix E).

Figure 15

The green-framed areas are the basic Tab controls; with Full Keyboard Access turned on, the orange-framed controls are included in the Tab order.

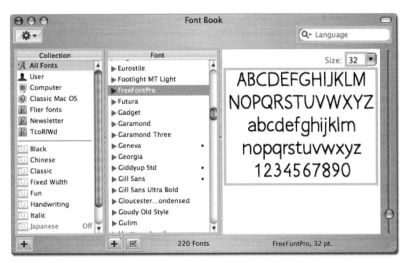

♦ **Up and Down arrow keys:** These keys move you in an activated Collection list, Font list, or Size menu. Page Up and Page Down also work in both lists, and you can type a few letters to jump to a list item.

♦ **Return or Enter:** Opens the Preview window for selected fonts when the Font list is active.

♦ **Return or Enter:** Activates a selected collection or library name for editing when the Collection list is active, and deactivates it after editing.

Install
New Fonts

Installing a font can be a simple double-click away—as long as you have simple needs and the default settings work for you! But if you want to prepare correctly for font installation, control where your fonts are stored, and take advantage of some of Font Book's other installation options, you need this chapter as a guide.

In addition, this chapter covers dealing with fonts in the Classic environment, and shows you how to print samples of installed fonts.

Get New Fonts

Install what fonts? From where? Some users are drowning in unwanted fonts; others just can't get enough. If you're in the market, you don't have to spend a cent to add to your font collection.

You may be disappointed that I've squeezed information about finding free fonts down to this little segment. But it's much worse for me: no more "But I'm *working*. No, *really!*" excuse for whiling away a few hours perusing the beauty of zillions of typefaces. But, after all, let's face it: you don't need a book to help you find fonts the way you would have before the Web—you can just search in Google for "free fonts" to find lots of offerings.

Many free-font sites are eyesores, with blinking banners and obnoxiously intrusive ads; lots of the hits you'll get on a Google search are sites that simply list other font sites (including those that list other sites that list…). In order for my countless hours of research not to go to waste (and to save you some trolling time), I offer some of my favorites—in no particular order—wherein I've forgiven an annoying ad or two that doesn't otherwise interfere with the overall interface:

◆ www.dafont.com   ◆ www.dingbatpages.com

◆ www.fontfile.com   ◆ www.fontgarden.com

◆ www.highfonts.com   ◆ www.1001fonts.com

◆ www.simplythebest.net/fonts/

◆ www.bancomicsans.com/fonts.html

If you're going to buy fonts, here are some guidelines to keep in mind:

◆ **Watch out for the font count:** The banner screams *Only $7.00 per font!* so you choose four, and your total comes to… $126? Three of those "fonts" had the standard four typefaces, and one of them had six, so you actually bought 18 "fonts." It all depends how you define font, and by traditional standards, a typeface *is* a font. Seven dollars per font *family,* now that's a bargain. (The sidebar *Fonts, Families, and Faces,* page 9, discusses the nomenclature issues.) Shame on the font vendors who don't make that clear for the less savvy customers, but they're not doing anything illegal.

◆ **Buy OpenType, not Type 1:** Adobe is converting, or has converted, their entire library; other houses may be slow to follow suit, but buy an OpenType version of whatever you need whenever possible.

◆ **Buy Windows TrueType, not the Mac version:** If you cringe when you read this, go back and read about Windows TrueType (page 6), and maybe you'll feel better.

◆ **Insist on Unicode compliance:** Okay, it's not as if you get to tell the vendor, "No, I want it in Unicode, please"; in fact, you may be surprised at how few fonts are even described as Unicode-compliant (or not). If you don't know, find out; if doesn't comply, try to find a similar font elsewhere does.

Be extra careful about any font that creates special characters—dingbats, mathematical symbols, phonetics, fractions—by simply replacing the standard alphanumeric characters (so the computer thinks you're typing an A, but the font is supplying a flower); it will cause trouble. Don't buy them; stick to Unicode-compliant versions whenever possible. (See *The Zapf Dingbats and Symbol Nightmare*, page 158, for an excruciating example of this problem.)

◆ **Try before you buy:** Some fonts have trial versions with grayed-out or missing characters; it's a great way to check out the character set, Unicode compliance, and just generally whether the font is really what you want.

TIP: A great place to shop. I called three graphic designers I know and asked: if they were to buy fonts on the Web, where would they shop? All three gave the same answer: MyFonts. (www.myfonts.com) (And that's without the up-to-fifteen-percent coupon at the back of this book!) It's a one-stop shop, providing downloadable fonts from many foundries with a wide array of search tools to find the kind of font you need. You can even upload a scan of a font that you saw in print and it's identified for you, and sign up for a newsletter or two about the latest in font design.

Before You Install

Don't rush headlong into font installation; a little preparation can save you time, and maybe even a lot of grief, later. Before you install any fonts, you should:

◆ **Organize your existing fonts:** Follow the directions in Chapter 2 to clean up your Fonts folders before you add new fonts.

◆ **Back up your Fonts folders:** I'm not suggesting you back up your Fonts folders prior to every font installation. But you should make archival copies of your "pure" Fonts folders before you add lots of your own fonts, and at occasional intervals if you have a large font collection that you'd rather not rebuild from scratch in case something goes wrong. (*Make Backup Archives*, page 41, explains how.)

♦ **Repack old suitcases:** If your suitcase files—whether TrueTypes or bitmapped PostScript companions—are relatively old, they might have more than one family inside. (See *Learn How to Pack a Suitcase for Mac OS X*, page 131.)

♦ **Decide (and follow through) on a font-tracking scheme:** Keeping track of the most recently installed fonts, or where they came from, is an invaluable troubleshooting technique; as a bonus, your fonts are more easily organized. (See *Stay Organized,* page 43.)

♦ **Learn the rudiments of Font Book.** Really, at least the basics of the interface, because Font Book opens when you install a font and you should know what you're looking at! (That's why the chapter *Get Acquainted with Font Book* came before this chapter.)

♦ **Set a default location for your fonts:** Use the guidelines in Table 8 to choose the standard destination for your fonts, and set it with Font Book's Preferences command; you'll be able to change the default at any time, or override it for specific fonts. (See *Set Font Book's Preferences,* page 51.)

♦ **Choose an installation approach:** Review Table 9 (page 68).

Install a Font From the Desktop

With all the background tasks—and the Font Book tour—out of the way, you can proceed to installing your fonts. Once you know the ins and outs of font installation, you can use whatever technique suits you best; I cover the entire gamut ahead, and round up the pros and cons of different installation techniques in **Table 9** (page 68). But the easiest, most convenient way to install a single font is with a double-click from the Desktop:

1. **Close applications:** More specifically, you must close applications that have font menus that don't accommodate font changes on the fly. Adobe programs can stay open; Microsoft programs cannot. This is not just an issue of whether an application's Font menu acknowledges the font changes; changing the font lineup behind an application's back can make it crash when you go back to it.

Table 8: Where to Install Your Fonts			
The situation	**Font usage is...**	**Store them in...**	**Comments**
You want to use fonts in Classic and Mac OS X		**Classic Fonts**	OpenType and Windows TrueType (.ttf) won't work in Classic
You're the sole user	Mild or wild	**User Fonts** or **Library Fonts**	When it's just you, either location works; pick one and stick to it
A shared (multiple-account) Mac at home	A few additional fonts for fun	**Library Fonts**, to be shared	Everybody likes playing with new fonts
	One member uses lots for fun or profit	**User Fonts**	Minimizes font menu clutter for others
A shared (multiple-account) Mac in office	Moderate: every user needs some extra fonts in common; a few use lots of fonts	**Library Fonts** for the extras that everyone wants	Avoids needing multiple copies of the same font, easier maintenance
		User Fonts for individual choices	Minimizes font menu clutter for all users
You're a graphics professional	Intense	**Adobe Fonts** for use in Adobe applications	User-defined libraries are covered in Chapter 7
		User Fonts for other frequently used fonts	
		User-defined libraries for "temporary" fonts	
Office network	Varies with users	**Network Fonts** for shared fonts	
		Library Fonts for fonts shared on a specific Mac	
		User Fonts for individual use	
Classic Fonts: `/System Folder/Fonts` Library Fonts: `/Library/Fonts` Network Fonts: `/Network/Library/Fonts`		User Fonts: `~/Library/Fonts` Adobe Fonts: `/Library/Application Support/` `Adobe/Fonts`	

2. **Open the font:** In the Finder, double-click the font file.

Font Book opens in the background and a Preview window appears so you can review the font (**Figure 16**). You can cancel the installation at this point by closing the Preview window; doing so will also quit Font Book.

PostScript Type 1 fonts: You can double-click either the suitcase or the printer file; for best results, the two files should be in the same folder. See Install PostScript Type 1 fonts (page 71) for more information.

Figure 16

Font Book's Preview window lets you view all the faces in a font file before installing it. The dimmed (Not Installed) note in the lower left is there because you can also open the Preview window by double-clicking on an installed font in Font Book's list; the note lets you know whether you're looking at an installed font.

3. **Change (or check) the default installation location:** In Font Book, choose Font Book > Preferences, verify that your desired location is chosen, check the box to validate fonts before installing, and close the window.

4. **Install:** Click the Install Font button.

This triggers a quick validation of the file's integrity; if it passes muster, a *copy* is placed in the default Fonts folder (the one selected in Font Book's preferences), and the Font Book window appears.

5. **Consider an extra validation:** If you have any reason to doubt the stability of your font (it's of dubious origins, or you acquired it back in, say, 1988), select the newly installed font in the Font list and choose File > Validate Font.

Font Book's automatic validation feature is not always reliable; see *Find your way around the Validation wind*ow (page 77) if you need help understanding the validation results.

6. **Check out your new font:** This is, of course, optional, but you can look at its entire repertoire of characters in the preview area.

7. **Quit Font Book:** Choose Font Book > Quit Font Book (Command-Q) or just close the Font Book window by clicking its close button or choosing File > Close (Command-W); to a single-window application like this, closing the window is the same as quitting.

8. **Put away the original font:** Since Font Book puts a *copy* of your font into the install location, the original is still sitting there where it started. Where you should put it depends on where it came from; in most cases, you can simply trash the original because you have a copy of the font in a Fonts folder.

Looking inside suitcases: This double-click installation method is the only one that opens a Preview window before the font is installed. So, if you're not absolutely sure what's in a suitcase font file—if there's even a remote possibility that it contains typefaces from more than one family—use this method so you can review the file. Beware of multi-family suitcases *(page 72) explains why.*

TIP: Unlocking font icons. You may find that you can't copy or install some older suitcase and printer fonts because they're locked; the padlock on the icon is a dead giveaway. To unlock the file, select it in the Finder, choose File > Get Info, and uncheck Locked.

Other Installation Options

With the basics of font installation under your belt, you can explore additional ways to install fonts to see what suits your situation and work habits. **Table 9** provides an overview of the pros and cons of your options.

Table 9: Font Installation Methods

Pros	Cons	Recommended for...
With Font Book		
Double-click on Desktop		
♦ Quick, easy ♦ Font preview ♦ Can see suitcase contents ♦ Can use or change default install folder ♦ Validation	♦ Tedious for multiple-font installs ♦ No chance to change default install folder	♦ One font, or a few, at a time ♦ When you're not sure what's in a suitcase file ♦ When you don't know what the font looks like and want to see a sample before installing
Add Font command or button		
♦ Can override default install folder ♦ Validation	♦ No font preview ♦ No suitcase preview ♦ Tedious for multiple-font installs unless it's an entire folder	♦ Many fonts at once ♦ When you know what's in a suitcase
Drag from Desktop		
♦ Can override default install folder ♦ Validation	♦ No font preview ♦ No suitcase preview ♦ Easy to drop on the wrong spot	♦ Many fonts at once ♦ When you know what's in a suitcase ♦ Installing a whole folder ♦ Creating user libraries
Create a library		
♦ Fonts remain in original location ♦ Validation	♦ No font preview ♦ No suitcase preview	♦ When fonts are used on short-term basis
Without Font Book		
Drag into a Fonts folder		
♦ The only way to add fonts to Application Fonts folder	♦ No validation ♦ Fonts are not copied, originals are moved	♦ Keeping fonts organized with subfolders ♦ Using Application Fonts folders ♦ Manipulating system fonts

Installation alternatives within Font Book

Font Book's three alternative install options all skip the Preview window, let you bypass the default install location, and still validate fonts before installation:

- **File > Add Fonts:** Adds the font to the currently selected library or collection.

- **The Font list ⊞ button:** Simply an alternative to using File > Add Fonts.

- **Dragging a font into Font Book from the Desktop:** Lets you ignore both the default install folder and the current item in the Collection list because you can drop the icon directly on any item in the list (**Figure 17**); you can also drop it in the Font list.

If a user-defined library is selected when you use the Add command or button, or you drop a file into the library, the font is not copied to any Fonts folder, but remains in its original location—that's the nature of user-defined libraries. (See *Create a Library for Temporary Fonts,* page 124.)

Figure 17

Dragging a font file directly into a Collection list item bypasses both the default install location and the current Collection item (Computer, *in this picture*).

Installation destinations

For some install procedures, it's obvious where the fonts are going: use an Add command with the User library selected, or drag a font into that library, and you've installed the font in ~/Library/Fonts.

But items like All Fonts, Computer, user-defined libraries, and collections don't represent single, specific locations. Where do fonts wind up when you drag them to these locations? The setup is logical, if not obvious, as you can see in **Table 10**.

Table 10: Font Destinations

Target		Result
𝒜	All Fonts	Default install folder
👤	User	`~/Library/Fonts`
🖥	Computer	`/Library/Fonts`
🎛	Classic Mac OS	`/System Folder/Fonts`
F	User-defined library	Font file remains in original location
▦	Collection	Default install folder
Font	Font list	Current item in the Collection list

Install a folder of fonts

Say you have an entire folder of fonts that you want to install, but you don't want to handle them individually; you don't even want to open them from the Desktop in a batch because you'll get a Preview window in Font Book for every last one of them.

As long as you want every font in the folder installed—including fonts in any of its subfolders—you can "install" the folder in either of two ways:

♦   **With Add:** Use Font Book's Add command or button and, while you're in the Open dialog, with the *folder* selected—not any of its *contents*—click the Open button.

Warning! This Mac OS X capability to open a folderful of documents when a folder is selected in an Open dialog can be pretty scary when, from years of habit, you select a folder and hit the Open button to open the folder to look inside, and—whoops!—you've opened everything in the folder instead.

Just imagine what happens if you happen to have, say, your drive selected in the Open dialog and you trigger the Open button: all the fonts on your drive are installed into whatever's selected in your Collection list. (Did I learn this from accidental experience? Nope, even worse: I did it on purpose to see what would happen.)

♦ **With a drag:** Drag the folder into the target spot in Font Book's Collection list—the User library, for instance. (If you're dragging it into a library above the line, make sure you drop it directly on the target: dropping it just above the line but not into an existing library creates a new library—as shown in **Figure 18**.)

Figure 18

Dropping a folder on a library (left) installs the fonts into that library. Dropping it under the last library (right) creates a new library.

Font Book may take a few seconds, or even minutes, to complete the installation because it's validating all the fonts; you'll see the in-progress gear spinning away.

Install PostScript Type 1 fonts

Installing a PostScript Type 1 font isn't much different from installing other fonts. Use any of the basic installation methods for Type 1 fonts, keeping these additional points in mind:

♦ **To install with a double-click:** When working from the Desktop, you can double-click either the suitcase or a printer file.

♦ **Choose from the Open dialog:** When you use the Add command or button in Font Book, only the suitcase file shows as selectable in the Open dialog, but both files are moved to their install destination when you open the suitcase.

♦ **To install the font by dragging it into Font Book:** Drag the suitcase, not a printer file; all the files are still copied to the correct folder.

♦ **One suitcase, many printer files:** There's seldom a one-to-one relationship between suitcases and printer files; a suitcase often holds several different typefaces for a family, while each typeface has its own printer file. So, your TektonPro suitcase serves as the companion to the printer files *TektoPro*, *TektoProBol*, *TektoProIta*, and *TektoProBolIta*.

♦ **Keep the files together:** Font Book can sometimes install PostScript Type 1 fonts when the suitcase and printer files aren't in the same folder, but you should keep them together or you might lose track of the originals.

♦ **PostScript fonts in the Preview window:** When you open a Preview window during or after installation, the typefaces shown are *only the ones with both printer files and bitmapped versions.* Typefaces in the suitcase that don't have matching printer files don't show, nor do typefaces for which there are printer files but no bitmapped equivalent in the suitcase.

Beware of multi-family suitcases

The suitcase font files that come with Tiger and current applications are neatly packed with only a single TrueType family, although they may include many typefaces. But older suitcases from previous systems or other font sources may contain more than one family, or even have bitmap fonts mixed in with the TrueTypes (**Figure 19**).

Figure 19

This multi-family suitcase file (as it appears in Mac OS 9) contains two different TrueType fonts (top row) and a set of bitmaps for a third font (bottom row).

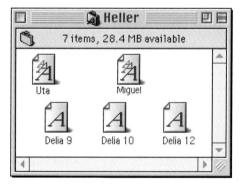

Double-clicking a multi-family suitcase opens multiple Preview windows in Font Book, and using the Validate File command on it displays a list of fonts. But *neither displays any bitmapped fonts* unless their Type 1 printer files are present; so when you see a bunch of Preview windows or a long validation list, don't be fooled into thinking you've seen *all* the contents of a suitcase file.

These multi-family suitcases, although usable, present several practical problems:

◆ You can't install a single family from the suitcase—it's an all-or-none proposition, since the file is moved into a Fonts folder, making all its fonts available. When the suitcase's multiple Preview windows open in Font Book, clicking the Install button in one of them often closes the others; if there are a dozen or so windows, you may have to click Install in three or four of them before they all go away.

◆ You can't remove a single family after the font's installed—they're all deleted at once because the single file gets moved to the Trash.

◆ TrueType fonts in multiple-family suitcases can't be disabled reliably; although marked as disabled in Font Book, they sometimes show up in font menus anyway.

◆ There's no indication in Font Book that these fonts are tied together by being in a single file, which makes it harder to avoid problems when you mean to disable or delete only one of them.

◆ Any bitmapped fonts in the suitcase—ones without their PostScript Type 1 chaperone—go along for the ride, and you won't know about them. But there they are, semi-installed, you might say, which can lead to problems. For one thing, the bitmapped fonts were never validated, since they came in under the radar, so they might be corrupted. For another, if a bitmapped font name matches a PostScript Type 1 font you're using, the accidental bitmap might be accessed instead of the companion bitmap you *think* is being used—and they might have different designs, despite their identical names. What fun!

In all, the only valid use of a multi-family font suitcase is as a companion to PostScript Type 1 fonts when you'd be using the "extended" family all at the same time, installing and removing them together: a suitcase, for instance, that contains the bitmaps for Futura, Futura Light, and Futura Condensed.

However, since Mac OS X doesn't provide any way to access a suitcase's contents, you might be stuck with a multi-family suitcase that you just *have* to install, even if only temporarily, no matter the consequences. Go ahead, if you must, but first see if you can manipulate the suitcase contents, as described in Chapter 8.

Tip: Expos(é)ing your fonts. If you open a stuffed-to-the-gills suitcase in Font Book, or choose to preview a whole library of installed fonts, the multiple Preview windows that open overlap, showing only the frontmost sample. To neatly tile the windows so you can scan the font samples, use Exposé's All Windows feature. (To set or change the trigger for this feature, use the Dashboard & Exposé pane in System Preferences.) With the Preview windows splayed across the screen, you can see all the fonts at once; just click on one to bring it to the top of the pile.

Tip within a Tip: Font Book has no Close All command, probably because Close is the same as Quit when the Font Book window is active. When you have *lots* of Preview windows open and want to close them without installing or removing the fonts, it's faster to quit Font Book and relaunch it than to close all the windows, even by holding down Command-W until they're gone.

The Forbidden Fonts

 Mac OS X officially handles only suit-cased TrueType and bitmapped fonts, not the "loose," single-font versions that were allowed under previous systems. (The single-font icon is a large A, shown here.) But say you have a loose TrueType font, or a PostScript Type 1 whose **bitmapped companion** is not suitcased, and you really, really, *really* must use it just for a little while. You may have tried installing the font by double-clicking on it on the Desktop or by opening it from within Font Book, to no avail—double-clicking doesn't work, and the files don't show up in an Open dialog. But you *can* install these fonts to use them in a pinch:

A loose TrueType font: Drag the font into any Font Book default library: User, Computer, or Classic Mac OS. You can also put the file directly into any of the Fonts folders, or into an application Fonts folder. Mac OS X adds the font to menus, and you can use it in any application, as if it were a suitcased font.

A loose Type 1 bitmapped companion: If you drag the font into a Font Book library, only the bitmapped file is copied into the target Fonts folder; the printer file remains in its original location. But you can drag them both directly into any Fonts folder, including Adobe's application Fonts folder, and you'll be able to use the font.

Tiger's attitude toward loose fonts has changed a little bit with each update, so these tricks may not work in updates beyond 10.4.7, where I last tested them, but you can try them.

As for loose bitmapped fonts that aren't Type 1 companions, you can put them in the Classics folder and access them in Classic applications, but you won't want to: they're jagged even at the designed sizes, and their very presence can trigger unexpected typing and formatting problems even when using other fonts.

Work directly with Fonts folders

There's nothing to stop you from dealing directly with various Fonts folders instead of going through Font Book, but here's what you give up by skipping the Font Book route:

♦ Easy access to buried Fonts folders.

♦ Validation of font files. Font Book's validation is less than rigorous, but it's better than none.

♦ The first line of defense against incorrect file types: Font Book just won't install bitmapped fonts without their printer files, non-suitcased fonts or some older Type 1's that don't function reliably.

♦ Protection, in the form of a warning dialog, from inadvertently removing a system font.

♦ The automatic "backup," since Font Book puts a copy of your font, not the original, in a Fonts folder.

Despite the Font Book advantages, you might want to, or have to, go directly to folders when:

♦ You want your fonts organized in subfolders inside a Fonts folder.

♦ You're dealing with application Fonts folders, which Font Book does not access.

♦ You want to manipulate system fonts, and *really* remove them from the `/System/Library/Fonts` folder instead of just from Font Book's Font list. (*Remove or Replace System Fonts*, page 87, explains how to do this.)

When you install fonts directly into any folder that Font Book accesses, validate the fonts before or after with the Validate Font command, described next.

Validate Fonts

Corrupted font files are an old, familiar problem to Mac users. They were corruptible because they were "writeable"—the system opened the files not just for use but also to change ID numbers in an effort to avoid conflicting IDs. That approach has, fortunately, fallen by the Mac OS X wayside, with font files strictly read-only now. Most font corruption reported under Mac OS X is either of old files, or a false report due to corruption in a font cache file. (See *Delete Caches and plists,* page 228.)

Validation is simply Font Book's way of checking font files for internal problems. It doesn't *fix* the problems; it merely reports them to you.

Font Book provides three ways of validating fonts:

- ◆ **Automatic validation:** Triggered when you install a font through Font Book, which is why installing more than a few fonts at a time can cause Font Book to seemingly seize up for anywhere from a half minute to several minutes: you'll see the "in progress" gear spinning as Font Book churns away at validating each and every font you just dragged in from that font CD.

- ◆ **File > Validate File:** For fonts that are not installed; you can choose a single font file, or an entire folder (which will include its subfolders in the checkup).

- ◆ **File > Validate Font:** For already-installed fonts; select one or more in the Font list.

Why would you need either of the "manual" Validate commands, when there's automatic validation of fonts on installation? If you install fonts by dragging them directly into folders, bypassing the automatic validation, you can check them beforehand with Validate File, or afterward with Validate Font. Validating in advance saves time, not so much for the install-and-then-remove a bad font, but because once the fonts are installed, it's time-consuming to pick them out of the Font list for validation. In addition, I've found that the Validate commands sometimes flag a questionable font that passes the automatic validation procedure.

With automatic validation, you won't see anything if the fonts pass inspection. With either of the Validate commands, the Font Validation window (**Figure 20**) opens even if everything's okay. It uses an equivocal, wimpy "Problems may have been found…. Please review…" comment even when everything passes muster.

Figure 20

The results of validating a group of installed fonts.

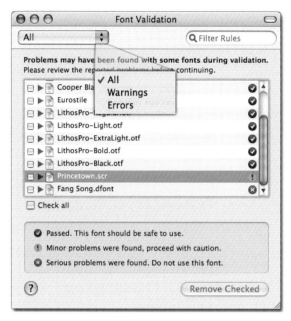

The pop-up menu winnows the list of fonts; in a serious lapse of parallelism, Warnings refers to the Minor problems description at the bottom of the window, and Errors to Serious problems.

The Remove Checked button is available when the fonts in the list are installed; if you are validating fonts that are not installed, the button is Install Checked.

Find your way around the Validation window

Inside the Validation window, you can:

♦ **See more info:** Use the triangles to expand the hierarchy: a font or suitcase name expands to its families, which expand to their faces, which expand to validated items (somewhere between 4 and 15, depending on the font).

♦ **Filter your results:** Choose All, Warnings, or Errors from the pop-up menu to filter a long list, as described in **Figure 20**.

♦ **Further filter your results:** Use the Filter field to winnow a list to commonly named items. (It does manage a little more than just using a font's name as the filter: you can type in OpenType or TrueType as the "rule." However, the results are erratic, especially with TrueType as the filter, which shows only files ending with .ttf, so Mac TrueType fonts aren't included.)

What to do about a reported problem

A font that fails validation is marked in the window as having minor or serious problems (**Figure 21**):

♦ **Minor problems… proceed with caution:** What does this mean—you should type *verrry slooowly* when using the font? Apple documentation originally defined this problem as "duplicate fonts have been found." This is patently false: try to validate a truly duplicate font, and no problems will be found; get a report like this on a truly problematic file and it's unlikely it will have a duplicate anywhere on your drive.

   You shouldn't ignore the warning; getting a fresh copy of the font in question would be prudent. But go ahead: use it if you need it, and consider it your chief suspect if you start having problems soon afterward. I have found several times that a "minor problem" font, though listed in Font Book, just doesn't appear in font menus; apparently another Apple document that states "Mac OS X… automatically deactivates corrupt fonts" might be true.

♦ **Serious problems…. Do not use this font:** You should probably take this warning seriously. But the first font that gave me this dire warning was Fang Song.dfont, carried forward from Jaguar. I can't say that I actually *used* this Chinese font, but I did play with it for weeks on two machines after finding the validation problem, and had no problems at all. If you get this result for a non-Roman font, it's possible the font is actually fine, and you should try using it if you need it. (Your mileage may vary.)

Figure 21

The number of items validated for a font differs from one font type to another. In these examples, a font in the list has failed validation with minor problems (yellow warnings, left) or major problems (red warnings, right).

In all, Font Book's validation procedure is somewhat like airport security—it's supposed to be important, it often looks like it's doing something, but its effectiveness is questionable.

And have you noticed that I haven't said anything about actually *fixing* problem fonts? That's because there's nothing to say—Font Book can't fix broken fonts. It must be an issue that's difficult to handle, because only one utility claims that capability along with its other font-management features: the $70 FontDoctor (`www.morrisonsoftdesign.com`).

Warning! The technical documentation available on Apple's Web site clearly state that fonts are automatically validated when you install them through Font Book. I haven't found that to be always the case, and, as a glutton for punishment, I purposely installed many problem fonts, multiple times. Font Book often blithely installed fonts that were reported as corrupted before or afterward with the Validate File or Validate Font command.

So, don't trust the automatic on-installation validation process; use a specific Validate command before or after installing any font of dubious provenance. And, okay, if you can't trust Font Book entirely on the validation issue, you can't really trust it at all. If you install a font (or two, or a hundred) and immediately start having problems, a corrupted font should be at the top of your suspect list even if Font Book says they're all healthy.

Bad-Font Detection

Here are two things you won't see very often: a heavy-duty font problem dialog and Font Book displaying the LastResort font.

I had set up a user library of all

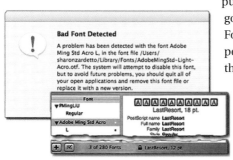

the Adobe application fonts, with no problem until I opened Font Book weeks later and got the Bad Font Detected dialog shown here for one of the Adobe fonts. I was puzzled: is font checking going on when you open Font Book? A little experimentation showed that as Font Book hit this font during its opening "roll call," it couldn't prepare the preview area sample, and that's when it

realized there was a problem. And that's what led to the LastResort font showing up.

Note that Font Book, with Adobe Ming Standard Acro selected in the Font list, is identifying LastResort as the current font (at the bottom of the window) and displaying it in the preview area. Ming was so corrupted it couldn't be used, so LastResort jumped in. See *Is It a Unicode Font?* (page 20) for an explanation for those framed A's along the top of the preview area.

Control Your Classic Fonts

There are only two reasons to install a font in the Classic Fonts folder (`/System Folder/Fonts`): you want to use it in a Classic application, or want it available in both the Classic and Mac OS X environments. Because this folder is somewhat of a "lowest common denominator," early Mac OS X users were often advised to use it when in doubt about where to put their fonts. But don't do it unless you actually work in the Classic environment, and the font is one that works there.

The two types of fonts you can install into Classic are Mac TrueType suitcases and PostScript Type 1's. Since Classic, in its heart, is OS 9, it can't use Windows TrueType, OpenType, or dfont fonts, so there's no reason to put them there, even though Mac OS X applications can still access them.

Third-Party Solution: Use your dfonts in Classic. Do you just love Baskerville or Herculanum, or other system-supplied dfonts, and want to use them in your Classic environment, too? There's not much difference between TrueType and a dfont, and the freeware dfontifier can change your dfont into TrueTypes, and vice versa (`http://homepage.mac.com/mdouma46/dfont/dfont.html`).

(Are you still trudging along in the Classic environment because you couldn't upgrade some program you love or QuarkXPress? Prepare to move on! How long do you think Apple is going to continue supporting the past? The new Intel-based Macs emulate the PowerPC environment, but they don't emulate the Classic OS environment, too.)

Installing a TrueType suitcase or PostScript Type 1 font into the Classic folder is almost identical to the operations for those fonts going into other libraries:

1. Quit all the applications running under Classic, or stop the Classic environment itself.

   You can stop Classic through the Classic preference pane in System Preferences, or with a command in the Classic menu if you've put it in your menu bar. (It's easier to navigate in and out of Classic if you install its menu in your menu bar, as described in *Easy-Access Classic,* just ahead.)

Use Font Book or restart Classic: *Note that stopping and restarting the Classic environment is optional when you install a font through Font Book; if you drag a font directly into /System Folder/Fonts, however, you may have to restart Classic to get it to recognize the font.*

2. Quit the Mac OS X applications that can't update their menus on the fly.

3. If you're going to install fonts by double-clicking their icons, in Font Book, set the install location to Classic Mac OS in Font Book's preferences window (choose Font Book > Preferences).

4. Install the fonts with any of the usual methods: double-clicking from the Desktop, adding from within Font Book, or dragging to the Classic library in the Collection list.

Once the fonts are installed, you can relaunch your Classic applications, or the Classic environment if you turned it off.

While a Classic restart is optional when you're installing a font, when it comes to removing a Classic font (either through Font Book or by dragging it out of the folder) you must *restart the Classic environment* before working in a Classic application. Otherwise, the removed font will still show up in Classic font menus—and you can imagine the mess you'll have on your hands at that point. (Some Classic fonts can't be removed without risking disaster in the Classic environment; see *The Classic Fonts Folder,* page 94.)

Classic fonts can't be disabled: *Disabling Classic fonts in Font Book has no effect on them in the Classic environment, but does prevent them from appearing in Tiger applications.*

Tip: Smooth PostScript fonts in classic. TrueType fonts in Classic applications are smoothly rendered by the operating system, but the bitmaps that serve as screen fonts for PostScript Type 1's appear in all their jagged glory unless you use ATM Light 4.6.2 or later, available at www.adobe.com/products/atmlight/.

Easy-Access Classic

Moving back and forth between the Classic and Mac OS X environments—and turning Classic on and off for font installation—is a lot easier if you keep a Classic menu in your menu bar; as a bonus, its icon indicates whether or not Classic is running. All you have to do is check the Show Classic Status In Menu Bar button in the Classic preference pane.

The menu bar icon tells you at a glance whether Classic is running (the half-darkened rectangle behind the 9, at the top of the menu in this picture) or not (the blank rectangle behind the 9, inset). As a bonus, you can jump directly to an application by using the Recent Items submenu in Apple Menu Items.

Tip: Jump-start Classic-folder fonts. Sometimes fonts installed in the Classic folder won't show up in Tiger menus until you give the system a little poke in the Start/Stop tab of the Classic preference pane: just click on System Folder under your drive's name.

If that doesn't do the trick, then start up the Classic environment (the Start button is in the same pane); you don't have to keep it running—you can quit it right away.

Print Font Samples

Mac OS X provides some built-in AppleScripts that let you do a few tricks with Font Book. The most useful is a routine that creates a list of font samples.

You can access Tiger-provided AppleScript routines in two ways:

♦ **From the menu bar:** If you haven't already, you can add the handy Script menu to the menu bar:

1. Double-click the AppleScript Utility program in /Applications/ AppleScript to open it.

2. Check both Show Script Menu In Menu Bar and Show Library Scripts.

    The little black AppleScript icon appears near the right of your menu bar, listing all the built-in scripts.

3. Close the utility window.

◆   **From the Finder:** Open the folder Library/Scripts, which is also accessible through its alias, /Applications/AppleScript/Example Scripts.

Menu/icon equivalents: A Script menu choice and its subchoice, like Finder Scripts > Add to File Names, is the equivalent of opening the folder Finder Scripts and double-clicking on the icon Add to File Names. If you are just experimenting with scripts, double-click on them from the Scripts folder; if you decide to use them on a regular basis, add the Script menu to your menu bar. Directions in this book assume you have the Script menu turned on.

To print font samples:

1. Open Font Book and select some fonts in the Font list.

    Samples are created for *selected* fonts, so start with a few to see what they look like before you print samples for all the fonts. (When you want to print all the fonts, click All Fonts in the Collection list, tab to the Font list, and choose Edit > Select All).

2. From the AppleScript menu, choose Font Book > Create Font Sample.

    An untitled document opens in TextEdit; you may wish to save and name it, as I've done in **Figure 22**.

3. Choose File >Print, to print the document.

Figure 22

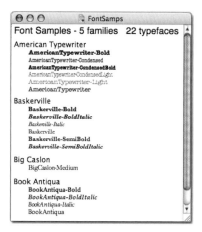

The script creates a TextEdit document with samples of each typeface you've selected. It doesn't differentiate between active and disabled fonts; if you have duplicates, it samples each duplicate face. You can select specific faces within a duplicated font family to limit the samples, but it's easier to let the script do its thing and then edit the document.

Third-Party Solutions: Printed font samples. Better font-sample printing solutions are available than the limited one you can get through AppleScript:

♦ **eBookfaces:** This freeware utility prints a traditional full-page sampling of a font (a single typeface per page) with different sizes (www.corpus-callosum.com/software.html).

♦ **Font Parade**: Download this free utility if you want a printout with a single line of sample text (The quick brown fox…) for each font; you can print subsets keyed to your Font Book collections (www.brightpebbles.org/fontparade/).

---

5 Remove Fonts You Don't Want

In this chapter, I discuss the two pressing issues of font removal. The first is how to remove fonts; working with the System Fonts folder takes some special trickery. The second is which fonts to remove (and, perhaps more importantly, which ones *not* to remove!).

And, in case you dragged fonts out of your Fonts folder but don't remember where you put them—but they're still *someplace* on your drive—this chapter also explains how to use Finder's Spotlight to track them down.

Use Font Book to Remove Fonts

To remove a font, select it in Font Book's Font list, and press Delete or choose File > Remove *FontName*. The font file is (usually) moved to the Trash, so if you don't want it erased the next time you empty the Trash, you have to drag it out and store it someplace. This isn't so draconian when you consider that a *copy* of the font file was placed in the target folder during installation, with the original left in place; so, you should already have a copy of any of your user-installed fonts. For system-installed fonts, you have to be more careful because there's no easy way to get fresh copies (see *Restore or Add Tiger Fonts*, page 235, for help with that).

I said the font file is "usually" moved to the Trash, because there are exceptions:

♦ A system font—one in /System/Library/Fonts—is removed only from Font Book's Font list; the font file is not removed from its folder.

♦ If you don't have administrative privileges, removing something from the Computer library in Font Book (regardless of whether the font's in /System/Library/Fonts or /Library/Fonts) removes it from the Font list, but the font file remains in its folder.

♦ A font from a user-defined library remains in its original location—which seems fair, since a copy of it was never placed in any Fonts folder in the first place. (See *Create a Library for Temporary Fonts,* page 124.)

Even when a deleted "font" is sent to Trash, which font files are deleted—and the effect on some of your other installed fonts—depends on what you've selected in the Font list and what kind of file(s) are related to the selection:

♦ **PostScript Type 1 fonts:** Removing a PostScript font moves all its printer files and the bitmapped suitcase to the Trash.

♦ **Suitcases:** If you remove a font that's in a suitcase (a TrueType font or a bitmapped font companion for a Type 1), all fonts in that suitcase are also removed—one of the gotchas of using suitcases with more than one family inside.

♦ **OpenType families:** Many OpenType fonts have separate files for each typeface; selecting the family name and deleting it puts all the related files in the Trash.

♦ **Individual typefaces:** You can use the Remove command on a selected typeface (instead of a family). If the typeface is a separate file, that's the only one removed; if all the faces are in the same file, the entire family is removed.

♦ **Duplicate fonts:** If you select the family name of a font with duplicates and remove it, *all the copies showing in the Font list* are removed. So, if All Fonts is the current library, every copy of a duplicated font is removed; if Computer is selected in the Collection list, copies in both

/System/Library/Fonts and /Library/Fonts are removed; if User is selected, only the copy in ~/Library/Fonts is deleted.

♦ **Collections:** Deleting a collection from the Collection list doesn't remove any fonts at all, since a collection is merely a convenient way of looking at a subset of installed fonts. (See Create and Edit Collections, page 117.)

♦ **Libraries:** Deleting a user-defined library from the Collection list removes the library and its list from Font Book, and removes the fonts in the library from use. The font files themselves, however, remain wherever you've been keeping them because they were never installed in a Fonts folder. (Learn more in *Create a Library for Temporary Fonts*, page 124.)

Font removal from Fonts folders: You can remove a font directly from its Fonts folder; its absence is reflected in Font Book's list almost immediately. But Font Book deletion is a better option because you can see whether you still have a copy of that font available in a different Fonts folder, and, in the case of PostScript fonts or OpenType families with separate typeface files, you won't have to select the multiple files yourself.

Remove or Replace System Fonts

If you've used Font Book to remove a system font, reinstalling it is tricky: although the font name disappears from Font Book's Font list, the font file remains in its folder—and how do you install a font where it already exists? (And where do you get it from?) In addition, Font Book doesn't provide any way of installing to /System/Library/Fonts anyway; items put in Font Book's Computer library go to only /Library/Fonts.

Warning! Do not remove these system fonts—some of which don't even appear in Font Book:

♦ *Keyboard.dfont*   ♦ *Geneva.dfont*

♦ *LastResort.dfont*   ♦ *Monaco.dfont*

♦ *LucidaGrande.dfont*   ♦ *Helvetica.dfont*

The next section, Trim the Font Fat, *provides details about these, and other fonts that you can, but probably don't want to, remove; for a roundup, see* **Table** *11 (page 91).*

Here's how to get a "removed" system font back in play:

1. Close Font Book.

2. In the Finder, open /System/Library/Fonts.

3. Drag the font file in question *directly* to the Trash.

    If you drag it anywhere else, a copy appears in the target spot, and the original stays in place.

4. Type your administrative password in the dialog that appears.

    The font goes to the Trash.

5. Open the Trash, and drag the font back into the Fonts folder.

    This triggers a dialog saying you can't do it because the folder can't be modified, but don't worry about that because it can be.

6. Click the Authenticate button and type in your administrative password.

7. Open Font Book (or, if you skipped the first step, close it and then reopen it) and you'll see the font back in action.

Tip: Un-remove the remove warning! As you can imagine, during the course of writing this book I gave Font Book quite a workout, adding and removing many fonts many times. I got tired of the confirmation dialog "Are you sure you want to remove this font?" making every font removal a two-step process. So, I finally checked Do Not Ask Me Again in the dialog. It wasn't long before I selected a font and, as I hit Delete, realized I had mis-clicked and selected the wrong font in the list. But Delete was already pressed, and, with no confirm dialog popping up, it was too late.

And then came another one of those annoying little interface problems. The Do Not Ask Me Again checkbox is only in the confirm dialog; since the dialog doesn't show up after you turn it off, you can't uncheck the checkbox to turn the warning back on.

If you've already made the same mistake (or do so in the future despite this warning), the solution is to quit Font Book and delete ~/Library/

Preferences/com.apple.Fontbook.plist. Prior to Tiger 10.4.3 with its Font Book 2.0.2, this would also make Font Book forget about any disabled fonts, re-enabling every single one of them, but that's no longer an issue.

Trim the Excess Font Fat

General users don't need to strip their systems of extraneous fonts—to a general user the fonts won't be extraneous. Pros and font fanatics, however, need to keep unnecessary fonts to a minimum, both to avoid problems and because the sheer number of fonts can become overwhelming to manage.

A "necessary" font, however, is often in the eye of the beholder, so for a complete list of the fonts included in your Tiger and Microsoft Fonts folders, with recommendations as to which ones you might want to keep (or not) for various reasons, see Chapter 2.

While that chapter gives specific directions for cleaning up your Fonts folders, it doesn't provide much in the way of "why" details. This section describes why you need certain fonts (or not), and gives you the opportunity to lighten your font load if you didn't do the thorough cleanup described earlier. (Appendix C rounds up the fonts you should preserve.)

Removing vs. disabling: *When you don't want to use a font, and won't want to use it again in the foreseeable future, you remove it. When you want it hanging around for easy access or a recurring project but don't want it cluttering your Font menus in the meantime, you can* disable *it instead, as described in* Turn Off Fonts Temporarily *(page 101).*

The System Fonts Folder

Table 11 (page 91) lists 12 font files that you should leave in /System/Library/Fonts. The six core fonts should never, *never* be removed (although one can be replaced by a different version), on pain of dire consequences. Not plagues-of-Egypt dire, but close, if you're on a tight deadline. At best, you'll have menus and dialogs with garbled text; at worst, your Mac might not start up at all and require a system reinstall. As for the other three fonts, one's "essentialness" is somewhat anecdotal, and the Preview application uses two. ***Don't disable the fonts in the table***, either, since that often causes the same problems as removing them.

Some of the fonts listed in the Table don't even appear in menus or in Font Book; others are difficult to remove through Font Book, which prevents you from accidentally removing them. But when you're serious about streamlining your font list, you may be working directly with folders in the Finder, so the Font Book safeguards won't apply. Watch your step!

In addition to the absolute necessities, you should keep these fonts because they are common on the Web and in cross-platform documents:

- ◆ Courier
- ◆ Times
- ◆ Symbol
- ◆ Zapf Dingbats

All the System fonts: *Table 2 (page 26) lists all the fonts that Tiger installs in your System Fonts folder, along with advice regarding which ones you might want to keep even though they aren't required.*

The Source of Misinformation

I've encountered a lot of misunderstanding among even reasonably knowledgeable users as to what can be safely removed or disabled, despite the fact that the list of necessary fonts is short and straightforward. One reason for the confusion is that the Mac OS X font capabilities and needs are continually evolving; the other is that, lacking reasonable documentation, users have turned to Apple's Tech Docs and misread some of their information.

One document "recommends" that certain foreign language fonts stay in /System/Library/Fonts; it goes on to list "required Japanese fonts," and so on. A more careful reading reveals that they're needed for international versions of the operating system and you should keep them because "you never know who might use your system or how it might be used in the future." Are you worried about that?

The more insidious problem comes from the lists of Mac OS X fonts with headings such as *Essential System Software; Installed: Always (cannot be disabled)* for /System/Library/Fonts. The heading actually refers to the installer process, wherein the fonts are included as part of the essential system software that's always installed, and it's a part of the installer package that can't be disabled. None of the terms applies to the *fonts* in the list!

Table 11: Do Not Remove or Disable These System Fonts	
Core fonts: Do not remove under any circumstances	
Keyboard.dfont* LastResort.dfont*	Keyboard holds many characters necessary for menus and dialogs (such as the symbols for Shift and Option). The cleverly named LastResort is a fallback font for when a needed Unicode character isn't included in any of your available fonts.
Monaco.dfont Geneva.dfont	Removing either of these fonts through Font Book triggers the "This is a system font… are you sure…" dialog, but you're allowed to remove it—at least ostensibly, because while it disappears from the Font list, it remains in the Fonts folder.†
LucidaGrande.dfont	This should be named LucidaMuchoGrande, because it contains so many different *scripts*—alphabets for different languages. It's used if a character isn't in the current font. If you try to remove it with Font Book, you're ignored; Lucida Grande remains in the Font list.
Core font: Do not remove unless you immediately replace it with another version	
Helvetica.dfont	Font Book treats this the same as Geneva and Monaco: try to remove it and it disappears from the Font list but not the Fonts folder.† You can remove this Helvetica as long as another version of Helvetica is available to your system.
Core font? Maybe, maybe not—but leave it alone	
AquaKanaRegular.otf AquaKanaBold.otf*	AquaKana is not on Apple's list of "do not remove" fonts. However, anecdotal evidence indicates that this font is needed even if you're not using any foreign language system. It doesn't appear in font menus; why would it be hidden unless you're supposed to leave it alone?
Fonts for Preview	
Helvetica LT MM/ HelveLTMM* Times LT MM/ TimesLTMM*	The operating system doesn't need these, but Preview does; new in Tiger, Preview uses them to render approximations of missing fonts in PDF files. You needn't worry about their conflicting with other versions of Helvetica or Times, since they're not included in the font-use hierarchy.
* These fonts don't appear in Font Book or in font menus. † Although these fonts remain in the Fonts folder after being removed from Font Book's list, the operating system can no longer access them.	

Hell-vetica and Other Publishing Favorites

Tiger supplies dfont versions of five stalwart standbys of the publishing business: Helvetica, Times, Courier, Symbol, and Zapf Dingbats. If you're a professional, you'll want to remove the dfont versions in `/System/Library/Fonts` to minimize the chance of their being substituted for your PostScript Type 1 (or, eventually, OpenType) versions. Put your replacements in `/Library/Fonts` or `~/Library/Fonts` to minimize the changes you make to `/System/Library/Fonts`.

Of these fonts, only Helvetica is essential to your operating system, but any old version will do, as long as it's in one of the system's Fonts folders. (The Classic folder doesn't count, nor does an application Fonts folder.) When you're replacing the system Helvetica, you have to replace it *right away*—think Indiana Jones swapping the bag of sand for the golden idol. In fact, put the new version in before you take the system version out; so many things go wrong when Helvetica is gone that it's difficult or impossible to get anything done.

The ubiquitous Helvetica stands out from this lineup in another way: it causes more problems than any single other font in computer history. Helvetica's troubled history is due to its very popularity, which resulted in dozens of versions being produced (*cheaper! better!*), which caused hundreds of font substitution problems *(reflow! reprint!)*, which led to thousands of headaches *(oy! ow!)*. But, come on, stop relying on Helvetica (yes, I'm talking to you font professionals): it's 50 years old, it's *tired*.

This is the Font Book Info view with and without Helvetica available.

The Library Fonts Folder

The Library Fonts folder (`/Library/Fonts`) is where Tiger puts nonessential fonts; so, by their very definition, all the fonts can be removed. But that doesn't mean you should get rid of them all:

♦ **Keep common Web fonts:** These fonts are ubiquitous on the Web because they're cross-platform and, with the exception of Times New Roman, easy to read on the screen:

- ♦ Comic Sans
- ♦ Times New Roman
- ♦ Georgia
- ♦ Verdana
- ♦ Trebuchet MS

You need either the Tiger-supplied or the Microsoft-supplied version someplace to keep your surfing smooth. Even if you're a font professional who's fanatic about getting rid of non-essentials to avoid conflicts, there shouldn't be any problem with these: you're not likely to be working with an OpenType or Type 1 version of any of these fonts for some professional job. (In addition, Office applications require Verdana for the definitions in its Reference Tools.)

When the Tiger versions are better: *Note that for viewing Arabic-language Web sites in Safari, you need the Tiger versions of Times New Roman (and Arial), even though the Microsoft versions offer more characters. You can keep both versions and enable or disable them as necessary.*

♦ **Keep common cross-platform fonts:** Arial and Arial Black may be overused, but you'll probably need them if you exchange documents with PC users.

♦ **Watch for application-installed fonts:** Applications sometimes install fonts into this folder; they're still typically expendable but you should check the application's documentation.

♦ **Mind your manners:** If you're on a multi-user Mac, keep in mind that this is the folder all users share; be polite and politic about removing these fonts.

The Library fonts: *Table 4 (page 39) provides a complete list of the fonts Tiger installs in the Library Fonts folder, along with more detailed advice to help you decide which ones you might want to keep, while Table 5 (page 40) lists the fonts that go into* /Library/Fonts *if you choose "Additional Fonts" when you install Tiger.*

The User Fonts Folder

The OS doesn't put any files in ~/Library/Fonts; the bulk of User fonts comes from Microsoft Office. While you can remove all of them because they're not essential to Office operations, that's not necessarily the wisest approach; the Microsoft versions of Tiger-supplied fonts are better in most cases. This is explained in *Microsoft Fonts* (page 108), and rounded up in Table 13 (page 109).

The other fonts in this folder are, presumably, the ones you put there, so they can be removed, too, assuming that you have copies someplace, should you ever wish to put them back.

The User fonts: In Organize the User Fonts folder *(page 27), I explain how to juggle the Tiger-supplied and Microsoft-supplied versions of certain fonts so you're left with the best versions in the right places.* Table 3 *(page 33) lists the Microsoft fonts and suggests which ones you should consider keeping.*

The Classic Fonts Folder

If you have Classic installed on your Mac, these fonts must stay in /System Folder/Fonts:

- ◆ Charcoal
- ◆ Geneva
- ◆ Chicago
- ◆ Monaco

Without these fonts, Classic applications, and the Classic environment itself, won't run properly. Font Book doesn't consider them system fonts, however, so you won't get any warning when you try to remove them.

Double fonts: You'll wind up with two versions each of Monaco and Geneva if you run Classic: TrueTypes in the Classic Fonts folder, and the dfont versions in the System Fonts folder.

Some argue that you need only Charcoal, despite Apple's admonitions about retaining these fonts; and that, furthermore, if you also remove Charcoal, the Classic environment will access a version that's buried in the Mac OS 9 System file. I say: What's the big deal? Are you planning an award-winning graphic design piece, or even a letter to your mother, using any of these four fonts? Leave them alone. You can disable the entire Classic Mac OS group in Font Book, anyway, because it won't affect how the fonts behave in Classic applications.

The Adobe Fonts Folders

How you handle the wealth of fonts supplied with Adobe applications depends on your general font usage. You may want to add to or delete from the Adobe Fonts folder, or even share the fonts with your other applications, as explained in the sidebar Create an Adobe Fonts Library (page 127). However, the issue at hand is which fonts you can dump. If you have Creative Suite, you have two main Adobe "private" folders, one of which has an important subfolder, while installing only Adobe Acrobat creates a single Fonts folder:

♦ `/Library/Application Support/Adobe/Fonts` holds most of the fonts that come with Creative Suite; you can remove any or all of them. But ***don't remove the folder*** because it has to hold the all-important subfolder described next.

♦ `/Library/Application Support/Adobe/Fonts/Rqrd/Base/` is a subfolder in the Adobe folder I just described. "Rqrd" means *required* and the fonts inside really are: some of the CS applications won't even run if these fonts are unavailable. The crossover in fonts between this and the main Adobe fonts folder—Courier, Minion, and Myriad—is surface only, because one set is PostScript Type 1 and the other OpenType. *Leave them alone.*

♦ `/Library/Application Support/Adobe/PDFL/7.0/Fonts` (or 5.0 or 6.0) comes along with Acrobat Professional (which is also part of the Creative Suite). There's lots of crossover between this folder and the Rqrd folder, but since different, specific applications access them, there's no problem with duplication. Leave them all alone if you value your Acrobat PDFs.

Outdated Adobe folders: *If you have a* `/Library/Application Support/Adobe/PDFL/7.0/Fonts` *in use, you might also have an outdated* `6.0` *and perhaps even a* `5.0` *version that can be trashed.*

The Microsoft Fonts Folder

The Microsoft folder `/Applications/Microsoft Office 2004/Office/Fonts` is somewhat of a red herring, because although it looks like an application Fonts folder, it's not: all its fonts are merely copied into a User Fonts folder the first time an Office application runs.

While you don't need this folder or its fonts, you should leave it in place, in case you set up a new user account as a troubleshooting procedure or need to reinstall the fonts for any other reason—for instance, if you deleted some of them in favor of the Tiger versions and realize the error of your ways after reviewing **Table** 13 (page 109).

Outdated Microsoft Office fonts: *When you install a new version of Microsoft Office, it makes a special folder to store the fonts that came with the previous version. Look for* `~/Library/Application Support/Microsoft/Old Fonts` *and get rid of the whole folder; even if you keep and run the previous Office version occasionally, it won't need those fonts.*

Dumping Duplicates

I describe how to handle the duplication in commonly installed fonts (those that come with Tiger, Microsoft Office, and iLife and iWork) in Chapter 2.

When it comes to fonts you've installed from other sources, the issues involved in deciding which version(s) of a duplicate font to remove are the same as those when considering which ones to disable; I cover these in *All Duplicates Are Not Created Equal* (page 105).

Keep in mind, however, that *disabling* a duplicate means it's still around if you change your mind (or your needs), which is not the case for fonts you've deleted.

Find Misplaced Fonts

Have you noticed that the Finder's Spotlight isn't entirely reliable, especially when it comes to searching for fonts? It occasionally seems to peek inside suitcase files, while other times it doesn't even list a font whose filename is the search criterion and you're *looking right at it in an open window!* But Spotlight's performance on font hunts is superb when you know how to focus the search, and you can choose to look just in suitcases, or for any type of font whose name you vaguely recall.

Say you want to install a PostScript Type 1 font and you have a handful of printer files that you know go together because of their similar names: *LaudaBld, LaudaBldItl, LaudaItl, LaudaNor.* You might not remember that the font is actually *Laudatio*, but at least you know it begins with *Lauda*. The real problem is that you can't find a suitcase, in your vast but messy font collection from previous Mac systems, that has a name anything like *LaudaWhatever*. You know, however, that it's in some multi-family suitcase because you often combined different bitmapped fonts in a single suitcase. Do you have to open a bunch of suitcases and check their contents until you find your font in the haystack? Not at all:

1. Start your search:

   ♦ If you have an idea of where the target suitcase is, start in that folder's window. Use Command-F to go into Find mode and select the folder's name in the window's header.

   ♦ Otherwise, use any open Finder window, or open a new one (Command-N) and use Command-F to go into Find mode. In the window's header, set the search scope to Home, Computer, or another volume as needed.

2. In the top row of pop-up menus (you won't be needing the second row, so you can ignore it or click the ⊖ button at its far right):

   a. From the first pop-up menu, choose Kind.

   b. From the second pop-up menu, choose Others.

   c. In the field that appears, start typing Font Suitcase.

      This creates a pop-up list with hundreds (literally) of choices. The menu's reaction can be excruciatingly slow, but when it's ready, you can either (finally) finish typing the phrase or select it from the pop-up list.

3. Type the name of the font you're looking for in the *Search for* field.

   Spotlight starts the search as soon as you start typing, but this is less likely to tie you up as when you do a more general Spotlight search.

And… bingo! You'll find the suitcase(s) holding your fonts, no matter what their names. **Figure 23** shows the result of a search like this.

Figure 23

This Spotlight search found the Laudatio font inside a suitcase named SynFliers. The path to the suitcase is at the bottom of the window; for this picture, I clicked the Info button (under the pointer at the right) to open the Info for the suitcase that was found. (The More Info button merely opens the standard Get Info window for the file.)

You might benefit from doing a slightly wider-ranging font search, one that doesn't grab only suitcases but is still limited to fonts. The following method rounds up all the related files in a font family because it looks inside all font files, not just suitcases, for the font name you provide. (Various font names—the PostScript name, the full name, and the family name, for instance—are all embedded in font files.)

1. Use Command-F in any Finder window to go into Find mode, and set the appropriate place for the search.

2. In the top row of pop-up menus:

   a. Choose Other from the first pop-up menu.

   b. Select Fonts from the list that appears and click OK.

   c. Set the second pop-up menu appropriately for what you think you know about the font's name: Contains, Begins With, Is.

   The default Contains may bring up things you don't want, but it's also more likely to include your elusive font.

   d. Type the name of the font you're looking for (or as much of it as you can remember). Don't type the name in the general Search For box—stay in the row with the pop-up menus, as shown in **Figure 24**.

Figure 24

This search for Laudatio *finds all the printer files, as well as the suitcase, because the full font name is embedded in each PostScript file.*

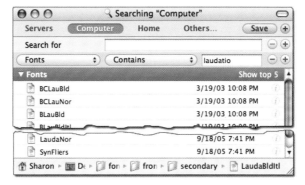

The result of this search is a list of any kind of font file (suitcase, printer file, OpenType, and so on) with your font's name in it.

Finally, one of my favorite font-management tricks: a sort of never-ending search procedure. It lets you track every font file on your hard drive, installed or not, so you can see what you have "stored," what you have multiples of, and so on. It provides an easily accessible list that's immediately updated anytime you add or remove a font from anywhere on the drive, and it shows where the font resides.

While you can't have a single list of all your fonts, you can have separate "live" lists for each type of font using smart folders:

1. On the Desktop, choose File > New Smart Folder (Command-Option-N).

   A new Finder window opens, already in Find mode. (If you perform a search in a standard Finder window without using the New Smart Folder command first, you can turn the search results into a smart folder by choosing File > Add to Sidebar when the search is complete.)

2. In the window header, click on Computer to set the scope of the search.

3. In the top row:

   a. Leave the first pop-up menu set at the default Kind.

   b. From the second pop-up menu, choose Others.

   c. In the field that appears, start typing Postscript Type 1 outline font.

   After you've typed a few letters, you'll see a pop-up list (there's often a delay while the list is compiled) with all the "kinds" listed.

    d. From the list, select *PostScript Type 1 outline font* instead of finishing the typing.

    Your PostScript printer files will be listed in the window within seconds.

4. Click the Save button at the top right of the window (**Figure 25**).

    If asked to confirm the save (which seems a waste of a dialog), do so.

5. Name the folder (maybe PostScript fonts for this one); set the location to Saved Searches and check Add To Sidebar. (You can, of course, access it in a variety of ways, but adding it to the sidebar makes it available for quick, frequent access.)

Your smart folders are always updated with the latest information from your hard drive.

To make folders for other types of fonts, create smart folders with Kind set to: OpenType font; Datafork TrueType font (for dfonts); Windows TrueType font; or Font suitcase. The last finds *all* suitcases—unfortunately, there's no differentiation between TrueType suitcases and the bitmaps that accompany PostScript Type 1's.

Figure 25

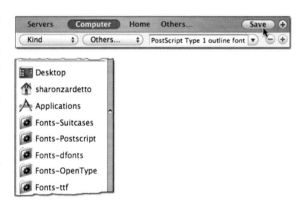

Save smart folder searches (top) to create "hot" lists of your fonts. If you like, add the resulting smart folders (the icons with the gear in the middle) to the sidebar to make them accessible from any Finder window (bottom).

6 Disable Fonts and Deal with Duplicates

You don't have to remove a font when you just want it out of commission temporarily (until, say, you have to do your monthly newsletter again): you can simply *disable* it through Font Book.

Disabling is one way to handle the duplicate fonts that find their way into your system, but it's not the only way. You can, for instance, let Tiger take care of handling the duplicates through its access-order hierarchy, or remove certain duplicates completely—as long as you know what *really* constitutes a duplicate, and know which duplicates to keep.

Turn Off Fonts Temporarily

Disabling a font makes it unavailable to applications without your removing it from a Fonts folder, letting you easily activate it again if you want to use it. (If you're *never* going to use it again, you can remove it.)

There are three reasons for disabling fonts:

◆ To shorten your Font menus by turning off fonts you don't use all the time.

♦ To force the operating system to use a specific version of a duplicate font so you can get at its special features or coordinate with another computer that will be using your document.

♦ On multi-user Macs, to "get rid of" fonts you don't use without actually removing them from a shared Fonts folder, so other users can still access them. (Fonts are disabled on a per-user basis.)

Warning! *Do not* disable *any font that can't be* removed *because the operating system uses it—disabling a font means the system can't access it. (See* The System Fonts Folder, *page 89.)*

Tip: Offload instead of disable. If you keep hundreds of fonts disabled at a time because your font collection is so vast, and you keep them disabled for long intervals, you're better off removing those fonts and putting them back in when you need them. The more fonts you have, the longer Font Book takes to open. More importantly, disabled fonts eat up memory. Off-loading isn't as time-consuming as it sounds, since you can keep your fonts in subfolders that can be dragged in and out of your Fonts folders. (Or, you might find that libraries, described in the next chapter, serve your situation well.)

Note: Disabled fonts still work in Classic applications. If you need a bunch of fonts for your Classic environment that you don't use elsewhere (maybe you're still stuck with a non-Mac OS X version of QuarkXPress), you can keep them from appearing in Tiger applications by disabling either individual fonts or the entire Classic Mac OS library.

The fonts are still available to Classic applications, because as far as Classic is concerned, Font Book exists only in the future.

Disable a Font Family

Say you installed an Adobe application and then decided you wanted to use some of its fonts in your other programs. Entranced by the possibilities of 32 typefaces in Warnock Pro, you copied its files into your

User Fonts folder; you were quickly disenchanted when you found that the Font menu in Word lists every single one of the faces separately. You want to temporarily turn off Warnock Pro so it clutters the menu only when you're using it:

1. Quit Word if it's open.

   Disabling or enabling fonts is analogous to removing or installing them, and many applications, like Word, choke if you change the font lineup while they're open.

2. In Font Book, select All Fonts or Users in the Collection list.

3. Select Warnock Pro in the Font list.

4. Click ☑ or choose Edit > Disable "Warnock Pro."

   When you disable a selected font family, it also disables all the type-faces *currently included in the list.*

Warnock Pro is now disabled, as shown in **Figure 26**.

Figure 26

After disabling, Warnock Pro is dimmed and marked with Off, and the button beneath the Font list changes to an Enable button. (In a ridiculous piece of design, when the button has a checkmark it's Disable; when it's a blank square, it's Enable. Wouldn't you think the checkmark means the font is going to be turned on?)

Target More or Less than a Family

You can disable or enable any font selection: a family, multiple families, a collection or library, or even an individual typeface (even if all the faces are in a single file).

Let's go back to the borrowed-from-Adobe-folder Warnock Pro situation. You've decided you want keep one of its variants—*Caption*—in your menus but turn off the others (Regular, Display, and Subhead) except for special projects.

Because there are so many typefaces, it's easier to turn them all off and then turn the Caption faces back on. So, you turn them all off as described previously, and then notice that the Caption typefaces, scattered throughout the typeface list, would require quite a bit of careful Command-clicking to select individually. Instead, you can use the Font Book search function to select them:

1. In Font Book, select All Fonts or the library that contains the Warnock fonts.

2. In the Search field at the upper right, type Warnock Caption.

   The Font list shows the Warnock Pro family name with only its Caption typefaces listed beneath it (**Figure 27**).

Figure 27

Searching for "Warnock Caption" finds all the variants of the font's Caption typefaces. Using the Enable button while the family name is selected activates only the listed typefaces.

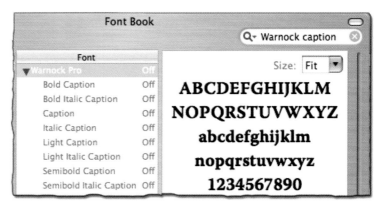

3. With the family name Warnock Pro selected, click the (Enable) button or use Edit > Enable "Warnock Pro."

   This reactivates all the typefaces *currently listed* under Warnock Pro—all the Caption variants.

You can disable an entire library or collection by selecting it in the Collection list and choosing Edit > Disable *CollectionName*. (Would it have killed Apple to put in another disable button, under the Collection list?) There are special considerations when disabling collections or libraries, described in *Disabled Collections vs. Disabled Contents* (page 121).

On the other end of the spectrum, you can disable an individual typeface, which then disappears from service. In InDesign, it won't show up in the font's submenu; in Word, applying, say, bold to a font whose bold face is disabled produces Word's faux bold instead of the real one. (See *Watch Out for Faux Styles*, page 146.)

Note: When fonts are un-disabled. If you open Font Book and find that all your disabled fonts have become enabled, it's not necessarily a problem with Font Book: it could be a feature. Three standard, general troubleshooting routines result in all fonts being enabled again:

- Starting up in Safe Mode

- Performing a Safe Login

- Cleaning up system-level caches

Each of these procedures (detailed in Chapter 13) either puts your user account's font caches in the Trash or erases them entirely. As a result, Font Book no longer knows which fonts were disabled, and on the startup after the procedure, everything's enabled. (Prior to Tiger 10.4.3, deleting Font Book's plist, a troubleshooting technique you might perform relatively frequently, also re-enabled all disabled fonts; that's no longer the case, though you may not have noticed the change!)

You can minimize the effort of re-enabling your fonts if you follow the advice in the tip *Overcome Erroneous Disabling* (page 120).

All Duplicates Are Not Created Equal

Duplicate fonts are not the bugaboo they were prior to Mac OS X, causing constant freezes and crashes. On the other hand, their current, generally peaceful, coexistence requires a new set of user skills and knowledge.

Theoretically, the existence of duplicate fonts should make no difference: the OS just grabs the first one in the access order and ignores the rest. And, of course, you may wonder why it matters at all which copy of a duplicate is being used: aren't they, after all... *duplicates?*

Font Book and the operating system define *duplicate fonts* as those sharing a name—which has nothing to do with the filename, but refers to the real name stored internally in the font file. This less-than-rigorous definition is the crux of many problems. Ostensible duplicates can be:

♦ **Different types:** OpenType, PostScript Type 1, Mac TrueType, Windows TrueType, dfont—it may not make any difference to you on your system, but if you're sharing fonts or documents, you may have to match the destination's font-handling capability. Windows TrueType and dfonts don't work on pre-Mac OS X Macs; PCs can't use Mac TrueTypes; a print shop might be using only PostScript fonts.

♦ **Different versions:** Older versions may not be Unicode-compliant; newer versions may offer more characters. One version—not necessarily the newer one—might have more typefaces than another. And, once again, matching the version of a font on the destination computer could be an overriding concern.

*The Tiger-Microsoft duplicates: The overlap of fonts from Tiger and Microsoft, detailed in **Table 13** (page 109), is for fonts of different versions, where one has more characters than the other. Replacing the Tiger versions with the Microsoft ones won't cause any compatibility problems, except for the one described in the note* When Tiger Versions are better *(page 93).*

♦ **Different designs:** Fonts with the same name but from different designers or foundries may be noticeably different in some ways, which can change the look of your document. Or the designs might be subtly different, especially in the font metrics that define the spacing between letters; these small differences can add up across a line of text so that a word gets bumped down to the next line, which changes the next line, and the next—your entire layout can implode.

Font Book's Info view provides all the information you need to differentiate duplicates for these three aspects—type, version, and designer/foundry. When you want to check if one version has more characters than another, use the Repertoire view and compare the character sets; the characters are always in the same order, so you can look at just the last part of the set.

And why can't you just get rid of your duplicates and have only one copy of each font? The reasons are built into the descriptions above, but all have to do with your Mac's connections to the outside world through font or document exchange: sometimes you need one of the duplicates, sometimes another. If your Mac is extremely isolated, then you *can* get rid of duplicates instead of shuffling them in and out of use as necessary—but make sure you keep the version that best meets your needs.

Table 12: Considerations in Disabling Duplicates	
Is the document going to be used on a non-OS X Mac?	The dfont format is for only Mac OS X machines; it will be substituted when opened on another platform.
Is the document going to be used cross-platform?	Keep the Microsoft-supplied version of a font active, since it's most likely to exist on the other platform
Do you need to match the font that will be used at a print shop? Are they insisting on PostScript Type 1 fonts?	You have to work with the same version (same foundry, same format, same version number) of the font that will be used for the print job.
Which copy of a duplicate font is the most recent version?	More recent fonts are more likely to be Unicode-compliant, and to have more characters. You can check the font's version number in Font Book's Info view, and look at its repertoire–its character set—in the preview pane.

Mac OS X Duplicates

If you've installed Classic on your Mac OS X machine, or have your Mac OS 9 fonts folder left from when you upgraded, you'll find some duplication between Classic and Tiger fonts:

◆ **Apple Chancery, Geneva, Trebuchet MS, and Skia:** The Tiger versions are dfonts and have later version numbers, but the designs and character sets for these fonts are the same.

◆ **Courier:** The Tiger version has nearly 300 more characters, chiefly accented letters.

◆ **Helvetica:** The Tiger version has over 600 more characters, including accented letters, Cyrillic and Greek letters, upper- and lowercase

Roman numerals, and full subscript and superscript sets. (I explain why built-in characters beat typed-in ones in *The Joy of Character-Rich Fonts,* page 154.)

♦ **Trebuchet MS and Verdana:** The Classic and Tiger fonts are the same, but the newer Microsoft versions outclass them, the subject of the next section.

 **Tip: How full is a font?** How can you tell if a font is chock full of characters? In Font Book it's easy to see the relative size of a font's character set. Use Preview > Repertoire to show a font's entire character set, and click on various fonts in the Font list. The size of the scroll box (well, it used to be an actual box, now it's a blue "lozenge," officially called a "scroller" by Apple) is keyed to the number of characters in the font.

In the screenshot here, the leftmost scroll bar, for Bodoni Ornaments, indicates a small character set, with almost all the characters already showing in the preview area; Arial Black, the center scroll bar, has a reasonably generous number of characters; the rightmost scroll bar, for Arial, promises a large character set.

Microsoft Fonts

Okay, let's be honest: many of us have a knee-jerk response to the very name *Microsoft.* The "other" operating system. The Evil Empire. Maker of… *idiosyncratic* but essential applications that we use because we must comply with company policy or coordinate with 90-some percent of the world's computers. So, we assume that the fonts Microsoft supplies are substandard in general, and specifically when the Mac OS also supplies a version. Well, you know what they say about *assume!* Because, in fact, the opposite is true.

Of the 12 fonts Microsoft Office 2004 and Tiger supply in common, 7 are different versions, and in every case the Microsoft version is later and better. (Some of the Microsoft Office X fonts were newer than the Tiger fonts, too, but in some cases have been updated in Office 2004, as noted in **Table 13**).

Does this really matter? Not all the time, but when it does, it could *really* matter. Maybe you typed the euro symbol, but the international monetary symbol showed up on the other end; or, an automatically substituted font for foreign characters worked fine on your end but comes up garbled or as boxes on the other machine.

Table 13: Fonts Common to Tiger and Microsoft Office 2004			
Font	**Tiger**	**Office**	**Difference**
Arial*	2.6	3.05[†]	More than six times as many characters, including: accented letters; Hebrew, Greek, Arabic, and Cyrillic letters; fractions for thirds and eighths; box pieces; mathematical symbols; dingbats, including card suits and musical notes.
Arial Black	2.35	2.35	
Andale Mono	2	2	
Arial Narrow	1.02	2.35	Three extra characters, including the euro symbol.[††]
Arial Rounded Bold	1	1.51	One extra character, the euro symbol.[††]
Brush Script	1	1.52	One extra character, the euro symbol.[††]
Comic Sans	2.1	2.1	
Georgia	2.05	2.05	
Impact	2.35	2.35	
Times New Roman*	2.6	3.05[†]	The same as Arial differences, above.
Trebuchet MS	1.15	1.26[†]	Approximately 250 more characters, including: accented letters, Greek and Cyrillic letters, fractions for eighths.
Verdana	2.35	2.45[†]	Approximately 450 more characters, including: accented letters, Greek and Cyrillic letters, fractions for eighths, superscripts up to 8, symbols like checkboxes and bullets.

* Microsoft versions of these fonts interfere with the rendering of Arabic Web pages in Safari.

† Office X supplied different versions: Arial 2.9, Times New Roman 2.91, Trebuchet 1.15, Verdana 2.35

†† The addition of the euro symbol ensures Unicode compliance; it takes the place of an existing character (the international monetary symbol), shifting that to another spot in the character map.

Use Font Book to Handle Duplicates

You may think that if you have two fonts that are the same, they're both duplicates, but that's not Font Book's approach, which defines all *but one* copy of a font as a duplicate; the one in use is not considered a duplicate. In fact, the definition is even a little more specific, because it's only multiple *active* copies of a font that are considered duplicates; if all but one are disabled, Font Book doesn't flag any duplicates at all.

The font that's considered *not* the duplicate is the one that's highest in the access-order hierarchy, discussed in *The Font Access Order* (page 15) but worth a quick repeat here. The system looks for fonts in this order:

1. The current application's Fonts folder

2. User-defined libraries, in reverse creation order (most recent first)

3. `~/Library/Fonts` (User fonts)

4. `/Library/Fonts` (Library fonts)

5. `/Network/Library/Fonts` (Network fonts)

6. `/System/Library/Fonts` (System fonts)

7. `/System Folder/Fonts` (Classic fonts)

Subverting this access order is the main reason for disabling duplicate fonts, since their mere existence is not always reason enough to turn them off.

In Font Book, duplicate fonts are marked with a dot (**Figure 28**), so it's the unmarked fonts and typefaces that are currently in use, or *active*. Don't forget that fonts in an application's Fonts folder don't show up in Font Book, so it won't indicate any duplicates you have in, say, your Adobe Fonts folder.

Figure 28

Duplicate fonts are marked with a dot in the Font list.

If the family is collapsed, the family name is marked (top); when you expand the list, the typefaces belonging to the duplicate font files are individually marked (bottom).

Disable Duplicates

When you want to use a specific duplicate font, you have to disable the copies higher in the font-access hierarchy; in practical terms, that means you disable all copies except the one you want to use. Unfortunately, because Font Book lets you disable individual typefaces, it also *requires* that you disable them individually—if you choose the Disable command while the family name is selected, *every* copy of every typeface is disabled. So, you have to select typefaces individually when you're disabling or enabling them. **Figure 29** shows an example of forcing a lower-order font into use by disabling the current one.

Figure 29

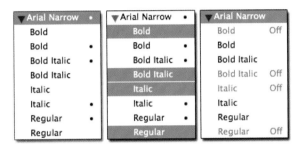

Left: Two copies of Arial Narrow are available; the faces without dots are the ones in use.

Center: Command-click the active typefaces to select them all at once.

Right: After using the Disable command, the faces previously in use are no longer available, and the ones that remain are "promoted" because they're the only ones available. (Note that once the copies have been disabled, the duplicate dot goes away.)

Tip: Typeface quick select. Here's a clever (if I do say so myself) way to select all the typefaces from a specific font copy without having to hunt and peck, and then check the Info view for each one's location.

Say you have two copies of Arial, one each in /Library/Fonts and ~/Library/Fonts, and you want to select the typefaces from the User folder:

1. Select User in the Collection list.

    Only one of the Arials shows in the Font list.

2. Expand the list of Arial typefaces in the Font list and select them all by clicking the first and Shift-clicking the last.

3. Select All Fonts in the Collection list.

Now the Font list shows Arial expanded, whether or not it was previously, and the typefaces belonging to the font file in the User Fonts folder are selected. The Collection list is still active, so if you want to use a Disable or Resolve Duplicates command on the selected typefaces, you have to press Tab to activate the Font list. *Don't click in the Font list,* or you'll lose the typeface selections.

Don't Trust the Duplicate List Orders

Figure 30 shows my triple Arial listing in Font Book, since there's a copy in three of my Fonts folders: Library, Classic, and User. Forget for the moment whether they're all the same type of font, or the same version. Just note that in each of the four typeface groupings (divided by the red lines in the figure), different ones are marked as duplicates: in the first two groups, the last typefaces are the active ones; in the third group, the first typeface is active; in the last group, it's the middle one that's still active.

Figure 30

The Arial faces marked with the arrows are all in User Fonts, even though they are in different spots in each grouping.

Arrows: AppleGothic
U+21E2 GID 2321

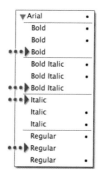

Does this mean that Font Book is picking and choosing which typefaces, from different folders, are the duplicates, in some Machiavellian scheme to make font management even more arcane? No, it's even worse than that: Font Book *does not list the typefaces in the same order!* In each group, the unmarked face is the one in my User Fonts folder, the one with the highest "use this" priority—there's just no logic to the list order.

If you don't stay aware of this interface glitch (yet another in Font Book's long list), you could be burned when you disable or remove fonts. If you check the file location of the first item and assume the first in each group belongs to the same file or is in the same folder, you could disable or remove the wrong duplicate. (It's easier to work with this if you use the technique described on page 111.)

Use the Resolve Duplicates Command

Font Book provides a quick way to disable all the copies of a font that are *not* being used with its Resolve Duplicates command. (It doesn't seem this should be necessary, since they're not being used—as I just said!—but some applications, like Word, are sometimes a little sensitive to the issue of non-disabled duplicates.)

You can use the Resolve Duplicates command in three ways:

♦ **Resolve unused duplicates in a family:** To disable the copies not in use.

♦ **Resolve all duplicates in the Font list:** To disable all font copies not in use.

♦ **Resolve duplicates within a family:** To disable all copies except the one you want to use.

Resolve unused duplicates in a family

Resolving the duplicates in a font family disables the copies that are not in use:

1. Select All Fonts in the Collection list.

   The Resolve Duplicates command works only on the *fonts showing in the Font list,* so they all must be displayed for the command to work properly.

2. In the Font list, select the font's family name.

   You can leave the typeface list expanded or collapsed.

3. Choose Edit > Resolve Duplicates.

While the net effect of this operation is the same as disabling one set of typefaces, it's much easier because you don't have to select the faces individually in order to disable them (**Figure 31**).

Figure 31

Resolve duplicates in a family.

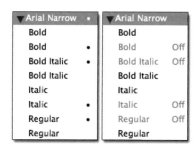

Left: The dotted faces are duplicates, so they're not in use.

Right: After using the Resolve Duplicates command with the family name selected, the duplicate fonts are disabled.

Resolve all duplicates in the Font list

You can resolve all your duplicates in one fell swoop, although the last font copy left standing is the one already uppermost in the font-access hierarchy and not necessarily the best version of a font:

1. Select All Fonts in the Collection list.

2. Tab to or click in the Font list and choose Edit > Select All.

3. Press the Left arrow key to collapse all the font families to just the family name.

    This step is **very important** if you don't want *all* your copies turned off. (That's *all the copies*—not just the duplicates!)

4. Choose Edit > Resolve Duplicates.

Warning! The Resolve Duplicates command disables all selected typefaces in an expanded font family. So, if you select all in the Font list and don't collapse the families, you'll be disabling every version of any font that has multiple copies, as if you had disabled them all.

Resolve duplicates within a family

Resolve Duplicates, when used normally, leaves the already-current copy of a font still in charge. But there's a special way to use it that changes which font is left in use; it's handy when you have more than two copies of a font installed. (When you have only two copies of a font, this procedure is no faster than using the Disable command to turn off one copy, as described earlier and shown in **Figure 32**.)

The key is to select the typefaces you want to *use*, rather than the ones you want to *disable*:

1. Select All Fonts in the Collection list to include all your duplicates in the list.

2. Select the target font in the Font list and expand it so you can see all the typefaces.

3. Select the typefaces belonging to the font version you want to use.

    Make sure you select typefaces from the same file. (You could use the procedure described in the recent tip *Typeface Quick Select,* page 111, to get to this point in the procedure.)

4. Choose Edit > Resolve Duplicates.

This disables all typefaces *except* the ones you've selected.

Figure 32

To change the active font for a family with more than two copies (left), select the faces you want to use (middle) and Resolve Duplicates. All but the selected faces are turned off (right).

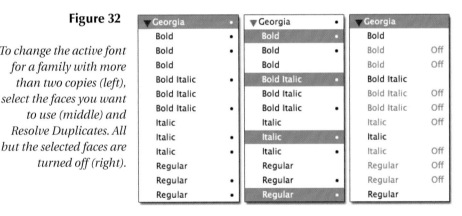

Work with Font Book Collections and Libraries

By creating and using Font Book *collections*, you can easily work with groups of installed fonts for targeted browsing, easy disabling and enabling, or quick exporting.

Creating Font Book *libraries* lets you access fonts no matter where they are stored on your Mac; so, when you want to use fonts on a temporary basis, you don't have to install them in the regular manner, into one of Mac OS X's Fonts folders.

Create and Edit Collections

A Font Book *collection* is a group of installed fonts with something in common. You get to define the commonality: it could be as simple as *Handwriting Fonts,* as general as *Sans Serif Fonts*, or as unique as *Ivory-billed Woodpecker Weekly Newsletter Fonts.* The collection itself is just a list, an arbitrary subset of your installed fonts.

Collections are for convenience in dealing with fonts:

♦ When considering just what font to use for a project, you can browse through a subset instead of your entire list.

- ◆ You can disable and enable an entire group of fonts at once.

- ◆ You can export the collection instead of individually selecting fonts for an export set.

- ◆ In applications that use the Font panel (mostly Apple applications at this point), a collection serves as a way to winnow the list of fonts you're selecting from, making it easier to get to the one you want. (Font Book collections and Font panel collections are spiritually connected on some higher plane, so creating or editing collections in one affects the list in the other.)

In the future, when Mac OS X gets its font act together (maybe as Mac OS XI), a collection could serve as a submenu, making Font menus more manageable; Apple's otherwise inconvenient Font panel interface uses this approach. (See page 142 for some ways to make the Font panel easier to work with.)

Create a Collection Based on a Font Face

Let's say that you often create fliers that need a variety of weights and widths in the type, but you never remember which of your fonts have condensed faces, which have bolder-than-bold faces, and so on, and you're tired of scrolling and clicking your way through your entire font collection when looking for type ideas.

Here's how to make a more limited browsing list for a specific style:

1. In Font Book, click the ⊞ button beneath the collection list or choose File > New Collection (Command-N).

2. Name the new collection Black.

3. Click on All Fonts in the Collection list.

4. Select Style from Search menu.

5. Type black in the Search field (capitals are ignored).

    You'll get several fonts from your Tiger set, such as Helvetica Neue and Hoefler Text. The family names are in the Font list with *only* their black faces listed.

6. Select all the fonts in the Font list (or be more choosey and select *some* of them) and drag them into your Black collection (**Figure** 33).

Figure 33

With the search set to "black" (shown in the Search field), fonts with black typefaces are found and listed in the Font list; they can all be dragged directly to the new Black collection.

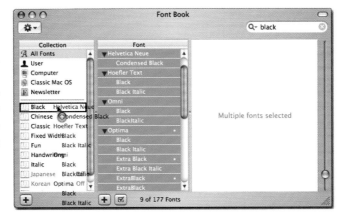

Create a Collection Based on Font Families

The procedure just described for collecting black faces, or any other style (condensed, for instance, or semibold) is great when the goal is a browsing list in Font Book. But if you're using Font panel, or some utility that provides font selection using Font Book's collections as groups, you don't want *only* the black faces in your Black collection: you want *all* the faces of any family that includes a black face. Luckily for you, your intrepid author doesn't give up easily when faced with these situations. Here's how to get the entire family into a style-based collection in Font Book:

1. *Before* you do any search, choose All Fonts in the Collection list.

2. Tab to the Font list and choose Edit > Select All.

3. Press the Left arrow key to collapse all the family names.

4. Create a new collection and perform a style-based search as previously described.

    The found fonts in the Font list are expanded to show the style faces found in the search. *Don't touch them.* Don't drag them to the collection yet.

5. Click the ⊗ (Clear) button in the Search field.

This shows the entire All Fonts list again. Don't worry—you haven't lost your found fonts. You might not be able to see them, but the fonts found in the search are still selected in the list. And, because you collapsed the Font list before the search, it's collapsed now, too, with only family names showing.

6. Scroll through the Font list until you can see one of your selected "found" fonts.

   Be careful! *Be very careful not to click anywhere and accidentally select anything, or all your found fonts will be deselected.*

7. Grab one of the selected, found fonts and drag it into your Collection list.

   All the selected fonts come along with it. Since the families are still collapsed, the entire family is put into the collection, instead of just the typeface style you searched for. **Figure 34** shows the results.

Figure 34

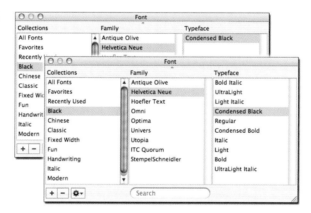

A standard style-based search turned into a collection makes only the found style available in Font panel (rear). In contrast, the results of a "collapsed Font list" style-based search provides Font-panel access to all faces of a found font family (front).

Tip: Overcome erroneous disabling. As described in *When Fonts are Un-Disabled* (page 105), certain troubleshooting procedures can re-enable all your disabled fonts. To minimize the time needed to disable them all again, make a collection specifically for fonts you generally keep disabled. Since fonts can belong to more than one collection, it doesn't matter if you've already put a font into some collection—it can also be dragged to your Disable These collection.

If you keep an entire collection turned off (maybe you keep the Asian fonts installed for their special characters, but you only enable them when you need the characters), you don't have to select the fonts in it to drag to your Disable These collection: working in the Collection list, drag the entire Asian collection (for instance) right into the Disable These collection.

When all your fonts are re-enabled by starting up in Safe Mode, you can, after returning to regular mode, open Font Book and disable everything in your Disable These collection instead of re-disabling various collections and single fonts.

Disabled Collections vs. Disabled Contents

One of the advantages of working with collections is the convenience of disabling an entire group of fonts at once, simply by selecting the collection and choosing Edit > Disable *CollectionName*. But disabling and enabling collections occasionally backfires, since Font Book is a little idiosyncratic when it comes to collections and disabled fonts:

◆ Disabling a collection turns off all the fonts in it, even if those fonts also belong to another collection. This sounds reasonable, but it's not the way most of us work: we might want to turn off Client A's fonts because the project's done for now, but still need to work with Client B's fonts—some of which are now turned off, too, because they were common to the other collection. You wind up having to disable Client A's Collection list and then enabling either the Client B collection or specific fonts in it—that is, if you remember that the font also exists in the other collection.

◆ Once a collection is disabled, turning on some, or even all, of the fonts in it directly (without turning on the collection specifically) *doesn't change the collection's disabled status*: its name remains dimmed and labeled *off* even though some of its fonts are on (**Figure 35**). This is particularly problematic when a troubleshooting technique re-enables all disabled fonts without changing the collection's status—you might not notice all the fonts are back on. It's also a problem because fonts can be turned on or off by manipulating them through other collections, as mentioned in the previous point, or directly in the Font list.

Figure 35

Just because a collection is marked as disabled (The Usuals, in this picture), that doesn't mean all its fonts are disabled.

♦ The reverse of the last point is also true: *disabling* some, or even all, of the fonts in a collection won't change its status from enabled to disabled. (Would it be so hard to indicate when *some* of a collection is on and some off?)

When a collection's status doesn't match its contents, it's harder than it should be to straighten out the problem. If, for instance, the collection thinks it's disabled even though its fonts are not, the only command available when you select the collection is *Enable*. If you want the fonts disabled, you either have to "enable" the collection (which does nothing except change the available command to *Disable)* and then disable it, or select all the fonts and disable them directly to match the collection's purported status.

Collection Quick Points

Here are a few details that can make working with Collections even easier:

♦ You can edit a collection name by double-clicking on it, or by selecting it and pressing Enter or Return.

♦ You can add fonts to an existing collection at any time, singly or in groups, regardless of where the font files reside.

♦   A font can belong to more than one collection; it might, for instance, belong in both *Sans Serif* and *My Favorites*.

♦   To delete something from a collection, select it and press Delete, or use File > Remove *FontName*. This *does not remove the font from Font Book*; it only removes its name from the collection.

Tip: Automatic collection creation. Wouldn't it be convenient if you could create a collection from the fonts you've used in a specific document? Then, before you give the document to someone else, you could double-check which fonts they're going to need, and use Font Book's Export Fonts command to gather copies of all the fonts to go along with the document.

Layout programs, or their add-ons, have long provided this capability, but Mac OS X has it built-in—although only Apple applications avail themselves of it so far. (But stay tuned, because there's a workaround in some cases.)

In an application like TextEdit, once you've created a document with various fonts, all you have to do is:

1. Select all the text in the document (or only some of it, if you want a collection of a subset of the document's fonts).

2. Choose TextEdit > Services > Font Book > Create Collection from Text.

3. Switch to Font Book and name the new collection (it initially defaults to the name of the first font in its list).

Tip within a Tip: This is all well and good if you're using an Apple application and Font Book Services are available. But if you want to do the same for, say, a Word document, you can copy the text from Word, paste it into a temporary TextEdit document, and continue the procedure from there.

Use Libraries to Control Your Fonts

Although Mac OS X offers many Fonts folders, you don't have to use any of them: you can store your fonts anywhere and make them available for use by creating libraries in Font Book (a feature new with Tiger).

The distinction between a library and collection is not always clear to users, but it's simple: a collection refers to a subset of your installed fonts, while the library *is* a group of installed fonts.

There are many advantages to working with user-defined libraries:

♦ The fonts are not installed in any Fonts folder; no copies are made—the originals, still in their original location, are accessed for use in Font menus and documents.

♦ When you remove a font from a library, or a library from Font Book, nothing is moved to the Trash—everything stays right where it is.

♦ In case of duplicates, the fonts in a library take precedence over everything except an application's Fonts folder, so you can be sure (okay, *most* of the time—there's always the application's folder) that the fonts you installed through a library are the ones being used by your programs.

♦ You don't have to make a collection, or a multiple selection from the Font list, in order to export the fonts you used on a job; if you have them all in a folder to start with, they're all ready to be sent to the other user.

Create a Library for Temporary Fonts

When you need a group of fonts for a short-term project, you don't have to clutter your menus with them forever, or go through the bother of individually removing them a short while after installing them. Creating a library in Font Book makes installing and removing groups of fonts a breeze. For example, with the fonts in question in a Desktop folder named FlierFonts:

1. Choose File > New Library (Command-Option-N).

2. Give the Library a name, such as *Flier.*

3. Drag the FlierFonts folder from the Desktop directly into the Flier library in the Collection list.

(Alternatively, you can just drag the folder of temporary fonts into the Collection list immediately above the divider line, making sure not to drop it into an existing item, as shown in **Figure 36**.)

Figure 36

Drag a folder of fonts directly under the last existing library, above the line (left), and you get a new library with all the folder's fonts in it (right). The new library takes the name of the folder and is alphabetized into the user-defined library list.

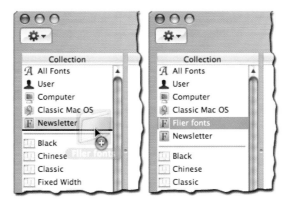

Your folder of fonts is still in its original location, and nothing has been copied anywhere: Font Book knows to look to the original location for the font files. This works whether you create a library from a folder, as in this example, or by dragging individual fonts into an existing library or into the User library area above the divider in the Collection list. And no matter how a font gets into a library, you can move it from its initial location, and *Font Book keeps it in the library, tracking its new location.*

It's important to note that if you create a library from a folder of fonts, *there's no live link* to that folder: putting fonts into the folder doesn't add them to the library. The live link is directly to the fonts themselves, which is why you can move them around and Font Book can still find them.

Because no copies are made when libraries are used, removing a font from a library, or a library from Font Book, doesn't send anything to the Trash; all items stay in their original locations.

The disappearing library list: *As of version 2.0.2, Font Book still has a bug that causes the list of fonts in a user-defined library to disappear if you rename the library. Although annoying, it's only a cosmetic problem; close Font Book and reopen it, and the list is visible again.*

Library Quick Points

Here are a few other things you should know about working with libraries:

♦ You can add fonts to existing libraries anytime.

♦ You can add fonts to a library with the other Font Book install methods. You can set a library to be the default install location with Font Book > Preferences and then double-click font files on the Desktop; or you can select the library in the Collection list and then use the Add button or command.

♦ Disabled libraries behave the same as disabled collections; the issues are described in *Disabled Collections vs. Disabled Contents,* earlier in this chapter (page 121).

♦ A library's fonts can be located in various places; they needn't all be in the same folder.

Although a user-defined library can include fonts from various locations on your drive, keep your sanity by limiting libraries to fonts in the same folder. Not all the fonts have to be included all the time—you can add and remove them from the Font Book library without moving them in and out of the folder—but don't have a library with fonts in different locations. And keep all the library folders organized by making a special folder to hold them all, keeping it in your Documents folder, on the Desktop, or in the Dock for easy access.

Create an Adobe Fonts Library

The fonts that come with Adobe applications don't show in Font Book because they're stored in an application Fonts folder. That means you can't browse the fonts in Font Book to see what you might like to use. More importantly, you can't identify duplicates between the Adobe fonts and your other fonts; this can lead to using one version of a font in, say, Word, which gets substituted when you import the document into InDesign. Here's how to get at those Adobe fonts in Font Book:

1. Create a new library named AdobeAppFonts, and keep it selected in the Collection list.

2. Choose File > Add Fonts and then go to /Library/Application Support/Adobe/Fonts. You can't just add the folder because the ../Adobe/Fonts/Reqrd/Base subfolder would come along with it, adding fonts that you don't want and can't use.

3. Depending on the view your using, either open the Fonts folder (in list view) or click in the column that lists the fonts.

4. Press Command-A to select all the fonts (Select All works in Open dialogs! Who knew? I found out experimentally for this procedure.)

5. Scroll through the list of fonts to find the Rqrd folder and Command-click on it to deselect it.

6. Click the Open button to add the fonts to the library. It could take up to a minute for the fonts to appear in the list because each file is checked for corruption.

If you're creating this library so you can use all the Adobe-provided fonts in your other applications, you can stop here. If you're making a reference list inside Font Book, then continue:

7. With the library selected in the Collection list, choose Edit > Disable "AdobeAppFonts." The fonts still work in Adobe programs, since those programs access the fonts from Adobe's folder.

Note once you turn off the Adobe fonts, whether singly or as a group, duplicates won't be marked (since Font Book marks only active fonts as duplicates).

8

Update Legacy Fonts

If you're not new to the Mac, you may have a few old font favorites, or even a vast collection that you have no intention of giving up. But there are a few things you *must* do and a few things you *should* do to use your old fonts in Mac OS X.

First, though, a little stroll down memory lane: Beginning in System 7, bitmapped and TrueType fonts were stored in the system's Fonts folder either as single-font files or grouped in suitcases. The suitcases frequently held several—or many—different font families, because the system had a limit to the number of font files that could be open at one time; stuffing a suitcase was the way to get at lots of fonts with only one *file* open. Bitmapped and TrueType fonts were often mixed in a single suitcase for several reasons: as a side effect of the stuff-the-suitcase philosophy; for backward compatibility with System 6 that could use the bitmapped but not the TrueType version; or because the bitmapped version accompanied the PostScript Type 1 file and the TrueType version looked better on the screen in some setups.

Although most of your old fonts are usable, many of them have to be manipulated first:

♦ Mac OS X can't use a single-font file for either bitmapped or TrueType; fonts *must* be in suitcase files, even if the suitcase holds only a single font. (But you can cheat and use some of these fonts: see *The Forbidden Fonts,* page 74.)

♦ You should trim down multiple-font suitcases, separating TrueType from bitmapped, and the bitmapped wheat from the chaff (the ones you need for PostScript fonts, and the ones you don't), as described in the sidebar *Learn How to Pack a Suitcase for OS X.*

Unfortunately, there's no way native to Mac OS X to manipulate suitcase contents. Even if you're in Classic, you can't open suitcase files the way you did in OS 9, because Classic is not really an operating system—it just plays one on your Mac. Manipulation issues aside, you can't even be sure of a suitcase's *contents*, because double-clicking it opens windows in Font Book for the TrueType contents, but not for all the bitmaps.

So, how *can* you handle this particular chore? You have two options:

♦ **Work directly in Mac OS 9:** Use your own Mac if it can boot into OS 9, or work on another machine. (Some apologies, or even begging, may be required if you've been giving friends a hard time about not moving up to Mac OS X.) I recommend this method, if possible, since it's the only one that lets you handle single-font files. (Details just ahead.)

♦ **Work in the Classic environment:** Install it on your machine if it's not there already, and get… ready for this?… Font/DA Mover 4.1, last seen with System 6. The details on this seeming outdated approach begin on page 133.

Note: Suitcase manipulation utilities. Two utilities handle suitcases under Mac OS X. Smasher can't handle single-font files, but does let you redistribute suitcase contents; despite several other handy features, its $49.95 price tag is outrageously steep (www.insidersoftware.com). Font Doctor can fix some corrupted fonts and automatically re-suitcase your legacy messes; in addition, it lets you manually create new suitcases, re-pack old ones, and work with single-font files. It's bundled with the font manager Suitcase Fusion, but is also available separately for $69.95 (www.extensis.com).

Learn How to Pack a Suitcase for OS X

Whatever your actual mechanics for repacking suitcases, these are your goals:

♦ Everything goes into a suitcase: no single-font files allowed. although single-font suitcases are fine.

♦ Separate the bitmapped fonts from TrueTypes, keeping them in separate suitcases even if they're the same family.

♦ Get rid of bitmapped fonts entirely if they are not companions for PostScript files.

♦ Limit a suitcase to a single family, with all its typefaces.

(The only exception: related families—I like to think of them as "cousins"—that will always be used or disabled at the same time, such as Nick, NickCondensed, and NickUltra.)

♦ Name the suitcase after the family it contains.

Work with Suitcases in Mac OS 9

If you can work in Mac OS 9 on your own or someone else's machine, it's easy to clean up your font suitcases. (Remember: that's a *real* OS 9, not the Classic environment on a machine running Mac OS X.)

You'll see up to four different font file types, easily identifiable by their icons (**Figure 37**):

♦ Single-font bitmapped

♦ Single-font TrueType

♦ PostScript printer files

♦ Suitcases with multiple fonts (although a single-font suitcase is possible, it probably never happened in the history of System 7 through Mac OS 9)

Figure 37

The Fonts folder in Mac OS 9 and its various font file icons.

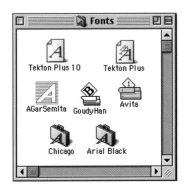

Top row: Single-font files; a bitmapped font (left) and a TrueType font (right).

Middle row: PostScript printer font icons vary from one vendor to another; Adobe's is at the far left.

Bottom row: Suitcase files for multiple fonts; the icon is the same no matter the contents.

Working with fonts in Mac OS 9 is straightforward. Start by opening the Fonts folder and Option-dragging the files out onto the Desktop, where you can work with the copies. (In general, it's a good idea to work on copies. And the system doesn't let you work on files in the Fonts folder, or even drag the originals out, if any application—even some subtle background item—is running.)

You need to know only a few things to manipulate suitcase contents:

♦ **Open a suitcase:** To open a suitcase file, double-click it. The suitcase window looks like a Finder window (as you can see in **Figure 38**), but it's not; the only things that can be moved in or out of it are font files.

Figure 38

This font suitcase window contains two TrueType fonts and four bitmapped ones. (The clue that this is not a standard Finder window is the suitcase icon at the left of the header.) These fonts are all in the same family, but a suitcase can hold a mixture of families and font types. Note that the names of the bitmapped fonts include their sizes.

♦ **Move a font file from one suitcase to another:** Open one suitcase and drag the font icon into the other suitcase—either its open window or the closed suitcase icon (as if it were a folder).

♦ **Make a new suitcase:** There's no way to create a new suitcase, an oddity much commented on since the advent of System 7 and these suitcase windows. If you need an empty suitcase—for a single-font file, for instance—make a copy of an existing one and drag everything out of it. (Really!)

♦ **Divide the fonts in a suitcase:** For a suitcase with two different font families, both of which you want to keep, creating a new suitcase for one family is not always the fastest route. Instead, duplicate the suitcase and dump one family from the original and the other family from the copy.

Use Font/DA Mover

If you don't have access to a native Mac OS 9 environment, but your Mac OS X machine supports Classic, you can work in the Classic environment with Font/DA Mover. (Relative newbies note: *DA* stands for Desk Accessory—the little programs like the Calculator, Scrapbook, and Puzzle, now inelegantly mimicked by widgets.) Try a search on the Apple site and you'll think the Mover doesn't exist anymore, although the 4.1 version is still available. Its address is so ridiculously long it would take three lines in this book to print it (and imagine the opportunities for typos!). So, use this address instead, which will magically redirect your browser to the Apple Web page you need: www.takecontrolbooks.com/resources/0037/font-da-mover.html.

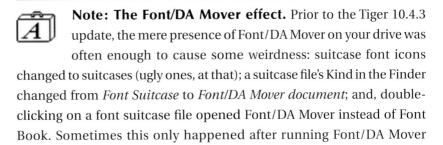 **Note: The Font/DA Mover effect.** Prior to the Tiger 10.4.3 update, the mere presence of Font/DA Mover on your drive was often enough to cause some weirdness: suitcase font icons changed to suitcases (ugly ones, at that); a suitcase file's Kind in the Finder changed from *Font Suitcase* to *Font/DA Mover document*; and, double-clicking on a font suitcase file opened Font/DA Mover instead of Font Book. Sometimes this only happened after running Font/DA Mover and/or restarting after using it.

If you haven't updated Tiger, you can get rid of these anomalies by getting rid of Font/DA Mover and restarting. If you're going to need Font/DA Mover again, use the Finder's Edit > Archive command to zip up a copy to keep around, and trash the unzipped version.

The Font/DA Mover interface is a little clunky, and in only basic black-and-white—but it was *always* oddly black and white and clunky, even in its day (**Figure 39**). However, it gets the job done.

Figure 39

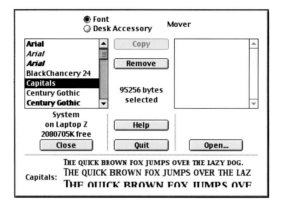

In the Font/DA Mover, bitmapped fonts (like Black Chancery in this picture) are listed with their point sizes, while TrueTypes are shown in their typefaces (the Arials and Century Gothics). Clicking a font provides a sample at the bottom of the window.

Follow these simple steps to work in Font/DA Mover:

1. In the Finder, take suitcases out of the Classic Fonts folder (the Fonts folder at /System Folder/Fonts).

   There's no reason to work on Tiger's suitcases, but if you've put other suitcases in the Classic Fonts folder, take them out before working on them. The Mover gets very confused if you make it look at anything in the Classic Fonts folder (see Step 3).

2. Launch Font/DA Mover by double-clicking it or by dropping a suitcase icon on it.

3. If you double-clicked the Mover to open it, click Close under the font list.

   Unless you start the Mover by dropping a suitcase on it, the fonts in the left panel are those in the Classic Fonts folder—the folder is being treated as one giant suitcase. *You can't work on the fonts this way.* Close the list and open individual, specific suitcases.

   If you try to open a suitcase that's in the Classic Fonts folder, you'll see all the fonts listed again.

4. Organize your suitcases according to the guidelines listed earlier in *Learn How to Pack a Suitcase for OS X* (page 131).

Here's how to manipulate suitcases and the fonts inside them:

♦ **Move fonts:** Manipulate suitcase contents by opening two suitcases (the button beneath each list changes from Close to Open depending on the context), selecting fonts in the list, and clicking Copy or Remove as needed.

♦ **Make a new suitcase:** It's not immediately apparent, but you can create new suitcases with Font/DA Mover: when you click an Open button, the dialog that opens includes a New button (**Figure 40**).

Figure 40

Create a new suitcase by clicking the Open button beneath one of the font lists and then clicking the New button in the resulting dialog.

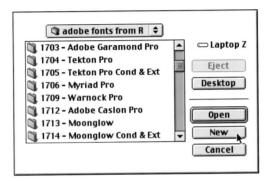

♦ **Deal with single-font files:** You can't open or manipulate single-font files with Font/DA Mover, since the program predates that whole concept.

♦ **Handle memory problems:** When a suitcase has a lot of fonts, Font/DA Mover can choke because of the limited amount of memory it addresses. If you run into that wall, you'll see the amusing dialog in **Figure 41**. (If you remember the thrill of MultiFinder, you've been around Macs for a while). Clicking the only available button quits Font/DA Mover.

Since the program doesn't actually seize up until you scroll toward the later fonts in a list, the way to get around this is to work on a copy of the fat suitcase, and remove as many fonts in the upper part of the list as necessary so you can get at the ones later in the list.

Figure 41

MultiFinder gave the illusion of multitasking back in its day.

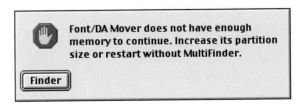

9

Master Font Menus and Font Formatting

Just pick a font from a menu and type, right? Not always: font menus differ from one application or utility to another, not only in the fonts they list but the order in which they list them. In addition, applying a character style often interacts with typeface selection.

You'd think locating a font in an alphabetical menu or list would be easy. And, in fact, if you're looking for something simple like Arial or Georgia, it *is* easy. But sometimes a font may be in an unexpected location in a menu, or seem to be missing. Or, your font selection might not format text the way you expect it to. In this chapter, I provide the background information you need to understand how font menus work and solve problems.

Find a Font in a Menu

To find some fonts—even a font with a name seemingly as simple as *Adobe Jenson*—you'll have to get used to how specific applications list them, or you'll waste a lot of time hunting for the font you want. Common programs, and even Apple utilities, take different approaches:

♦ Font Book lists items alphabetically in its Font list—until you look past Zapfino and see a second group of alphabetized fonts, starting with those whose names begin with #, followed by alphabetical listings of fonts identified by foundry or company: Adobe, Apple, Monotype, and so on. The Font panel (found in most current Apple applications, and some others) uses this approach, too.

◆ Character Palette uses a single, all-encompassing alphabetical list, with the #-prefixed fonts at the top and the foundry-specific fonts included in their alphabetical slots.

◆ Word and InDesign both use initial alphabetical lists followed by groups of foreign language fonts. But they don't agree on the alphabetization in the main group (the general issue is whether to include foundry or company names: Adobe Jenson might be listed as such, or as Jenson), what constitutes a foreign language font, in what order to list groups, or even how many foreign characters to use in a foreign font's name.

What's a "menu"? *For the most part, when I talk about font "menus," I really mean anyplace you encounter a list of selectable fonts: submenus, toolbar menus, the Font panel, pop-ups in utilities or dialogs.*

Short of overriding every application's font organization approach (which you can do with some third-party utilities described in *Better Font Menus* on page 141), the best you can do with this situation is familiarize yourself with the habits of the programs you use the most. **Table 14** shows examples of how Font Book, Character Palette, InDesign, and Word handle some standard and foreign language fonts.

And here's a tip that's not worth any special highlighting: if you don't see your font right away in a menu, keep looking! When you're really sure it's not there, check *Font Menus and Font Panel Problems* (page 271) for troubleshooting suggestions.

Table 14: Examples of "Alphabetization" in Font Menus and Lists

Font	Font Book*	Character Palette	InDesign†	Word†
Adobe Jenson	second group, under A	under A	under J	under A
Monotype Corsiva	second group, under M	under M	under C	under M
Apple LiSung	second group, under A	under A	language, under A	language, under A, listed as Apple LiSung Light
Ayuthaya	under A	under A	under A	language, under A
#PilGi	second group, before A	before A	language, before A	language, listed as ヒラギノ丸ゴ Pro W4
Hiragino Kaku Gothic Pro 4	under H	under H	language, under H	language, listed as #필기체

*Second group: alphabetized list after main group
†Language: segregated in group with other fonts from same language

Where Do Microsoft Word CE and CY Fonts Come From?

If you've installed the Tiger supplied additional foreign language fonts, you have Charcoal CY, Geneva CY, and Helvetica CY in your /Library/Fonts folder, and in your menus.

But even if you haven't installed any additional fonts, you'll find other CY (Cyrillic) and CE (Central European) fonts in Word's Font menu—and you'll have a devil of a time figuring out where they came from. They're not in other font menus, they aren't listed in Font Book, and you won't find any such font files in any of your Fonts folders.

The additional CY, and all the CE, fonts are each part of a parent dfont, as noted in this list. The italicized fonts in the list have their own font files, from Tiger's "Additionals," foreign language fonts installed optionally (listed in **Table 24**, page 293); the others are required system fonts. (Only some older programs, like Word X and AppleWorks, need these fonts.)

Listing in Font Menu ....From Font File
Charcoal CY ....*CharcoalCY.dfont*
Courier CE...Courier.dfont
Geneva CE ....Geneva.dfont
Geneva CY ....*GenevaCY.dfont*
Helvetica CE..Helvetica.dfont
Helvetica CY..*HelveticaCY.dfont*
Lucida Grande CE, Lucida Grande CY ....LucidaGrande.dfont
Monaco CE, Monaco CY ....Monaco.dfont

Get to Your Font Faster

Ever-scrolling font menus and lists are time-consuming at best, crazy-making at worst. Cut them down to size or use some navigational tricks (or both):

♦ **Get rid of fonts you don't use.** Whether you remove them completely or disable them temporarily, fewer fonts mean shorter, easier-to-navigate Font menus.

♦ **Use a hierarchical Font menu utility.** The shortest distance between your mouse and your font is a system of submenus keyed to your Font Book collections, provided by either of the utilities described in *Better Font Menus* (opposite).

♦ **Use keyboard shortcuts.** System-wide keyboard shortcuts are described below; details about keyboard control of the Font panel start on page 142.

Use Keyboard Shortcuts for Font Menu Selections

Some programs have shortcuts for font selection, but for any application with fonts available from the menu bar (even from a submenu), you can use these under-appreciated, system-level keyboard menu controls:

1. Press Control-F2 to activate the menu bar; this also selects the Apple menu.

2. Type enough letters to identify the menu you want (*fo* or *fon* for Font, for instance, depending on other menus present); or, use the Right and Left arrow keys to move through the menu names.

3. Open the menu with Return, Enter, the spacebar, or the Down arrow key.

   To close a menu when nothing is selected in it, use Return, Enter, Esc, or the spacebar.

4. If the fonts are in a submenu, type a few letters to get to the submenu's name, or use the Down arrow key to get there; then use the Right arrow key to open the submenu.

Better Font Menus

Two utilities offer better Font menus for Mac OS X. Both provide typeface submenus, with options to use Font Book collections as a top-level grouping, although both seem reluctant to update collection changes. Neither works with Font Book libraries, a significant drawback to productivity.

FontCard: Get hierarchical menus *everywhere:* not just in your menu bar, but also in dialog pop-up menus

and Keyboard Viewer. FontCard works flawlessly in Word; in fact, it gives Word the capability to update menus on the fly, so you can install and remove fonts without quitting Word—this alone could be worth the price of admission. A handy menu item at the top tracks recently used fonts; at the bottom, there's an All Fonts submenu. The FontCard main menu is too wide (about twice as wide as shown here); as a result, you often slip before you slide over to a font choice. With that fixed and the addition of Font Book library handling, it might well be perfect; as it is, it's only terrific (www.unsanity.com/haxies/fontcard/, $17).

You Control: Fonts: You can put the YC:Fonts menu on either end of the menu bar, and it remains accessible no matter what program you use. Extra features include: a submenu of typeface samples in a range of sizes; an optional user-defined Favorites group in addition to a standard Recent group; and an option to list font families in the main menu grouped according to Font Book collections instead of using submenus. One drawback is a main menu item named Collections that provides a submenu of Font Book collections; you must slide through *four* menus to get to your typeface instead of the three it takes in FontCard (www.yousoftware.com, $19.95).

5. Type enough letters to jump to the font you want; if you're close, use the Up or Down arrow key to move up or down in the menu.

6. Press Return, Enter, or the spacebar to choose the font and close the menu.

   If you change your mind at any point about using a menu, press Esc to cancel the whole thing.

That's a lot of steps, but they go quickly for a decent typist. For more about handy system-level keyboard controls, including how to change the keyboard combinations that trigger them and special PowerBook concerns, see Appendix E.

Learn Shortcuts for the Font Panel

The Font panel, Apple's Font menu replacement, sometimes seems like a step backward in interface design because of its mouse-only approach, but you can avail yourself of some keyboard shortcuts.

Some basic keyboard options are always available:

♦ **Activate the Font panel for keyboard control. Click in one of its three editable areas:** the sample text, or the Size or Search field. Otherwise, all your keystrokes are passed through to the document window. (If you don't have a sample text area, choose Show Preview from the Action menu at the lower left of the panel.)

♦ **Move from one element to another with Tab and Shift-Tab. The tab order includes:** the sample text; the Collections, Family, and Typeface columns; the Size field and Size list; and the Search field.

♦ **Select something in a list with the Up and Down arrow keys. But that's it—no typing a few letters to select collections or font names.**

♦ **If you have the Mac OS X Full Keyboard Access turned on (that's described in Appendix E), you have more keyboard controls:**

♦ **Focus on the Font panel:** Press Control-F7 to activate the panel (so you don't have to click on it) and Control-F4 to move back to the document window.

♦ **Tab to almost any control:** Almost everything is added to the tab order: all the controls in the Effects area, the Size slider, the Add and Delete buttons, and the Action menu (**Figure 42**).

Figure 42

The Font panel normally supports tabbing to the areas in the green rectangles; with Full Keyboard Access turned on, the items in the orange rectangles are added to the tab order.

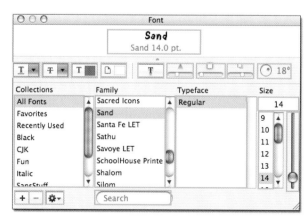

- **Navigate menus:** If the selected element has a menu, you can open it with the Up or Down arrow key or the spacebar. Move to menu items with the Up and Down arrow keys, or type a few letters to jump to an item. Use Enter or the spacebar to "activate" a chosen menu item. Use Esc to get out of the menu without choosing anything.

- **Click a button:** Use the spacebar to "click" buttons like Add and Delete, and Text Effects.

- **Manipulate the Effects sliders and dial:** Use the arrow keys to slide or spin these controls when they're selected.

Whatever keyboard shortcuts you use in the Font panel, you can keep it from getting in your way when it's open by minimizing its size. Change it to a "font bar" that shows a series of pop-up menus instead of lists by dragging the resize control upwards as far as you can (**Figure 43**).

Figure 43

Use the resize control in the lower right corner of the Font panel to change it from its full size (background image) to a minimum font bar (foreground). You can't use the Zoom button to shrink the panel like this, but the button works to enlarge it again.

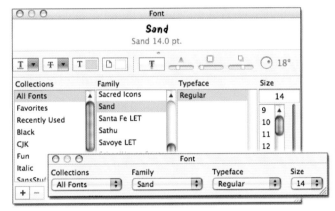

Manage Character Style-Typeface Interactions

Maybe you've never thought about what really happens when you apply a bold style to plain text—that you are specifying a *typeface* in the font. Maybe you've been well aware of that all along, or perhaps it's just beginning to dawn on you as you peruse Font Book's hierarchical Font list or find yourself clicking on a font family name and then a typeface name in the Font panel.

No matter how or when you reached this point, here is where you learn how to access a specific typeface in the font you're using. This is important so that you can:

♦ Get to the typeface you want quickly and easily.

♦ Understand why bold and italic styling can't be applied to some fonts in certain programs.

♦ Understand why some font formatting is lost when you paste text, or import documents, between applications.

Specify a Typeface When There's No Submenu

Programs take one of two approaches to listing fonts:

♦ **Hide the basic typefaces behind a single menu entry:** This was the original Apple method, and is still the Microsoft approach. To get at a typeface, you select the font and then apply styles—bold, italic, or both.

♦ **Gang the family members together in a submenu:** This has long been available in layout software, and in all Adobe programs; Apple's Font panel uses this approach with its Font and Typeface lists. You usually select a typeface directly, but applying bold, italic, or both styles to the base font also changes the typeface.

In a program with no typeface submenus, it's easy to access the nuclear family of faces—regular, italic, bold, and bold italic. But what about something like the Tiger Baskerville font with its six faces: the four basics plus Semibold and Semibold Italic? Word has a quandary: how do you let a user choose from two different bold weights (with or without italics) when the only way she can get even the standard bold face is by applying the bold style to the base font?

Word may not be pretty, but it's not stupid, either. It breaks the family members into two groups: Baskerville and Baskerville Semibold. As shown in **Figure 44**, the first item lets you get at any of the four basic faces, while the second provides access to the other two typefaces in the family.

Figure 44

The six faces of Baskerville shown in Font Book (left) are reflected in two listings in the Word menu (right).

The four basic faces (red dots) are rolled into one menu entry, as usual, while the other two (purple squares) are available from the second menu choice.

More typefaces mean more groupings and less predictability. Your Helvetica Neue (that's German for *new,* pronounced *"noyeh"*) has ten faces. Word once again lumps the nuclear family of four into a single menu item; it represents the other six faces with four additional listings. **Figure 45** shows how the menu listings interact with style commands.

Figure 45

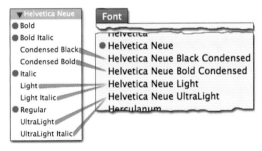

The ten faces of Helvetica Neue listed in Font Book (left) are combined into five listings in Word (right).

You access the four basic faces (red dots) through the first menu item. The next two menu items represent single typefaces. The last two menu choices provide two faces each: the named face and the italic variation you get when you apply the italic style.

Note: Using "sort of" bold or italic typefaces. The apply-a-style-and-get-a-typeface method works for faces other than bold and italic under specific circumstances. If a family has *no bold typeface*, but has a weight heavier than the regular one, like a semibold or black variant, applying a bold style almost always gives you that heavier face.

Similarly, for a font without an italic face but with something comparable, like Oblique, applying the italic style substitutes the analogous typeface.

Only two character styles work for typeface selection: *The only character styles that interact with typeface selections are bold and italic—due to a combination of legacy formatting procedures and the ubiquitous use of the typeface styles.*

You can't, for instance, use Word's Condensed style or InDesign's font tracking to change American Typewriter to American Typewriter Condensed.

Watch Out for Faux Styles

In font-savvy applications like InDesign, applying a bold style to a base font that doesn't have a bold typeface (or a substitutive face like semibold) gives you... nothing. The font stays at the plain base font because there's no bold typeface available.

Try the same thing in Word, and you get... a bold typeface. Sort of. Word creates a "faux" bold by superimposing copies of the text, offsetting each by just a few pixels. This means you can "bold," or thicken, even fonts that are already semibold or black. So, Baskerville Semibold with bold styling becomes a little darker, and "bolding" Helvetica Condensed Black makes it even blacker (though less condensed, since the offset copies spread the text horizontally). The same kind of thing happens if you use italic styling on a font that doesn't have an italic face: you get a fake italic that slants all the letters, forgoing the hand-tooled changes to certain letters that are a part of a true italic face, as you can see in **Figure 46**.

Figure 46

Real: Georgia **Georgia bold** *Georgia italic* ***Georgia bold italic***
Faux: Georgia **Georgia bold** *Georgia italic* ***Georgia bold italic***

The real Georgia typefaces (top) and Word's faux versions (bottom). The faux bold is lighter, and has extra spacing between letters, and wider spaces between the bold words (because the space is also "bolded"). In the italic face, note the entirely different letter shapes for the lowercase g *and the* a *in the real version, and that the faux italic is more slanted overall than the real one.*

Why should you care whether you're using a faux style or a real typeface?

♦ **The aesthetics of it all:** You don't have to be a purist to see that many faux typefaces aren't as nice as the real ones. But if you're working solely in Word and need bold for a heading, or italic for emphasis, you might not care whether they're real typefaces. The faux stylings aren't acceptable to a professional (they are, in fact, a possible trigger for severe anaphylactic shock), but they're serviceable. Besides, judiciously applied faux bold styling can thicken dingbats a little (like the

bottom line of these characters from Monotype Sorts), which might be just what you need to better match them to surrounding text.

♦ **Faux styles are application-specific:** If you work in Word and then paste or import into InDesign or Quark, the faux stylings are lost entirely (and, okay, good riddance) because those programs deal strictly with existing typefaces.

And that brings us to: how can you tell if Word, or any other program, is slipping in a faux style, since the real bold and italic are always hidden behind a family name? If you can't tell by looking—and sometimes that's difficult—you can check lists or submenus of real typefaces in several places, so use whichever of these is most convenient: Font Book, Keyboard Viewer, or Character Palette's glyph view (the latter two are covered in Chapter 11).

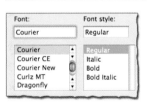

Tip: Don't trust Word's font dialog. Word's Font dialog seems to list typefaces, but don't be fooled: it always offers the four basic character styles, regardless of what typefaces are available. The snippet here shows Courier selected, but Tiger's Courier.dfont has no italic or bold italic faces.

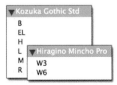

Tip: Asian font typefaces. The letters and numbers used to identify Asian fonts (this shows Font Book's listings) are easy to decode. A *W* followed by a number indicates the weight (boldness): a higher number is a heavier face. Other faces are identified by letters alone, but still describe weights, as for Kozuka Bold, Extra Light, Heavy, Light, Medium, and Regular.

Master Your Multiple Masters

Some font formats are about to fall by the wayside, but Multiple Master fonts got there first, abandoned even by Adobe years ago. If you depend on some of yours for specific jobs, find replacements as soon as possible.

In the meantime, you'll find that using a Multiple Master font is not as straightforward as you'd expect, given that Apple claims to support them in Mac OS X. (Installing the two Multiple Master font files is the same as installing any other PostScript font.)

For this example, I used a Tekton MM suitcase and its two PostScript files, TektoMM and TektoMMObl (oblique). The unadulterated files include nine variations each for the regular and oblique bases. I created additional faces—*instances*—with PageMaker 6.5 under Mac OS 9.

With the files installed in any Mac OS X Fonts folder, the results are consistent and fairly predictable:

Word: The menu lists all 18 original variations, but no matter which you select, you get only the base font (Regular or Oblique).

Apple applications: Programs like TextEdit are more reasonable: they also let you access only the two base faces, but they don't list all the others just to tease you.

InDesign: The way InDesign handles Multiple Master fonts depends on whether they're in a Mac OS X Fonts folder or the Adobe Fonts folder (read on!).

When You're in Adobe Programs...

For a Multiple Master font stored in a Mac OS X Fonts folder, Adobe applications show all the core variations of the two Tekton families (Regular and Oblique) and let you access each variation from the typeface submenu (below, left).

But even InDesign doesn't show the additional faces that were created under OS 9 when the fonts are in a Mac OS X Fonts folder. However, Adobe programs *can* see the custom-made faces if you put the files in the Adobe fonts folder (/Library/Application Support/Adobe/Fonts). In the picture at right below, the smaller menu shows the choices when the font files are in any standard Fonts folder; the longer menu shows the result when the files are in the Adobe Fonts folder.

Left: InDesign choices when fonts are in a Mac OS X Fonts folder.

Right: An InDesign menu with fonts in a Mac OS X Fonts folder (the short one) and in the Adobe Fonts folder (the long one).

10 Learn about Characters in Fonts

Most of this chapter qualifies as background information, but don't think that means you don't really need to know it! It helps you make the most out of 21st-century fonts because it

explains the glyph approach to font characters; describes how applications handle characters that don't have Unicode IDs (which is why some characters might disappear as you move them from one application to another); and shows you why you should care about alternate characters available in your fonts (genuine Small Caps *are* better, as are designed fractions, superscripts, and subscripts!).

The World According to Glyphs

A glyph, in fontspeak, is a single entity of a particular shape. You can refer to an uppercase A as a letter or a character, but there's only one such animal; it does, however, come in many different designs, or shapes. All the characters in this picture are A's, but there are 13 different glyphs.

A glyph doesn't always represent a single character. It can be a double-letter ligature, a triple-character fraction, or a multiple-letter Roman numeral. (The Zapfino font has a separate, single glyph for the word Zapfino.) No matter how many characters seem to be in a glyph, it is always a single entity in a font; it might take multiple keystrokes to generate it, but a single backspace will delete it (like the accented letters covered in *Use Keyboard Viewer to Type Accented Letters*, page 167).

The Unicode system provides for a single instance of a character in each script (written language): there is one capital A in Unicode, and its ID is U+0041. A font, on the other hand, can have multiple representations of a single character: alternate capital A's, standard and Small Caps versions, and so on. A font can also contain glyphs that have no relationship to any Unicode character.

Since every character you see and store on a computer must be represented by some sort of numeric ID, and so many glyphs fall outside the range of Unicode characters, there's a whole 'nother identification system, in addition to Unicode: the glyph ID (GID). Each glyph in a font has a GID, even if it also has a Unicode ID. There's no standardization for this: the GIDs for three alternate A's in one font won't match those for alternate A's in another, and a fancy flourish in one font is unlikely to have a counterpart in another.

Even the most basic of characters across fonts don't necessarily have the same GIDs: the question mark might have a GID of 34 in one font, 36 in another, and 1141 in a third. This doesn't affect your usage at all because each question mark still has a Unicode ID of 003F. But it can become a problem when you're using non-Unicode characters: an alternate A in one font might have a GID that's assigned to the @ symbol in another.

Because a GID reference is not always the best guide to what a character is supposed to be, some non-Unicode characters include additional information about "who" they are. If a non-Unicode character is related to a defined Unicode character—as is the case with alternate capitals, for instance—it is "mapped" back to that Unicode ID. Then, if using a character's GID might not make sense (as when the font changes), or in the absence of the capability to interpret a GID, a program can use the fallback mapping and turn an alternate capital A into a plain old A in whatever font is being used.

Did you catch that "absence of the capability to interpret a GID" in the last paragraph? Some programs don't handle GIDs at all, pretending they just don't exist. Word, for instance, knows nothing about GIDs. (In the interest of fairness, however, let's note that even Photoshop is not as glyph-savvy as InDesign.)

But "handling GIDs" is a rather vague phrase, and the "handling" is not always the same. Apple and Adobe programs take rather insular attitudes in regard to font technologies. As a result, the success of font format changes and copy/paste (or import) operations sometimes depends on whether you're using Apple TrueTypes (including dfonts, a variety of TrueType) or Adobe OpenTypes with Apple or Adobe programs. The core technologies, described in the sidebar *Fonts with Smarts* (page 9), are not fully interpreted by each other's applications.

Apple Fonts in Apple Programs

Type Zapfino's four different capital A's in a well-behaved, glyph-savvy program like TextEdit or iWork's Pages; select them and change the font to something that doesn't have four different A's, like Verdana. What do you get? Four Verdana A's, all the same.

Copy the original four Zapfino A's from the Apple program, paste them into Word, and you get four Zapfino A's—but they're all the same Zapfino A.

In the case of the font change, TextEdit gave precedence to a character's Unicode ID; when there was no Unicode ID available, it used the fallback Unicode mapping for the alternate A's, ignoring their GIDs completely. This is an intelligent move, because if you had used an alternate A for a fancy drop cap, you'd like it replaced by another A, and not just whatever character happened to have a matching GID in the new font.

Because Word doesn't understand glyph IDs, it does the best it can with the Zapfino A's: it gives you four of them, using the Unicode ID for the first, and then the fallback information for the others—which is all the same U+0041 for the letter A (**Figure 47**).

So far, so good!

Figure 47

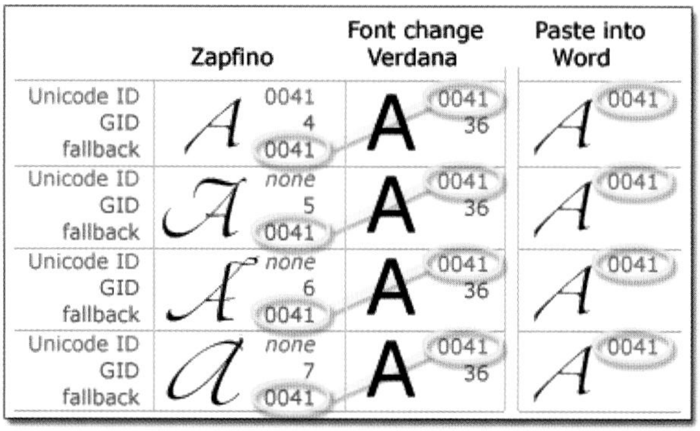

Apple font, Apple program. In TextEdit, changing the four Zapfino A's to Verdana results in four identical Verdana A's because the fallback Unicode ID of 0041 is given precedence over GIDs. Pasting the Zapfino A's into Word gives you four Zapfino A's; once again, the fallback Unicode IDs are used (Word can't see the GIDs, anyway!).

*Apple applications are not quite as sensible when using Adobe fonts: try this in TextEdit with the alternate A's in Caflisch Pro and the fallback Unicodes are dumped in favor of the GIDs. (****Figure 48*** *shows what happens when GIDs win out over the fallback IDs.)*

Apple Fonts in Adobe Programs

Now try the same the exercise in InDesign, and you get entirely different results. Enter the four Zapfino A's, change the font to Verdana, and you get **A"#$**; change it to Adobe Jenson Pro, and you get **A$%&**. Copy the Zapfino A's, paste them into Word, and you wind up with a single A.

There's actually a method behind this seeming madness. The madness is that InDesign can't seem to read the underlying fallback mappings for the alternate A's, and so treats them as if they had no Unicode IDs at all.

Now, for the method: InDesign uses the Unicode ID for the first A, which it can see, and the GIDs for the other letters, which it thinks have no Unicode IDs. In all three fonts (Zapfino, Verdana, Jenson), the first A is Unicode ID U+0041, so the first character remains an A no matter what font you use. The GID of the second A in Zapfino is 5; in Verdana, GID 5 is assigned to the straight quotes, and in Jenson, it's the dollar sign. Similarly, the third and fourth Zapfino A's have GIDs that are assigned to entirely different characters in the other two fonts (Figure 48).

When it comes to pasting the A's into Word, the only Unicode ID copied from InDesign is for the first A; since Word doesn't handle GID-only characters, it "sees" only the first A when you paste.

Figure 48

	Zapfino	Font change to Verdana	Jenson	Paste into Word
Unicode ID / GID / fallback	*A* — 0041 / 4 / 0041	A — 0041 / 36	A — 0041 / 34	*A* — 0041
Unicode ID / GID / fallback	— none / 5 / 0041	‖ — 0022 / 5	$ — 0024 / 5	
Unicode ID / GID / fallback	— none / 6 / 0041	# — 0023 / 6	% — 0025 / 6	
Unicode ID / GID / fallback	— none / 7 / 0041	$ — 0024 / 7	& — 0026 / 7	

Apple font, Adobe program. *InDesign gives precedence to the standard Unicode ID, but then uses the GID instead of the fallback Unicode mapping. As a result, changing the four Zapfino A's into another font gives you a single A and then various characters whose GIDs match those of the alternate A's.*

Copying the Zapfino A's from InDesign copies the Unicode ID for the first letter and the GIDs for the others (ignoring the fallback Unicode ID); pasting them into Word results in a single A because Word doesn't handle GIDs at all.

Using Adobe OpenType fonts in InDesign gives the more circumspect, expected behavior shown in **Figure 47** *for TextEdit and Zapfino: underlying Unicode fallback IDs are used instead of GIDs.*

Adobe Fonts in Adobe and Apple Programs

Both previous examples started with an Apple font, the Zapfino dfont. It seems that TextEdit and Pages behave properly, accessing fallback Unicode IDs when needed to preserve the sense of the original input, and that InDesign drops the ball when it comes to font changes and copy/pastes.

But there's more to this situation than the previous examples might indicate: start the exercise with the two capital A's in Adobe's Caflisch Script Pro, and you'll see the "vice-versa effect." InDesign behaves properly, correctly reading the fallback Unicode ID for the alternate A's, providing two A's in whatever font you choose, and copying two A's to be pasted into Word along with their fallback Unicode IDs. TextEdit, on the other hand, gets confused if you start out with an Adobe font. Change the two Caflisch A's to another font, and it substitutes a question-mark "unknown" character for the second A, so it looks like this: **A◆**. Copy the two Caflisch A's to Word, and only a single A is pasted in, because TextEdit doesn't pass along the fall-back Unicode ID for the second A (as it would with a non-Adobe font).

So it's not that one vendor's programs behave better than another's: it's that neither completely "understands" the other's font technology.

What you can do about this: *Nothing—if by "doing" you want to make things work differently. But you can avoid these problems no matter which programs and which fonts you use by choosing a font for a project* before *you do a lot of work on it—which is the smart way of doing it regardless of ID glitches.*

Yet Another Character ID Scheme

Unicode: 2603
UTF8: E2 98 83
CID: 8218

I didn't want to bother you with this, but you may run across it when you're in Character Palette: yet another way of identifying characters. The picture here shows the Character Palette help tag for an adorable little snowman. (Snowmen actually have a Unicode ID, although snowwomen don't have a similar acknowledgement.) The bottom line in the help tag? It's not your eyes, it's not a typo:

it's **C**ID, not **G**ID. That's for *character ID,* a scheme that Adobe came up with in the mid-90s to solve the problem of Asian fonts having so many characters that they needed double-byte numbers to identify them. (This was before the two major computer platforms wholeheartedly embraced the Unicode approach, described in *Explore the Unicode Universe,* page 16.) To keep track of tens of thousands of font characters, Adobe created files of "character maps" that worked

with information in the font and assigned a character ID (the CID); with that, an application could find the character based on a CID.

What does this mean for *you?* Just that sometimes you'll see a character identified with a CID—sometimes *only* a CID, in which case it's unlikely you can use the character in any but an Adobe program. It also explains why you'll find CMAPS folder in /Library/Application Support/ Adobe/PDFL/7.0—it holds the CID mapping files.

The Joy of Character-Rich Fonts

I've mentioned several times that fonts can have non-Unicode characters in them; this isn't exactly true, since every character has a Unicode number. More accurately, fonts can include non-defined characters: that is, the Unicode ID scheme has "slots" that aren't defined to contain an A (slot 41), or a Clockwise Top Semicircle Arrow (slot 8631) but are left empty for "private use." In fact, there are over 6000 free slots in the first 65K of Unicode IDs.

Nothing's more fun (typographically speaking) than finding that a font is jam-packed with all sorts of useful alternate characters. These extra Small Caps, special ligatures, and so on. The major types of special alphanumeric glyphs, and why they're better than the ones faked from standard characters, are described here. (Professionals will recognize many of these descriptions as the additional characters that were once available in special Adobe fonts called Expert Sets. These sets included a base font and several coordinating sets of swashy alternate capitals, "old style" numbers, and Small Caps; now all these characters can be squeezed into a single font.)

How do you type all these nifty characters? Well, sometimes you don't— type them, that is. Sometimes you must use special input methods, like Character Palette, or an application's Typography panel or equivalent. Sometime you can't input extra-special characters at all because a program just doesn't recognize them. All of this is covered in Chapter 11.

Alternate Letters. When it comes to alternate letters, initial and final letters with great swashes come to mind. Some OpenType fonts contain multiple alternates for every letter—enough to both satisfy picky designers and almost guarantee unsightly combinations by amateurs (remember ransom-note layouts in the San Francisco font?).

A Large, Kind Zoo
A Large, Kind Zoo

Standard (top) and alternate capital letters (bottom) in Papyrus.

Alternate Numbers. Alternate numbers usually means you have a choice between monospaced numbers that end neatly on the baseline (even proportional fonts almost always have monospaced numbers) and elegant "old style" numbers that have proportional spacing and ascenders and descenders on certain numerals.

1234567890
1234567890

Standard (top) and Old Style (bottom) numbers. OS numerals are usually smaller than the standard ones; these are from the same font, in the same point size, as those in the top row.

Ligatures. Ligatures are letters tied together in type for easier reading (or for good looks); you're so used to seeing them in printed materials like newspapers that you don't notice them. The most common ligatures are for fi and fl, since they make particularly awkward partners when the letters aren't altered. (And, of course, there's the fj ligature for when you're writing about fjords.) Some fonts offer dozens of ligatures—sometimes even alternates for the same pairs of letters.

firefly firefly

Top: The f-i and f-l combinations without any ligatures (left) and with them (right).

Bottom: Separate s *and* t *characters and a fancy ligatured version; standalone and ligatured g's.*

Superscript and Subscript. When numbers or letters are superscripted or subscripted by your application, you wind up with characters whose strokes are much thinner in comparison to the main font; adjusting the characters to the proper height—even if you know what that is—can be an exercise in frustration. Designed superscript and subscript numbers and letters coordinate with the font's main characters and are placed at the proper height.

10^{100} 10^{100}
H_2O H_2O 1st 1st

In each example, the smart-font version is at the right. (The first example is a famous, if misspelled, Web site.)

Fractions. So many people settle for typing fractions like this: 1/8. It's not great, but it's easy to read unless it's accompanied by an integer: 1 1/8 or 1-1/8. You can superscript the numerator and make the denominator smaller, but their weights will be too light and that slash is just too vertical. Built-in fractions are the answer (although this isn't strictly a rich-font feature—almost every font has some basic fractions).

$2^{1/2}$
$2\frac{1}{2}$

Built-in fractions are obviously superior to the roll-your-own variety; the number on the right is the designed glyph.

Small Caps. When a font doesn't have genuine Small Caps included, the style is created on the fly from two different point sizes, resulting in mixed stroke weights.

SMALL CAPS
SMALL CAPS
SMALL CAPS

The stroke difference in faked Small Caps is very obvious in some fonts (top). In others (middle), the stroke weight is less significant, but the relative heights and overall spacing are ungainly compared to the designed one (bottom).

All Caps. When it comes to All Caps, real designers prefer designed All Caps over just pressing Caps Lock and getting capitals because of the better punctuation positions and spacing.

¿QUE PASA?
¿QUE PASA?

The designed all-caps letters (bottom) have the leading character placed correctly, better spacing between words, and better overall letter spacing.

Font Fun Sampler

You should spend some time browsing through the character sets of the fonts you own, either in Font Book's Repertoire view or in Character Palette's Glyph view to see what's available besides standard letters and numbers. Here are samples of some of the gems you'll find. And if you like these, check out the treasure trove buried in Asian fonts—see the *Asian Font Fun Sampler* (page 162).

Lucida Grande is ubiquitous on Mac OS X, with its multiple language scripts, but it also has Mac OS symbols, rounded-rectangle enclosed numbers, and not-so-run-of-the-mill fractions.

Times New Roman (version 3.65 from MS Office, not the Tiger-supplied one) offers several language scripts, building blocks for boxes, and these readily recognizable symbols.

Apple Symbols has a rich, albeit cutesy, character set that includes a gazillion arrows, full chess sets (white and black), cards, dice, music, weather, and business/office items.

Papyrus is well on its way to being overused; enjoy its alternate capitals while you still can.

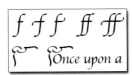

Apple Chancery has lowercase alternates; you can even roll your own ligatures. Some corner characters can automatically nest letters that follow.

Zapfino goes beyond the tired, staid pointing hand, and includes an adorable mouse among its myriad symbols.

The Zapf Dingbats and Symbol Nightmare

Mac OS X ushered in major problems with two tried-and-true favorites: Zapf Dingbats and Symbol. Why? Because their characters, under Unicode, have IDs that aren't accessible from your standard keyboard; they are, in effect, foreign language characters that you can't type. Ironically, the confusion has been compounded by the individual efforts of applications that either adhere strictly to the rules or try to help with the problem; all of which was made even worse by Adobe's somewhat misguided attempts to provide backward compatibility. Unfortunately, although I can describe the problem, I can't give you an easy solution.

The Zapf Dingbats Situation

Try typing in Zapf Dingbats in an Apple program like TextEdit and you get alphabetic characters, even though Zapf Dingbats doesn't include any alphabetic characters. This is the way it's supposed to work: when you type characters that aren't in the current font, another font is substituted—and there are no ABC's in Zapf Dingbats. Sure enough, if you check the font being used, it's LucidaGrande, despite your having selected Zapf Dingbats; when you pressed the A key, it generated the code for the letter A, not for the little Zapf flower you used to get from the A key. Try to look at Zapf Dingbats in Keyboard Viewer, and you see only alphanumerics—Keyboard Viewer is telling you what you're going to get if you type while Zapf Dingbats is selected.

But choose Zapf Dingbats and type in Word 2004 and, by golly, you get that little flower when you hit the A key: Word is aware of the font you've chosen and is helpfully translating the press of the A key from its usual code for the letter A to the number necessary to get the flower (**Figure 49**). Nice, but potentially confusing—especially because it feels right, especially to long-time Mac users who've pressed the A key to get the flower for many years.

Confounding the issue is the difference between compliant and noncompliant versions of Zapf Dingbats—an issue I explain in regard to the Symbol font (coming right up) and illustrate in **Figure 51**.

Figure 49

Set the font to Zapf Dingbats in TextEdit, press the A key, and you get a Lucida Grande a; in Word, the same setup provides a Zapf Dingbats flower.

The Symbol Situation

The Symbol font seems to behave erratically, providing different symbols from different keys depending on the programs you're using:

♦ **Typical behavior:** Type Option-V and Option-/ in almost any program in Symbol, and you get the square root symbol and the division sign. In fact, you get those characters from those keys in any Unicode-compliant font when a Roman-language keyboard is active because you've generated the codes 221A and 00F7, the IDs for those characters.

♦ **In Adobe InDesign CS1:** Use the same keypresses in Symbol in InDesign CS1, and you get a script P when you expect the square root symbol (Option-V), and the square root symbol when you expect the division sign (Option-/); this is where those symbols have always been in the PostScript Symbol font, unlike their positions in other fonts. Copy the two characters from InDesign, and they change when you paste them into Word or TextEdit—from P and square root to square root and vertical line.

♦ **In Adobe InDesign CS2:** Type Option-V and Option-/ in InDesign and you get the square root and division symbols, the way you do nearly everywhere else.

Several factors contribute to this mess, starting with the fact that, although you're likely unaware of it, you're using two different fonts: non-Adobe programs use the Unicode-compliant system font Symbol.dfont, while Adobe programs access the Type 1 version in the Adobe Reqrd folder (see *The Adobe approach*, page 14). That Type 1 font is not Unicode-compliant; it uses the old method of slapping characters into a matrix of ID numbers that really belong to the basic alphanumerics.

In most programs, typing Option-V puts the code 221A into a document; that's the ID for the square root symbol, and that's what you get in almost every font. In an Adobe program that's using the Symbol Type 1 font, however, code 221A retrieves the script P character instead. Copy it and paste it into Word, and it's the code that comes across—and 221A in the Symbol font that Word is using (the system dfont) is correctly interpreted as the square root symbol.

In fact, it's not the Adobe programs at issue, but the Type 1 font, and if you use the Type 1 Symbol font anywhere, you'll run into the problem of which keypresses produce which characters.

So, here's Adobe's dilemma: update the Symbol font and everything already done in Symbol totally breaks—open an old document, and the Symbol characters will change because it's always been codes that are stored in the document, not characters.

Here's Adobe's solution: in new applications, such as the CS2 suite, align those Symbol symbols with the standard keypresses so that Option-V and Option-/ produce, respectively, the square root and division symbols (the way they do on all fonts). But, to keep the backward compatibility, make those keypresses actually generate the nonstandard codes needed to retrieve the symbols from the noncompliant Type 1 Symbol font (**Figure 50**). To further protect the user from the mess, reinterpret imports and copy/paste operations as necessary to preserve the illusion of Unicode compliance. Wow! It almost works all the time, too. (Unless you always used the Type 1 Symbol font and you type, out of habit, Option-/ to get the square root and InDesign substitutes the standard division symbol. Or if you use the Type 1 font in any program besides a new Adobe one.)

Zapf Dingbats has the same problem of being non-Unicode compliant in the Type 1 version used by Adobe programs (**Figure 51**). But the internal font names are different for the system's ZapfDingbats.dfont and the Type 1 ITC Zapf Dingbats in the Rqrd folder that Adobe programs use (see *The Adobe approach*, page 14). So, two distinct fonts appear in your font menu, making it easier to tell which is being used.

Figure 50

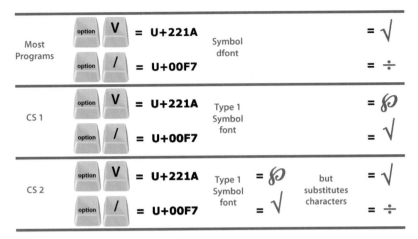

Top: *Most programs use the Symbol dfont that provides the checkmark and division sign in response to the Unicode symbols produced by the key combinations Option-V and Option-/.*

Middle: The same codes are assigned to different characters in the Type 1 Symbol font accessed by Adobe programs; CS1 programs produce those characters.

Bottom: CS2 programs also produce the incorrect characters from the Type 1 Symbol font but substitute the correct ones before displaying them.

Figure 51

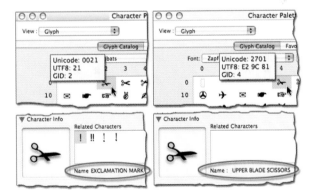

ITC Dingbats (left) has it all wrong internally. The first scissors character has an ID of U+0021, which really belongs to the exclamation mark. Character Palette reports the character's name as Exclamation Mark *and shows the related characters as other types of exclamation marks. The Tiger Zapf Dingbats dfont (right) gets it right, using the correct Unicode ID for the dingbat characters.*

What to Do When You Need Dingbats or Symbols

In the end, here's all you can do about the Zapf Dingbats and Symbol nightmares:

- ◆ Know which font you're using, which one was used in older documents, and which one is going to be used by anyone else looking at your document.

- ◆ Hope that Adobe will bite the bullet by updating its versions of the fonts, letting users suffer a little in the short-term transition instead of long-term with workarounds.

- ◆ Consider using different symbol and dingbat fonts when you can: Apple Symbols comes with Tiger, and Monotype Sorts—with almost the same repertoire as Zapf Dingbats—comes with Microsoft Office.

Asian Font Fun Sampler

Have you ever felt limited by the Zapf Dingbats circled numbers, which end at ten? How would you like circled numbers up to one hundred, with options for leading zeroes? How about numbers in double circles or rounded rectangles—all in white-on-black *and* black-on-white? How about upper and lowercase Roman numerals? And arrows: hollow, filled, curved, squiggly, dotted, dashed…? All these characters are in a single Asian font: Hiragino Kaku Gothic Pro, which also includes fractions way beyond the usual: sixths, sevenths, tenths, elevenths(!), and twelfths. This font is installed with your basic Tiger fonts, so take a look at its character set in Font Book or Character Palette.

The Tiger "Additional Fonts" collection includes Asian fonts with the nifty characters shown here. (If you didn't install them initially, *Restore or Add Tiger Fonts,* page 235, tells you how to add them now.) This is only a tiny sampling of the things you'll find in Asian fonts. If you view the repertoires in Font Book or Character Palette, make sure you scroll past all the Asian characters because some of the best items are at the end of the character list.

DFPLeisho: Beautiful Latin elements and matching numbers.

#GungSeo: Little icons, dingbats, and arrows galore.

#PCMyungjo: A dagger collection and a myriad of dingbats.

#Pilgi: Enclosed letters and numbers, and 170 or so arrows.

Control Character Entry

Character entry? Isn't that what we used to call "typing"? Yes, but how can you "type" characters that may (or may not) be accessible from your keyboard—assuming you can even *find* the one you want out of the many hundreds packed into every font?

Luckily, you don't have to learn the myriad of text-entry options Mac OS X provides if you have a few targeted needs. Start with Turn On the Tools (next page) so you have Keyboard Viewer and Character Palette at your beck and call, and then check the information you need:

♦ If you can't remember where basic characters like • ™ © √ ¢ are—or if you didn't know you could easily type them in any font—read *Use Keyboard Viewer to Find Special Character*s (page 165).

♦ If you type almost entirely in English but need basic accented letters so you can meet *Chloë* at the *café* for a *tête-à-tête mañana*, read *Use Keyboard Viewer to Type Accented Lett*ers (page 167). If you use less common accented Roman-based letters, such as å ğ Ę đ ķ (I don't even know what to call those characters, but you'll recognize them if you need them), you'll find that information there, too.

♦ Not typing in English? Check out *Use Alternate Keyboards for Foreign Languages or Other Special Inpu*t (page 188).

◆ Learn how to get at every character in a font's repertoire—including the special characters described in the last chapter—in *Find and Enter Characters with Character Palette* (page 176). Or, if you're working in an amenable program, you can automatically type special ligatures and fractions, as described in *Utilize Smart-Font Technology* (page 172).

Turn On the Tools

Mac OS X provides several tools (known collectively as *input methods)* to help handle the input problems resulting from two issues: not all the basic characters are printed on your keys (where the heck is that © character?), and many fonts have characters that can't be typed from the keyboard. The three basics tools are:

◆ **Keyboard Viewer,** accessible through a Preferences pane (where it's hiding in embarrassment at how little it has changed in 20 years from the old Key Caps utility). Use it to see what character a key combination in a specific font produces.

◆ **Character Palette** provides access to the hundreds of characters that you can't type from the keyboard. Use it to both browse through character sets and insert a character into your document.

◆ **Input keyboards** let you type in foreign languages and with non-standard methods like the Dvorak keyboard arrangement.

You can access all these system-wide text tools from the Input menu, which you'll find at the right side of your menu bar—its "title" is a flag, keyed to the operating system language. If you don't have an Input menu, turn it on:

1. Go to the Input Menu tab of the International preference pane.

2. Check Character Palette and Keyboard Viewer in the list.

3. At the bottom of the window, check Show Input Menu In Menu Bar.

The Input menu (**Figure 52**) should now be on the right side of the menu bar.

Figure 52

Activating items in the Input menu list creates the menu itself, which includes a shortcut back to the International preference pane.

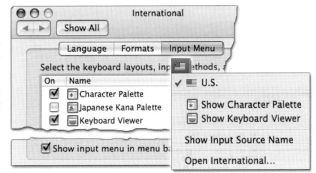

Character Palette access: *Character Palette is also available from several places besides the Input menu: in the Finder and Font Book, and other programs that strictly follow Apple guidelines, Edit > Special Characters opens Character Palette. (Apparently the guidelines don't call for direct choices like "Edit > Character Palette.")*

Note: Input Asian characters with special input methods. The cast of characters (so to speak) in Asian languages is so vast as to make typing solely from the keyboard impossible, and entering items from Character Palette unmanageable. Mac OS X provides special input methods for these languages; I'm not covering them in this book, but you can check out the basics at several Web sites, including www.yale.edu/chinesemac/.

Use Keyboard Viewer to Find Special Characters

Since the dawn of the Mac, we've been able to access up to four characters from each key on the keyboard: with and without the Shift key, with Option, and with Option-Shift. Many of the Option and Option-Shift characters—especially the ones you're likely to use often—are easy to remember because some thought went into their placement: there's often a relationship between at least one of the characters printed on a key and the hidden Option or Option-Shift character.

You can check out the entire Option and Option-Shift character sets, and look up the characters you can't remember, with Keyboard Viewer. Open it from the Input menu, and hold down Shift, Option, or Option-Shift to see the characters those modifiers produce.

You can type directly in your document while Keyboard Viewer is open, or click on its keys to enter a displayed character, but your best bet is to learn what key combinations produce the characters you use often, and come up with some clever mnemonics so you'll remember them. **Table 15** provides some examples of easy-to-remember patterns for common symbols.

*U.S.-centric key combos: The key combinations in **Table 15** and described elsewhere throughout this section hold for only the U.S. keyboard. If you use a different input keyboard (described in* Use Alternate Keyboards for Foreign Languages or Other Special Input, *toward the end of this chapter) or a different Mac OS X system language, even some common characters can be in different places.*

Table 15: Common Option & Option-Shift Characters

Seen		Hidden		Comment
Plain	**Shift** ⇧	**Option** ⌥	**Option-Shift** ⌥⇧	
2	@	™	€	Both begin with T; trademark is **2** letters
3	#	£	‹	# and £ are both "pound" signs
4	$	¢	›	(American) money
8	*	•	°	Basically round characters
r	R	®	‰	R's
v	V	√	◊	V-shaped bottoms
-	_	–	—	Hyphen, underline, minus sign, em (long) dash
=	+	≠	±	(You do the math)
,	>	≥	˘	Greater than, greater than or equal to
.	<	≤	ˇ	Less than, less than or equal to
/	?	÷	¿	What's the question?

Keyboard symbols: Sand. Shift: U+21E7, GID 339. Option: U+2325, GID 355.

Use Keyboard Viewer to Type Accented Letters

The Mac has always provided an easy way to type a letter with one of five common accent marks for use in words like *déjà vu, naïve, rôle,* and *El Niño* through the use of *dead keys*: keys that don't type anything until you type a second letter. All the dead keys are Option-key combinations. To type an accented letter:

1. Type the Option key combination that produces the accent. The accents and their key combinations are:

   ` grave accent: Option-~

   ′ acute accent: Option-e

   •• umlaut/dieresis: Option-u

   ^ circumflex: Option-i

   ~ tilde: Option-n

   The dead keys are only half-dead in most applications now, so you'll probably see the accent in your text, with a squiggly line under it or some type of highlighting to signify you have to type another letter; the exact look depends on the application.

2. Type the letter that's going with the accent.

   Accenting is often restricted to certain letters—you can't just put an umlaut on a capital X because you feel like it.

So, all you have to do is type Option-e for the acute accent, and then the *e*, and you get *é*. Behind the scenes, your application has substituted the single Unicode accented *e* character for the two that you typed.

Using dead keys is, in fact, just a clever way to type characters that are otherwise unavailable from the keyboard. (You could enter an é in other ways—through Character Palette, for instance, or with a foreign language keyboard—but why bother when this method is so easy?)

Dead keys in early Mac systems: *In the old days, the accented-letter trick worked because the accents themselves were specially designed to fall outside* the rectangular area within which a character's shape is defined. So, when you typed an accent, you couldn't see it—it was beyond the bounds of its character space—but when you typed the next letter, they both, in effect, occupied the same space and appeared superimposed. Under this system, it took two backspaces to delete the accented letter because it was composed of two characters.

When you need one of these accents but can't remember the key combination, Keyboard Viewer can help. It shows both the accent keys and the accentable letters, as described in **Figure 53**. If you keep Keyboard Viewer open while you're typing, you can click its keys to enter the accents and letters in your document. It doesn't matter if the font selected in Keyboard Viewer is the same as the one you're using in your document because nearly all Roman-based language fonts have these accented letters available.

Keyboard Viewer's font: *The font you choose in Keyboard Viewer displays characters for that font, but even if you "type" by clicking the Viewer's keys, characters are entered in the document's current font.*

Figure 53

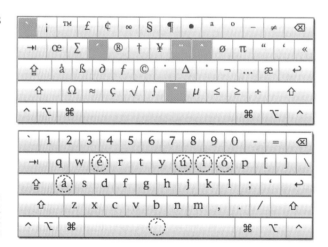

Dotted circles:
#PilGi
U+25CC
GID 1215

Keyboard Viewer highlights the accent keys when you hold down Option (top).

With Option down, type an accent; release Option and you'll see the letters that can go with the accent (bottom). They're easy to miss because they blend in with the rest of the letters—the red circles are only for this illustration.

Hold down Shift when the accented letters are displayed to see the capitals that can take the accent. (Note that the Viewer shows that if you want to type an accent by itself, you type a space after the Option combination.)

Note: When Keyboard Viewer won't show accents. The results shown in **Figure 53**—accented letters appearing in Keyboard Viewer after you click on an orange accent key—usually appear only when you're working with editable text, when typing or clicking a Keyboard Viewer key enters text in the current window.

If, for instance, a Safari window is open but neither the URL field nor the Google field is active, you can press Option and click one of Keyboard Viewer's orange keys; but, when you release the Option key you won't see any accented letters, because you're not working with "live" text. On the other hand, if you're in the Finder and you're not actually typing anything (editing a file's name, say, or typing in the Spotlight search field), you'll still be able to see the accented letters even though you're not entering text anywhere.

Type More Accents with the U.S. Extended Keyboard

Roman-based languages use many more accents than the five basics that Mac dead keys have always provided. In keeping with the Unicode lots-of-characters spirit, Mac OS X provides *19* dead-key accents with the special U.S. Extended input keyboard. (I explain input keyboards in more detail in *Use Alternate Keyboards for Foreign Languages or Other Special Input*, page 188.) Here's how to activate it:

1. Go to the Input Menu tab of the International preference pane.

   Shortcut: Choose Open International from the Input menu.

2. In the list of keyboards, check U.S. Extended, and close the Preferences window.

   Shortcut: Click on the Name column title to sort the keyboard names in reverse alphabetical order so the U.S. keyboards are conveniently at the top of the list.

3. Choose the U.S. Extended keyboard from the Input menu.

   Its menu bar icon differs from the standard U.S. keyboard by the little add-on U for Unicode.

If you choose a keyboard from the Input menu while Keyboard Viewer is open, it may not register the change (look in its title bar to see what keyboard it thinks it is). Sometimes just choosing the same item again from the Input menu makes Keyboard Viewer catch up; sometimes you might have to close and reopen it to display the new input keyboard.

Use Keyboard Viewer to access the larger selection of accents and accentable letters:

1. Open Keyboard Viewer.

2. Choose your current document font in Keyboard Viewer's pop-up font menu.

    Since not all the extra accented letters are available in all fonts, you need to see what your current document font has to offer.

3. Hold down Option to see the all the dead-key accents, highlighted in orange.

4. With Option still down, press a key, or click a key in Keyboard Viewer, to get the accent you want.

5. Release the Option key.

    Keyboard Viewer now shows the available accented letters, which you can type or click to insert into your document. Accented characters that aren't available in the current font are slightly larger and bold, as shown in **Figure 54**. (Note that Keyboard Viewer's current font doesn't automatically change to match what you're using in your document, so if you skipped Step 2, you won't see what's available in your document's font.) You can still use these "unavailables," but they are entered in your document in a font other than the one you chose—one that actually contains the character. (This phenomenon is explained in *Type in a foreign language without changing fonts*, page 192.)

Why not* always *use the Extended keyboard? *Because it giveth with one hand and taketh away with the other. With all the accents given over to the Option key, you lose standard Option characters like the √ on Option-V.*

Figure 54

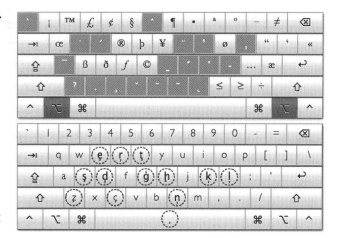

Circles: InaiMathi
U+25CC GID 277

Hold down Option (top) to see available accents highlighted in orange. Click or type one of the accents and then release Option to see the available accented letters (bottom, after the cedilla—the third key in the bottom row—was clicked). Finally, click or type the desired character.

The larger, slightly bold letters on the keyboard (circled here in red) show which accented letters are not available in the current font (the one selected in Keyboard Viewer). If you type or click an unavailable letter, the accented character is inserted in your document in a different font. Characters available in the current font (circled here in purple) are shown accented, but with no special emphasis.

Tip: Apply after-the-fact accents. In some applications, and with certain fonts (yes, that's vague, but with so many variables the best I can give you is a "more often than not"), you can type a letter first and then use an Option-Shift-accent combination to add the accent when you have the U.S. Extended Keyboard active.

So, in Word or InDesign, for instance, you can choose Lucida Grande, type an n and then press Option-Shift-U, and wind up with a dieresis over the *n*. (My colleague Joe Kissell points out that this is a necessary combination to properly spell Spïnal Tap.) You can check www.homepage.mac.com/thgewecke/diacritics.html for a list of the Option-Shift combinations you need for applying accents this way.

Utilize Smart-Font Typography

Using Keyboard Viewer and Character Palette (described in Chapter 11) lets you get at all the characters fonts contain even when they're not easily typed—or at all available—from the keyboard. But wouldn't it be more… technologically advanced… if you could just type away and get the special glyphs you need in context of the surrounding text?

Well, you can, sometimes. But before I show you how that works, consider the not-so-advanced usual method of inserting ligatured letters. If a font includes the common *fi* and *fl* ligatures, you can type them with Option-Shift-5 and Option-Shift-6; likewise, the *æ* can be typed *æsthetically* using Option-". These are each single glyphs, and once they're inserted, a single backspace removes them.

Layout programs like QuarkXPress and the late PageMaker provided "automatic" ligatures many years ago: type the two letters and the program would replace them with the single ligature character, much the way most programs replace straight quotes (") with curly ones (").

But OpenType fonts provide a whole new level of ligature access: just type the standard letters (*f* followed by *i*, for instance) and the proper ligature is inserted in the document. But *backspacing deletes a single letter at time*, and when you delete one of the letters, the remaining one reverts to its standalone shape. This happens because the substitution is not a single-glyph ligature like the one you enter with Option-Shift-5; instead, special glyphs for each of the component letters are being used, and they're separate characters.

You need three things to realize this typographic potential:

♦ Mac OS X

♦ Fonts designed with appropriate characters *and* special substitution rules attached to them

The rules are along the lines of: "If the glyph right before/after me is the same as I am, then switch to…"; and "If I'm at the beginning/end of a word…"; and "If I'm next to a T, then…".

♦ An application that can interpret the built-in font rules

The application also has to understand GIDs. Presumably, any application that can handle a font's internal typography rules also knows how to display non-Unicode characters, since most of the substitutions use glyphs that have only GIDs.

Applications that provide special font substitutions offer them as options, usually in a piecemeal fashion: you can turn on common ligatures, or fancy ones, or special fractions, and so on, exclusive of one another. Some substitution options are turned on as defaults, so you may not realize you have a choice (or that they're not just automatic).

TrueType/OpenType smart substitutions: The following examples all use Apple fonts in TextEdit, so you can try them out. Many OpenType fonts have lots of smart substitutions available, too, which have been accessible in Adobe programs. But, starting with Tiger, Mac OS X lets you get at the built-in OpenType features in other programs, too.

Type Common Ligatures

The specifics of accessing special typographic features vary from one program to another. Here's how to turn on typographic features in Apple programs and to type common ligatures:

1. With a TextEdit document open, display the Font panel by choosing Format > Font > Show Fonts, and choose the Baskerville font.

   You might also want to set a large-ish font size—about 36 points—so you can clearly see the ligature results.

2. From the Font panel's Action menu (the gear at the lower left), choose Typography.

   The controls in the Typography palette vary with the font you've chosen—they depend on what's available in the font.

3. In the Typography palette, expand the Ligatures section (the only one available for Baskerville) and check Common Ligatures (**Figure 55**).

4. Type f followed by i.

   Watch the *f* change, its top stretching over to shelter the *i* and the crossbar reaching out to touch it; the *i* doesn't have its usual dot because its next to the *f.*

   If you backspace once, you'll erase the *i*, and the *f* reverts to its standard glyph.

Figure 55

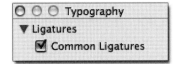

When Common Ligatures is activated in the Typography panel, TextEdit replaces the primary character glyphs with alternates when they're typed next to each other.

From left to right, notice Baskerville's primary f, i (top), and l (bottom) glyphs, the non-ligatured pairs, and the ligature substitutes.

Type Special Ligatures

Tiger's Zapfino font is especially rich in typographic options and is perfect for experimentation in features beyond common ligatures.

Here's how to include *fancy* ligatures in your text:

1. With a TextEdit document open, choose Zapfino in the Font panel.

2. Open the Typography panel from the Font panel's Action menu.

    Zapfino's built-in typography options far outnumber the Baskerville ones, as you'll see when the Typography panel opens to list them all.

3. Expand the Ligatures section if necessary and check Special Ligatures.

4. Type the word stress.

The *s* and *t* as standalone letters are one design, as you can see in **Figure 56**, but type them next to each other and they both change; the *e* changes subtly when you type the following *s*, which differs from both the first and the last *s* in the word.

Figure 56

Letters change automatically as you type in Zapfino with the Special Ligatures option active.

Type Editable Fractions

The smart-font technology that gives you automatic ligatures also provides automatic fraction formatting.

With many fonts in many applications, if you type 1/2, a ½ is substituted; you can tell it's a single glyph because a single backspace erases it. But with well-defined fonts, you can build any kind of fraction at all, and edit any of its constituent numbers. Here's how to type amazing fractions in TextEdit:

1. With a TextEdit document open, choose Zapfino in the Font panel.

2. From the Font panel's Action menu, choose Typography.

3. Expand the Vertical Position section and click Contextual Fractions.

4. Type 14/212.

    Zapfino is "watching" for numbers typed on both sides of a slash, so when you type the first 2, the fraction formats itself, as shown in the red rectangle in **Figure 57**. You can continue typing a larger denominator, past the first 2, because the fraction is being built on the fly; it's not a substituted glyph.

5. Backspace once and watch the fraction change to 14/21.

    Since the fraction isn't a single glyph, you can edit it; you could even erase just the 4 and the formatted fraction would change to 1/212.

Figure 57

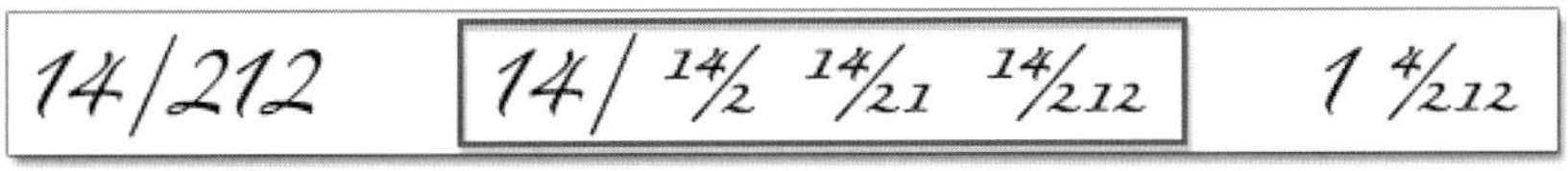

The first "fraction," (top left), was typed without the Contextual Fractions option active. When it's on, typing a number on each side of a slash (in red rectangle), signals a fraction, which is automatically formatted: even the slash changes to a shorter, less vertical form. You can edit any part of the fraction, like inserting a space between the numerator's 1 and 4 to get the final number (right).

Note: Smart fonts aren't just for looks. All the examples provided here as benefits of smart-font capabilities have to do with looking good—typographically speaking. But the benefits of smart fonts go far beyond looks. Many languages have complex scripts that require different letter shapes for certain circumstances. A simple example is Hebrew, which has five letters that take different forms if they're the last letter of a word. With a smart Hebrew font, you wouldn't have to press any special key combination to get the final-letter form; you could just type the regular letter and the font would substitute the final form if it's at the end of a word.

The benefits increase as the language script gets more complex; languages like Arabic and Hindi have characters whose shapes, and sometimes positions, depend on the characters that come before and after them.

Find and Enter
Characters with Character Palette

Some programs provide ways for you to enter characters beyond the ones you can type, like InDesign and its Glyph table; in most cases the application-specific tool is the easiest and best approach when you already know which character you're looking for and what font you want to use.

But you always have at your disposal Apple's system-wide solution, Character Palette, available from the Input menu (if you've activated it, as described in *Turn on the Tools,* page 164). It's not overly friendly: there's a lot in it, but none of it is intuitive. It's invaluable, however, for browsing through font character sets and selecting characters to insert into documents.

Character Palette offers four types of views for different ways of working. They differ not only in the way they present characters, but also in *which* characters are displayed: some views show only Unicode characters, others show a font's entire repertoire, including non-Unicode glyphs (**Figure 58**). **Table 16** provides a roundup of the differences; it's followed by details about working in each view. (Except for the PiFonts view, which is not worth your time. It purports to list *picture* fonts but severely limits which fonts are included—no Zapf Dingbats, nothing from the Hoefler Text typeface Ornaments. Use the Glyph view instead.)

Figure 58

The Character Palette interface

Circled numbers:
Hiragino MinchoPro
Starting at U+24F5

1. *View menu:* The first five menu choices, for specific language scripts, are subsets of the sixth choice, All Characters.

2. *View area:* This changes based on the View menu choice.

3. *Character grid:* Glyphs are arranged according to the view chosen.

4. *Character Info:* This collapsible section includes the character well and a list of related characters.

5. *Font Variation:* This collapsible section is not available in views like Glyph, where you work with a specific font.

Table 16: Character Palette Views

View	Shows Glyphs…	Glyph Order	Use For
Generic views*			
Category†	…included in Unicode	Unicode categories	Browsing by character type; looking at a specific character in many font variations
Code Tables	…included in the selected encoding scheme	Selected encoding scheme	Browsing Unicode set; inserting special character when you know its Unicode or other encoding
Font-specific views			
PiFonts	…in selected font, including those beyond Unicode	Unicode ID	Nothing; use Glyph view instead
Glyph	…in selected font, including those beyond Unicode	Glyph ID	Browsing and selecting from character set of specific font

* Generic views can show glyphs only if they exist in at least one installed font

† The five language-specific views and All Characters

Find a Character in a Category View

Using a category view is a good way to become familiar with what kinds of characters are available in many Unicode fonts. It's also a great way to find a specific character when you know *generally* what you want, like a circled number or geometric shape. You start with the general category, find a specific character, and then select the actual glyph from the fonts you have installed. For example, try these steps:

1. Choose All Characters from Character Palette's View pop-up menu.

2. In the left pane, expand the Symbols category by clicking its triangle.

3. Click on the Arrows subcategory.

    Scroll through the character grid to view the various arrows and arrow-like characters.

4. Select the right-pointing hand that's in the middle of the fourth row. In **Figure 59**, it appears in the third displayed row because the first row is scrolled out of view.

5. Expand the Character Info section by clicking on its triangle.

    This area displays the character well holding a gratifyingly large version of your selected character, and the Related Characters list.

6. Expand the Font Variation section by clicking on its triangle.

    This section is your best friend when you're looking for just the right version of a character you've selected: you'll see the current character in every font that contains it. For the pointing hand, you can select from fat or skinny hands, with or without cuffs, and so on, as shown in **Figure 59**.

Unicode-only views: Since category views show only Unicode characters, you won't see some of the best pointing hands available, in the Zapfino font, because they aren't Unicode characters and have only GIDs.

Figure 59

A category view in
Character Palette

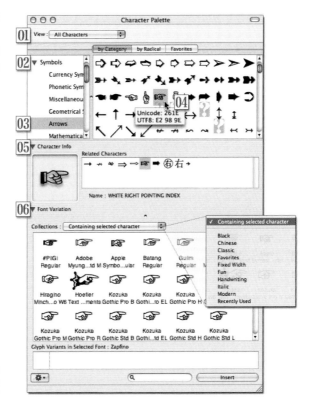

Boxed numbers:
Hiragino MinchoPro
Starting at CID 10767

1. *The View menu's All Characters choice encompasses all your installed fonts.*

2. *In a category view, the View area displays a list of categories (some of which are expandable) and the character grid. The By Radical tab is for use with Asian languages.*

3. *The Arrows subcategory under Symbols includes pointing hands.*

4. *Gray boxes or question marks in the character grid are placeholders for Unicode characters that are unavailable in your installed fonts, so Character Palette can't display them.*

5. *The Related Characters list, next to the character well, is empty much more often than not; but when characters are available, you can click on one to make it the current selected character.*

6. *The Collections pop-up menu lists Font Book collections; selecting one narrows the scope of the font samples.*

Browse the Unicode Repertoire in Code Tables View

The default Code Tables view displays the same set of characters as the Category views—Unicode characters—but presents them in Unicode ID order. Use Code Tables view to familiarize yourself with the breadth of the Unicode repertoire, or to find a character whose Unicode ID you already know. To get started, try this example (the numbers in **Figure 60** are keyed to these steps):

1. Choose Code Tables from the View pop-up menu.

2. Scroll through the list at the top of the window and select Letterlike Symbols.

   The hex numbers in the leftmost column identify the first ID assigned to a block of characters; the entire block is highlighted in blue to the left of the character grid.

   If you use this view to look at a specific character whose Unicode ID you already know, you can scroll through this list watching the numbers instead of the category names; or, you can scroll through the character grid to get to the area with that ID.

   Missing scrollbars: If scrollbars are missing from any area in Character Palette, resize it vertically until they reappear.

3. In the grid, click on the symbol that looks like a backward euro symbol.

   There's nothing in Related Characters for this character, but its name, Unicode ID, and UTF-8 encoding are all identified beneath the panel— the area circled in **Figure 60**. (I picked this character as a sample in case you ever wondered what a *scruple* actually looks like.)

As in category views, the Font Variation section shows how the character appears in various fonts.

Figure 60

This is the Unicode option in Code Tables view (the numbers are keyed to the steps in the text). There are other encoding views besides Unicode; the only non-Asian one is the charmingly named ISO-8859-1.

Numbers:
Hiragino MinchoPro
Starting at CID 11578

Pick a Font-Specific Character in Glyph View

If you use Character Palette for browsing or inserting characters in a specific font, Glyph view is the one you'll use most because it lets you view a font's entire repertoire, including the glyphs that aren't in the Unicode set.

Say you liked the Papyrus alternate capitals shown in the *Font Fun Sampler* (page 157) and want to see how many letters have alternates. Follow these steps (illustrated in **Figure 61**):

1. Choose Glyph from the View pop-up menu.

2. Choose Papyrus from the Font pop-up menu. (There's nothing available in the typeface menu besides Regular because Papyrus has no face variants.)

3. Scroll through the character grid until you see the glyphs you want.

As in the other views, there's a Character Info area with the character well and the Related Characters list; there's no Font Variations section, since you've already picked a specific font.

Figure 61

The Glyph view for Papyrus. The red-circled numbers are keyed to the steps in the text.

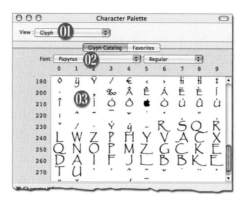

Numbers: Hiragino MinchoPro
Starting at CID 10505

ISO and UTF-8 Encodings

If you're wondering what the ISO-8859-1 encoding choice in Code Tables view refers to, or what those "UTF8" labels in Character Palette's pop-up help tags are, this is the sidebar you've been waiting for.

Remember all that stuff at the start of this book about encodings and the history of ASCII? The ISO-8859-1 standard is the first that subsumed the 128-character ASCII group and defined a full 256-character set. Also referred to as *Latin-1*, it's what the Windows character set (*WinLatin1* or *Windows-1252*) was based on. It's an old setup, and for the most part, the character IDs match those in Unicode.

UTF-8 encoding is a little more complicated. Unicode provides for just over a million characters, and 8-bit numbers top out at 255; it takes more than 20 bits, or a 6-digit hexadecimal number, to represent the highest Unicode ID numbers.

A "double-byte" number is needed to represent numbers in the upper Unicode range; that's a binary string of 16 digits, or a hexadecimal 4-digit number (see Appendix D if this sentence hurts). But the underlying Unix environment for Mac OS X—like most other computer systems, applications, and communications—expects character codes to be single-byte chunks, a two-digit hex number called an *octet*.

The solution: 8-bit UCS Universal Character Set Transformation Format, or UTF-8, a way to represent Unicode numbers in octets. The number of octets needed depends on the Unicode ID: a single octet can describe the first 128 characters—the original ASCII set; two or three octets can describe the rest of the 65K characters in a Unicode set; and four octets are needed for the characters in the planes beyond the first one. The UTF-8 encoding scheme is so clever, in a

Zen-like, self-referential way, that a character's code includes a way to determine how many octets are being used to describe the character.

So, UTF-8 encodings don't assign new codes to characters; they merely represent a character's Unicode ID. The acute-accent e (*é*), for instance, is represented by C389 in UTF-8. If you were just translating that hex number into decimal, it would be 50,153. But it's not supposed to be calculated into decimal: it gets transformed into the hex value 00E9 (decimal 233), the Unicode ID for the acute-accent *e*.

The majority of our English communications—in email, on Web pages—still use the original 128 characters, all of which are described by a single UTF-8 octet, so, in a serendipitous side effect, the characters we use the most are transmitted more quickly than those further in the code set.

Insert Characters

Finding a character in Character Palette wouldn't do you much good if you couldn't *do* anything with it. There are several ways to insert the current character into your document; when an application balks at one method it often cooperates with another. To insert the selected character:

1. Set the desired font in your document.

   Despite the "Insert With Font" button name, Character Palette font information seldom overrides that of your document.

2. Use any of these methods to insert the character; the "click" options insert the character at the current document insertion point, while dragging lets you drop the character anywhere in the document:

   ◆ Click the Insert With Font button.

   Sometimes the button is titled just Insert, and both versions are dimmed more often than not because so many of the glyphs you see in Character Palette can't be used in certain applications (as described in *The World According to Glyphs,* page 149).

   ◆ Click on the character well or drag the character from it.

   ◆ Double-click on the character in, or drag it from, any area that displays it: the character grid, the Related Characters list, or the Font Variation area.

Tip: *Really* **insert with font.** Character Palette's Insert With Font button doesn't always do what it says, even when the selected character is an "insertable" glyph. To increase the chances of its working, set the font you want in your document, too.

If you're dragging a character from Character Palette, taking it from the well means it will be formatted with the font that's in use at the spot where you drop it in a document; dragging the character from the Font Variation area almost always brings the font formatting with it no matter where you drop it in your document.

Find Characters with the Search Function

Character Palette lets you search for characters in three different ways:

♦ **By Unicode ID:** Say you want to get at the dotted-circle character used in the Keyboard Viewer picture in Figure 53 on page 168; the caption notes that its Unicode ID is U+25CC. Use 25CC for the search (the Search field doesn't understand the U+ part), and it finds a dotted circle in the Geometrical Shapes group.

♦ **By a typed or pasted character:** You don't have to go through views or character grids to select a character to see its variations in other fonts. Type the character (a bullet, say, with Option-8) directly into the Search field, and Character Palette displays all the bullet characters from all your fonts: you'll see tiny ones, fat ones, and even splotchy blobs from some of the less formal fonts.

♦ **By Unicode name:** While it's unlikely that you know the Unicode names for characters you want, partial-name searches usually work very well, and using some descriptive name almost always comes up with *something*.

Say you want to put a checkbox—already checked—as a graphic element in a document. You assume (rightly) that at least one of your fonts has such a character, so all you have to do is find it (the numbers in **Figure 62** are keyed to these steps):

1. Set Character Palette's View menu to All Characters.

   You can start in any view, but the character grid in All Characters is arranged by "similarity," so it's the best when you're looking at shapes—you'll see items similar to the one that showed up from your search.

2. Click in the Search field (at the bottom right of the window), type check, and press Return.

   A list pops up with several suggestions and samples of checkmarks and other items with "check" in their names.

   Use the Return key: Character Palette starts looking for the search item as soon as you start typing (the way Spotlight works in the Finder). You don't need to press Return for the search to work, but you do need it to "deactivate" the Search field. If the field remains active, clicking on a character to enter it into your document enters it into the Search field instead!

3. Choose "Ballot Box With Check" from the list.

Selecting something from this list is occasionally an exercise in frustration: the list disappears suddenly or treats you as if you'd clicked on a different item. Your best bet is to use the Up and Down arrow keys to select the item you want and then press Return or Enter. **Figure 62** shows the result of this search.

Experimenting with Character Palette's search feature familiarizes you not only with what it can do, but also with Unicode names (*Is it a circled digit or an enclosed number?*) and font repertoires. Try these search words to sample the possibilities: *life, bullet, dash, asterisk, sesame, heart, earth.*

Figure 62

The numbers in this figure, keyed to the steps in the text, were not rotated graphically; many Asian fonts have Roman characters in this orientation to work with the native orientation of the font.

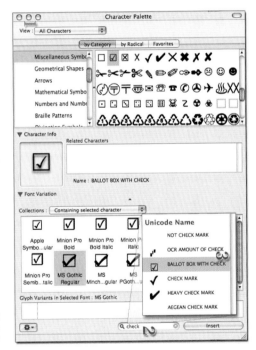

Numbers:
Hiragino MinchoPro
Starting at CID 8737

Searching for "check" in Character Palette provides a list of six Unicode symbols with that word in their names (inset). Selecting one from the list shows you what it looks like in various fonts. The first and last items in the found list have no sample next to them because no installed font with those characters is available.

Character Palette Fine Points

The more you use Character Palette, the more you'll benefit from knowing these small but useful details:

- **Included fonts:** Character Palette is limited to the *active* fonts in Font Book: disabled fonts, and any fonts in application-specific Fonts folders, are not included in searches or the pop-up Font menu in Glyph view.

- **Decode character grid numbers:** Some Character Palette views use a grid to identify a character's code in decimal or in hexadecimal (**Figure 63**). In either case, you derive the ID by combining the numbers labeling the rows and columns.

Figure 63

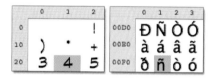

Left: A decimal-number grid; the selected character's ID is 21.

Right: A hex-number grid; the selected character's ID is 00F1.

- **Recover screen real estate:** Character Palette's zoom button shrinks it down to just the character well. You can make this shrinking automatic as you leave one application for another by choosing Minimize Palette On Application Switch from the Actions menu.

- **Open Font Book from within Character Palette:** Use the Manage Fonts command in the Actions menu. (Apparently the Open Font Book command was already taken.)

- **Help tags offer differing information:** Character Palette seems a little erratic when it comes to the information it shows in its pop-up help tags. Sometimes there's both a Unicode ID and a glyph ID, and sometimes there's only one or the other; the UTF-8 encoding, when it's included, varies from one to four pairs of hex numbers (**Figure 64**).

But it's not being capricious: sometimes a character has just a GID. Only those with Unicode IDs can have UTF-8 encodings, and lower Unicode IDs need fewer UTF-8 digits. And sometimes it can't show a GID because you're in a view that shows a "generic" character that has a different GID in each font where it's available.

Figure 64

Help tags in Character Palette give varying character ID information depending on the font, the character, and the Character Palette view being used.

You might occasionally see a CID number in a help tag; that possibility is limited to Adobe PostScript Asian-language fonts (see the sidebar *Yet Another Character ID Scheme,* page 154.)

◆ **Be careful about Unicode ID references:** Character Palette pop-up help tags always use hex numbers. Some programs—Word's Symbol palette, for instance, as shown in **Figure 65**—may refer to a Unicode ID with a decimal number in an effort to confuse you.

Figure 65

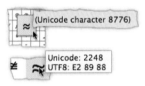

Word reports the symbol's Unicode ID as 8776 (top), but Character Palette (bottom) says it's 2248. The apparent discrepancy results because Word uses a decimal number while Character Palette reports a hex number: 8776 in decimal is the same as 2248 in hex.

This is a good reason to always use the U+ prefix, which indicates not only that it's a Unicode ID but also that it's a hex number. (See Appendix D for a tutorial on hex numbering.)

◆ **Put frequently used characters in the Favorites collection:** Character Palette lets you collect characters in a scrapbook-like collection of Favorites. When a specific character is selected, you can use the Action menu's Add To Favorites command and later access the character through the Favorites tab. So, for instance, you can round up the white-on-black circled numbers from 1 to 20 and then save time when you access them.

Unfortunately, the feature is poorly implemented. The Favorites collection shows only a generic version of the character—there's no font information attached. You can't reorder the items, and to remove them you must use the Action menu's Remove from Favorites command instead of a simple select-and-delete action. It's better than nothing, but you may find that the applications you use the most provide better, more convenient ways for repeatedly accessing special characters, as Word does with its AutoText feature. (See the sidebar "Easier Character Entry," on the next page.)

Easier Character Entry

Character Palette is overwhelming not only in its features but also in its size: even at its smallest, it takes over a laptop screen or bites a goodly chunk out of a regular screen, floating on top of everything else and generally getting in your way. But what else can you do when you need to go through a character set to find something special and Keyboard Viewer is so lame? Or when you repeatedly need certain non-typeable characters and your application doesn't support any kind of "favorites" glossary?

PopChar X: This $29.99 utility ($24.99 with the coupon at the back of this book) from Ergonis Software has been around just this side of forever. Its tiny menu nestles unobtrusively in the menu bar; click on it and the characters in the selected font are arrayed according to your choice of Unicode groupings, alphanumerics, or accented characters. Choose a character, and it's inserted into your document—in a size and style of your choosing. The 3.x version puts Character Palette to shame. Its price tag may seem a little hefty at first for a "tiny" utility, but it could be well worth the investment if you input non-standard characters on a regular basis; try out the partially disabled demo version (`www.macility.com/products/popcharx/`).

SpellCatcher: Although not made with Unicode in mind, when comes to entering special characters easily, nothing beats the $39.95 SpellCatcher from Rainmaker Software (get it for $29.95 with the coupon at the back of this book). Because its Shorthand feature lets you define a short sequence that's automatically replaced as you type (so "fb" turns into "Font Book"), you can type z1 and it's replaced by the Zapf Dingbats circled 1, or have cA and cB replaced by the circled A and B characters available in an Asian font. It works everywhere, in every application… oh, and it checks your spelling on the fly or after the fact, too, along with some other nifty features (`www.rainmakerinc.com`).

Use Alternate Keyboards for Foreign Languages or Other Special Input

Let's get this out of the way right up front: I'm no xenophobe. I know that what's a foreign language to me is native to someone else. For any user, all but a few of the languages and keyboards in Mac OS X are foreign. Since I'm using a Mac with an English—more specifically, a U.S.—operating system, everything else is, by definition, foreign. (Not that there's anything wrong with that.)

Alternate keyboards (or *input keyboards* or *keyboard layouts* or, sometimes, just *keyboards*) alter your typed input so your keypresses are translated into something other than what you usually type with each key. You might use an alternate keyboard to:

♦ **Type characters not available from your standard keyboard:** You can't use Character Palette to enter more than an occasional foreign language character unless you put aside a full day to write a letter home; Option character sets and dead keys provide only standard, Latin-based accented letters. When you want to type in a foreign language, you need to be able to really *type,* and foreign language input keyboards let you do that.

♦ **Match your input to a foreign hardware keyboard:** Whether you're practicing for a move, or learned on another system and want to continue using it, you can make your (presumably American) Mac keyboard respond as if it were from someplace else.

♦ **Use a rearranged keyboard layout to suit your typing habits:** Of course, this mainly refers to the Dvorak layout for more ergonomic typing, but that's not the only alternate layout in the world.

Understand Alternate Keyboards

Prior to Mac OS X, many foreign alphabets were simply fonts with appropriately arranged characters. Pressing Shift-A generated a numeric code that was passed along to the application, which said to itself "Okay, a 41... let's see, that's an A, so I'll display an A." If you had chosen a Greek font, the internal dialog remained the same, but *alpha* was displayed because the font was designed with an alpha in A's spot. In a Hebrew font, code 41 retrieved *aleph,* and in Cyrillic fonts an *ef*—but these were just funny-looking A's as far as the system was concerned. (Mac OS 9 provided special language kits, and "keyboard layouts" for more intensive foreign language typing, but the older approach I describe here—the only one used for many years—still worked under Mac OS 9 and many users never saw a need to switch to something that, while more sophisticated, was also more complicated.)

With the shift to Unicode, this approach presents a problem. The code for A is still 41 (U+0041) but many characters formerly accessed with the Shift-A combination now have different IDs: the Greek *alpha* is U+0391; the Hebrew *aleph* is U+05D0; the Cyrillic *ef* is U+0424.

What you need is something that translates your press of Shift-A into the correct code for the character you really want, in the context of the language you're working in. And that's exactly what you have with Mac OS X *input keyboards*, software that interprets the signal coming in from the hardware keyboard, translating the keypress according to the input keyboard you've chosen. With a U.S. keyboard active, pressing Shift-A generates a code that's interpreted as U+0041, the Unicode ID for A; select a Ukrainian keyboard, and pressing Shift-A ultimately generates U+0424, the Unicode ID for the Cyrillic *ef.* (See **Figure 66**.)

Figure 66

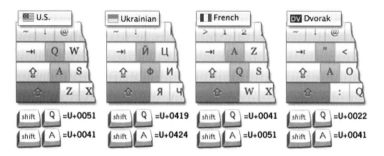

Using an input keyboard, or keyboard layout, from the Input menu is like putting an overlay on your hardware keyboard that lets you type characters other than the ones printed on the keys.

This picture shows which Unicode IDs are generated by pressing Shift-Q and Shift-A when various input keyboards are in use.

An input keyboard is not just an interpreter; it's also a specific arrangement of characters commonly used in a language. Usually, this means the setup matches the hardware normally used in the country where that language is spoken. (That's why there are both American and British keyboards, even though we speak the same language. More or less.) Sometimes the keyboard provides access to the characters most often used in a language but arranged to help native English speakers type more easily, like the QWERTY options for Armenian and Hebrew. And sometimes the input keyboard might have nothing at all to do with a foreign language, as with the Dvorak keyboard arrangement for more efficient typing.

Access an Alternate Keyboard

Once your Input menu is activated (described in *Turn On the Tools*, at the beginning of this chapter), it's easy to access a new keyboard:

1. From the Input menu, choose Open International.

   This is a shortcut to the International preference pane.

2. Scroll through the list of keyboards and check those you want to use.

3. Select the keyboard from the Input menu.

   The Input menu's "title" changes to the flag that represents the chosen keyboard (inset in **Figure 67**).

Figure 67

Keyboard Viewer shows the result of activating a Ukrainian keyboard in the Input menu (inset) and selecting the Cyrillic font Helvetica CY.

Tip: Select a keyboard from the keyboard. You don't have to go to the Input menu (a long trip on some big, wide screens) to select a keyboard. Command-Space sends you back to your previous input keyboard, which effectively toggles you back and forth between two keyboards in the list—an extremely handy shortcut when you're bouncing back and forth between languages to intersperse your basically English text with a few *bon mots* in, say, Russian.

Option-Command-Space cycles through all the keyboards listed in your Input menu. (But, as described in the sidebar *Clash of the Keyboard Shortcuts* on page 195, you might have trouble using that default key combination.)

Type in a Foreign Language without Changing Fonts

Mac OS X lets you type in many foreign languages without ever switching to a language-specific font, and sometimes without even switching keyboards.

Type in Roman languages

You don't have to change fonts or input keyboards to type in Spanish or French or any language that uses the Latin alphabet. All the characters you need to type *Répéter cela en français s'il vous plaît* are readily available—in every font you have—without switching fonts or keyboards. (Typing these kinds of accents was covered in *Use Keyboard Viewer to Type Accented Letters*, page 167.)

But if you're typing more than a few phrases here and there, you may not want to fuss with dead keys and multiple keystrokes to access accented characters. Switching keyboards lets you type the accented characters specific to a language more easily, since they'll be right up top instead of buried, as shown in **Figure 68**. (Okay, the French AZERTY instead of QWERTY might cause more problems than it solves, but you get the idea.)

Figure 68

The French keyboard puts frequently used accented characters on unshifted keys (the top row changes to numbers with the Shift key).

Type in non-Roman languages

As long as you change to an input keyboard that specifies the characters you want to type, you don't have to change fonts—you can let Mac OS X find the appropriate characters for you. Say you want to type:

The Hebrew spelling for shalom is שולם.

Here's the no-muss, no-fuss way to do it (assuming you've installed a Hebrew keyboard in the Input menu):

1. Type the English part of the sentence in some standard font, like Verdana.

2. Choose the Hebrew keyboard from the Input menu.

3. Type the four characters for Shalom.

   Never mind, for the moment, that since you're inserting this in an English sentence you have to type left to right, which is backwards for Hebrew; that's not the point. The point is: *you haven't changed fonts but the Hebrew letters appear.*

As Arthur C. Clarke said, any sufficiently advanced technology is indistinguishable from magic! This particular magic works because you used a Hebrew keyboard, so your application received codes for Hebrew letters. The characters don't exist in your current font, Verdana, so Mac OS X looks through your active fonts to find one that contains the letters you're trying to type. When it finds one, it substitutes that font for those letters. The system font Lucida Grande, which contains alphabets for many different languages, is usually the pinch hitter. (If no available font has the characters you typed, you'll get boxes instead.)

And, sure enough, if you go back and select those letters, you'll see they're in Lucida Grande (or possibly Times New Roman since it also contains the Hebrew alphabet). Try to apply a different font, and you just can't do it: the letters stubbornly (or cleverly) remain in the automatically applied font. You can change the font only if the new one also includes the Unicode Hebrew characters.

שלום **שלום** **שׁלוֹם**
שלום שלום **שׁלום**
שלום **שלוֹם** שלום

So, with automatic substitution available, why would you want to specify a font when you switch to a non-Roman language? For the same reason you change fonts when you're typing in English: for the look.

Third-Party Solution: Roll your own keyboard. Since keyboards trigger Unicode IDs for characters, wouldn't it be nice if you could make your own keyboard so you could easily type ancient Sumerian characters by generating the correct codes? Well, you can, with the free Ukelele, from SIL Software.

First, let me say that my spelling checker is annoyed that this utility isn't named *Ukulele*. Next, let me say that's the only thing wrong with this program. All you have to do is drag characters from Character Palette onto a keyboard layout in Ukelele; you can stick to basics or venture into multilevel dead keys. Ukelele makes the keyboard, and you stick it in ~/Library/Keyboard Layouts. On your next login, your new keyboard is listed in the Input Menu tab of the International preference pane. I used Ukelele to make keyboard shown here; it generates the circled letters available in several of the Tiger-supplied Asian fonts (http://scripts.sil.org/cms/scripts/page. php?site_id=nrsi&item_id=ukelele).

Use the Unicode Keyboard

Prior to Character Palette's introduction in Tiger, the Unicode keyboard was the only system-level way to enter characters that couldn't be typed because the keyboard couldn't generate their Unicode IDs. It's not as necessary now, but if you have the keyboard already available in the Input menu, it can still be faster and easier than dragging out Character Palette when you already know the ID of the character you want to type:

1. Add the Unicode Hex Input keyboard to the Input menu by checking it in the International preference pane's Input Method tab.

2. Choose the keyboard from the Input menu to activate it.

3. While holding down the Option key, type the Unicode ID *in hex, not decimal.*

Clash of the Keyboard Shortcuts

In case you haven't noticed, the Interface Police skipped their Cupertino patrol several times during Mac OS X development.

The default keyboard shortcuts to move to the previous keyboard in the Input menu or to cycle through all its listed keyboards are Command-Space and Command-Option-Space. The default keyboard shortcuts to activate the Finder's Spotlight menu bar option or its window are... guess what? Command-Space and Command-Option-Space. Really.

To use a shortcut to change Input keyboards, you must change the key combo for one or the other of these pairs.

Change Spotlight's shortcut: Go to the Spotlight preference pane and turn the shortcut on or off with the checkboxes at the bottom of the window. The two

options (for the menu and for the window) use pop-up menus that seem to limit your choice of key combinations, but you can click on the current one and press any keys you want to use. You can also edit these shortcuts through the Keyboard & Mouse preference pane.

Change the shortcut for Input keyboards: In the Keyboard Shortcuts tab of the Keyboard & Mouse preference pane, find

Input Menu in the list and expand it. Use the checkboxes to turn the options on or off, and change a keyboard trigger by clicking directly on it and typing the new combination. (You can just ignore the pane's directions to *double*-click on the existing shortcut to change it.) Yellow warning icons, as shown in the picture here, mark commands whose keyboard shortcuts are duplicated elsewhere.

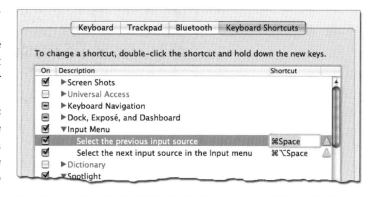

As soon as you finish typing the four digits, the character appears. For instance, entering 2042 produces an *asterism*, a triangle made of three asterisks. (Playing with Unicode can greatly expand your vocabulary.)

If the character whose code you input doesn't exist in the font you're using, it will be inserted in a different font, as long as there's an installed font that contains the character.

The unshifted and shifted letters of the Unicode keyboard are the same as a standard U.S. keyboard, so if you need to intersperse a few special symbols in standard text, you can conveniently type the standard alphanumerics with the Hex keyboard still active. (The Option and Shift-Option keys are blank.)

Override a balky Character Palette: Occasionally, I've found that even when Character Palette's Insert With Font button is active and I'm in an application that should accept the Unicode character I'm trying to use, I can neither use the Insert button nor drag the character into a document. In most of these cases, using the Hex Input keyboard worked to insert the character.

Third-Party Solution: Hex-decimal conversion. If you find yourself needing to convert hex numbers to decimal or vice versa when trying to access a specific character (or perhaps defining it in a Web page), let the free Hex Toaster do it for you (`www.toast442.org/hextoaster/`).

Watch Out for Keyboard Commands on Foreign Keyboards

When you're using a keyboard that, like the French one, doesn't have a Q in the expected place (from a U.S. perspective) or keyboards for non-Roman languages that don't have a Q at all, what happens when you press your usual Command-Q for Quit? If the foreign keyboard is designed with the native English-speaking computer user in mind, the program quits as usual, and other common keyboard sequences, like the ones for Cut, Copy, and Paste, also work as expected.

You're familiar with how a modifier key changes what the alphanumeric keys do: press Shift and get capitals, press Option and get special characters, and so on. The Command key is also a modifier, and a keyboard can be designed so that the character set available with the Command key is the basic Roman alphabet no matter what the typeable keys produce. So, as shown in **Figure 69**, pressing Command while using a Hebrew QWERTY keyboard temporarily "rewires" the keys to the Roman alphabet so that pressing Command-Q still generates the code that means "Quit."

The French input keyboard, on the other hand, with its AZERTY key arrangement (shown in **Figure 68**, page 193) doesn't change when you press Command; pressing Command-Q on your American hardware is interpreted as Command-A, so you get a Select All instead of Quit!

Figure 69

The QWERTY Hebrew keyboard uses Roman letters when you press Command; this doesn't affect typing since the sequence doesn't get passed through to your application or document, but it's what you need to use Command-S for Save.

Make sure you use Keyboard Viewer to check where your Command keys are when you switch to a foreign keyboard (just hold down Command while Keyboard Viewer is open). Improperly designed input keyboards, including most homegrown ones, may have no Command character set at all, requiring you to either use menu commands or switch keyboards to execute keyboard commands.

Warning! Log-Out Lockout with a foreign keyboard: *If you use a foreign keyboard, make sure you log out (an actual log out, or a shutdown or restart of the system) with the U.S. keyboard selected, not the foreign one. At log in, the system uses whichever keyboard was active when you logged out, so your password is typed with the characters from that keyboard. If you're lucky, the foreign keyboard will at least let you access the characters you need—but you still have to know how to access them. (It could be as easy as a British keyboard needing Option-3 instead of Shift-3 for the # sign. It could be—but it won't be.) See the* You logged out with a foreign keyboard active and now you can't log in *(page 262) for preventive measures and solutions for this problem.*

It's easy to log out with a foreign keyboard mistakenly activated: the keyboard command for logging out is Command-Shift-Q, and the one for changing the keyboard is Command-Spacebar. It's easy to hit Command-Spacebar with the thumb that's going simply for the Command key—you might not even notice the keyboard's switched.

12 Synchronize with the Rest of the World

You take your newborn home from the hospital wrapped in the 21st-century equivalent of swaddling clothes—a car seat. You're determined to protect her not just from harm but from the slightest distress. And yet, one day—whether it's day care, a playgroup, or the school bus—there she goes: out in the world and away from your protective care.

So it is with your documents once they leave the cocooned (relative) safety of your own computer. Out in the world, they face the onslaught of foreign systems and applications that can't always provide what you did when they were safe at home: just the right fonts.

Supply Fonts When You Can

The only way to be sure that the documents you send to another machine will use the exact same fonts you did is to send the fonts along with the document. But not all your fonts will work on other platforms—even on other, pre-OS X, Macs. **Table 17** rounds up your options.

Unfortunately, using the same font—even the same font *file*—is still no guarantee that a Mac-designed document will look the same on a PC but it's the best chance you have of getting the details across that great divide.

Disclaimer: The information in this chapter does not take into account copyright issues when discussing exchanging fonts between platforms or even embedding them in PDF files. We're all adults here; you know what you're not supposed to do.

Table 17: The Font Exchange		
Font Type	**Usable By**	**Comment**
dfont	Mac OS X	You can transform a dfont into a TrueType for older Mac systems with the freeware dfontifier program.
Mac TrueType	Macs, back through System 7	This should cover every Mac in use.*
Windows TrueType (.ttf)	Mac OS X and PCs	They've been available on the Windows side for many more years than on ours, so older versions of common fonts may be in use on that end.*
PostScript Type 1	All Mac systems; different files needed for PCs	The font files themselves are unique to each platform, so are not exchangeable.
OpenType	Mac OS X and PCs	Any Adobe offering is likely to be identical everywhere because of their recent decision to convert all their fonts to this format.
*If the user at the other end thinks her version of the font is the same as yours—just because the names are the same—and doesn't use the one you provided, your document may be affected.		

Minimize Document-Exchange Problems

While even Mac-to-Mac document transfers can't be depended upon to preserve font information, there's no doubt that it's the Mac/PC interchange that really causes problems. Understanding the most common problems helps avoid them—or at least minimize their impact.

Avoid Special Characters (Unless)

Avoid special characters unless a Unicode font is available on the other end. Unfortunately, "special" includes what we now think of as basics, like bullets and curly quotes.

The crux of Mac-PC font problems began not with the different fonts employed on the platforms (after all, an A in one font was always rendered as an A in another font on the other platform), but with the extended character sets used by each platform's fonts, and the way those characters were encoded.

As you may recall from the early pages of this book, the original ASCII scheme of assigning a number to every letter began with 128 numbers; the next 128 numbers were eventually standardized, but with a separate standard for each platform.

Macs used *MacRoman* encoding; PCs went with *WinLatin1*. The two are identical for the first 128 characters, which encompass the alphanumerics and basic punctuation. But while there's some overlap in the second 128 characters, the Mac standard has 23 characters you won't find on PCs (such as pi and the apple) and PCs have 17 unique characters (such as some superscripted numbers and fractions). As for the characters in common, many are assigned different numbers on each platform. So, type something innocent on the Mac—something including curly quotes, a bullet, and a degree symbol—and watch it turn into gibberish on the PC side (**Figure 70**).

Figure 70

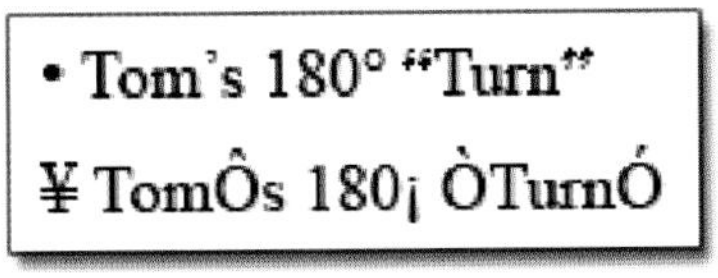

Type a seemingly straightforward phrase on the Mac (top) that uses characters from the "high" ASCII set, and a Windows machine may display them according to its own encoding scheme (bottom). A bullet is #165 in MacRoman; that number is assigned to the yen symbol in Windows; similar encoding problems occur with curly apostrophes, quotes, and the degree mark in this example.

Unicode solves all these problems since it uses the same character codes everywhere, but if Unicode isn't in use on the PC side, you may encounter character substitution problems like those shown in **Figure 70**. So, if you think Unicode's not on the other end (that is, your counterparts are using an operating system earlier than Windows 2000 or XP), stick with the "lower ASCII" set of characters: straight quotes and apostrophes, no bullets, and so on—ugly documents guaranteed.

Leave Room for Font Enlargement

PCs usually render the same point size at a larger visual size (without enlarging other aspects of a document, like graphics).

Wouldn't you think that since Mac screens started out at 72 dpi (dots per inch) and PC screens at 96 dpi, the same point-size font on a PC would appear *smaller?* It doesn't, however, because early PC programs, and the Windows operating system, corrected for that potentially smaller-looking font by upping its apparent size. This approach is so entrenched that many programs still do it, so even today with screens of varied resolutions, a font defined as 12 points on a PC looks about the same as one set to 15 points on the Mac. (And you thought all those Web sites with tiny text were because of your aging eyes, but they are, in fact, a result of development on a PC platform!)

Since this font resizing is independent of screen resolution and anything else in the document, a neatly designed PowerPoint presentation, a nicely laid-out Word document, or a painstakingly arranged FileMaker layout might have problems with how text relates to graphics or to a page or screen when it's viewed on the other platform—regardless of which font you use and whether the same one is available on the other end. In programs whose layouts use text boxes (like PowerPoint and FileMaker), make sure the boxes are big enough to accommodate the larger type, as shown in **Figure 71**.

Preserve Typefaces with "Style-linking"

Preserve the typeface you want in your document by applying character formatting from the keyboard instead of selecting from a submenu. Otherwise, your bold and italic variations may disappear.

On the Mac, many programs let you select a specific typeface for a family by selecting from a submenu *or* by applying a style like bold or italic, whichever is more convenient to your work habits. (Details are in *Manage Character Style-Typeface Interactions,* page 143).

On the PC side, getting a typeface by applying a style to a base font is called "style-linking," and it's often the only choice on Windows platforms (as it

Figure 71

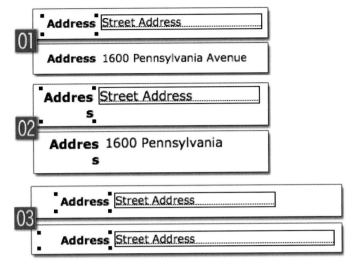

Numbers:
Hiragino Kaku Gothic Pro
CIDs 11579, 11581, 11583

1: A simple FileMaker layout element, a field with a label, is satisfactory on the Mac. (Top, Layout mode; bottom, Browse mode.)

2: When opened on a PC, the font with the same defined size is larger; the label's text box and the field are both too small.

3: The original layout setup (top). The adjustments to the layout needed to allow for expansion on the PC (bottom).

is in Word on the Mac side). Oddly enough, the Windows programs seem to care how the font formatting was done originally: select a typeface from a submenu for a Mac document, and it often reverts to the base font when viewed in the Windows environment. Use the style-linked formatting approach (applying bold or italic styles to selected text) on the Mac side whenever possible to cut down on potential interpretation problems.

Stick to the Safe-as-Possible Fonts

While there are no guarantees that certain fonts will always be found on both sides of the Mac/PC equation, you can maximize the chances by sticking to certain fonts. List the fonts installed by each system and add the Microsoft Office fonts, and you get two dozen reasonably "safe" choices.

These are the fonts in common; you may have two versions of the asterisked ones: one each from Tiger and Microsoft Office 2004. Use the ones that came with Office, not only because those are the versions

Windows users will have but also because they're better, as detailed in **Table 13** (page 109):

Arial*	Helvetica
Arial Black*	Impact*
Arial Narrow*	Monotype Corsiva
Book Antiqua	Tahoma
Bookman Old Style	Times
Century	Times New Roman*
Century Gothic	Trebuchet MS*
Comic Sans MS*	Verdana*
Courier	Wingdings
Courier New	Wingdings 2
Garamond	Wingdings 3
Georgia*	Zapf Dingbats

Of course, fonts in common doesn't *guarantee* anything: you can still run into problems with different font versions, and then there's that pesky size differential. But it's a start.

Can you PDF it? *If things are only going to be read—onscreen or printed—so that you don't need a "live" document that can be edited, making a PDF of your document is the best way to ensure that what you created is what they see. In Mac OS X, every Print dialog has a PDF button.*

Tip: Testing 1, 2, 3. This is actually less a tip than a stern warning: Test on the target machine! If you're creating a Web site, an important PowerPoint presentation, or a cross-platform FileMaker solution, there's no excuse for not finding a way to view your work or perform a test run on the target platform. If you don't test it, you'll deserve your fate when it explodes.

When You're on the Receiving End

You might be able to totally reformat a report written in Word, or tweak a few PowerPoint slides, when the creator's use of fonts is not as carefully considered as yours would be. But some documents are, by their very nature, non-editable, meant only for your viewing pleasure.

When it comes to the ultimate in one-way document exchange—Web pages—there *is* something you can do that might miraculously clear up a garbage-ridden page. That other one-way document vector, the PDF file? Well, at least I can reassure you that, except for one possibility, the problems aren't on *your* end.

Refine Your Web-Page Reception

Pity the poor Web designer, whose best-laid plans are so easily thwarted by a user's font collection and preferences settings. And spare a little for the surfers (especially the ones hanging ten on their Macs), who aren't up to juggling font issues that affect how a Web page looks.

Encoding issues—and their historic differences on the two platforms, as described a few pages ago in *Minimize Document-Exchange Problems*— cause most of the Web-page problems you run into. If the designer knows what he's doing, you shouldn't have problems, because each of his pages will contain information that tells your browser what encoding to use. But there are thousands of less-than-knowledgeable people churning out Web pages, so you won't always have this particular get-out-of-jail-free card.

In the absence of the proper embedded encoding information, a page created on a PC using its default WinLatin1 encoding can have problems on a Mac using *its* default MacRoman encoding. The difference in IDs and the presence or absence of specific characters in each encoding standard results in gibberish for characters beyond the basic alphanumerics.

Take, for instance, the display of the lyrics to the Oscar-winning song from *The Lord of the Rings*, "May It Be," which includes a few Elvish words. (Please don't send me email to complain about that generic species reference; I know Tolkien defined more than one Elvish tongue, and these words are in *Quenya*):

Mornië utúlië; believe and you will find your way.
Mornië alantië; a promise lives within you now.

A WinLatin-encoded page with these lyrics viewed under MacRoman encoding displays the problems shown in **Figure 72**.

Figure 72

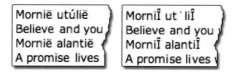

The text as typed in on the PC side for the page, with no special encoding instructions, defaulting to WinLatin1 (left), and its appearance in a Mac browser using MacRoman encoding (right).

Luckily, Macs are not limited to MacRoman encoding (nor are PCs limited to WinLatin1!). You can change the encoding Safari uses, both on a global and a page-specific level:

♦ **Define the default encoding scheme:** In Safari > Preferences, use the Default Encoding pop-up menu at the bottom of the Appearance pane (**Figure 73**). This tells Safari which encoding to use in the absence of encoding information in the page itself.

♦ **Redefine the encoding scheme for the current page:** Use the View > Text Encoding command and the page changes instantly (usually to something much more reasonable).

Figure 73

Choose a default encoding scheme from Safari's Appearances preference pane.

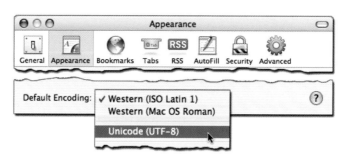

Whether you're choosing default or page-specific encoding, for English and Western European languages, the ones to try are:

♦ **Western (ISO Latin 1):** The WinLatin1 PC standard. On browsers other than Safari, an equivalent might be listed as ISO 8859-1, WinLatin1, or Windows-1252.

♦ **Western (Mac OS Roman):** The MacRoman standard prior to Mac OS X.

♦ **Unicode (UTF-8):** An international standard. (The UTF-8 scheme is described in the sidebar *ISO and UTF-8 Encodings,* page 182.)

"The ones to try are…"? What kind of advice is that? It's hard to be specific, because you'll never know ahead of time what encoding any particular Web page uses. (**Figure 74** shows how the same page can look under your three basic browser encoding choices.) But here's some more-specific advice:

♦ If your browsing is primarily of cutting-edge, techie, or up-to-date sites, set your default encoding to UTF-8.

♦ If your browsing is more wide-ranging and includes lots of older, amateur, or made-for-Windows-users sites, set your default to ISO Latin 1.

When specific pages don't render correctly, override the default setting with the page-specific encoding option.

Other encoding choices: *The descriptions here assume you are dealing with English or a Western European language. There are dozens of encoding choices specific to non-Roman languages when UTF-8 doesn't work for a page.*

Figure 74

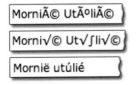

More variations on a theme: the same page viewed with a Safari encoding set to ISO Latin 1 (top), Mac OS Roman (middle), or UTF-8 (bottom). Note that the letter/accent combos are interpreted as two separate characters in the first two examples.

Note: The Unicode "replacement character." In Figures 72 and 74, the browser may be showing incorrect characters, but it's *unaware* that its interpretation isn't correct—it's just doing what it's told. Sometimes, however, it stumbles on something that it doesn't know how to interpret in the defined encoding scheme; that's when it substitutes the Unicode "replacement character" shown here.

> Morni◆ ut◆li ◆

Put Up with PDF Peculiarities

Another way to "supply" fonts is to embed them in a document. On the PC side, several programs—notably PowerPoint—can embed fonts in documents, but only other PCs can see the embedded fonts. On our side, embedding is possible for only PDF documents.

Creating PDFs with full-fledged PDF-writing software is a mixture of art, science, and voodoo—and a topic for another author. Mac OS X makes the production of basic PDFs incredibly easy for users with the PDF button/menu in the Print dialog.

Embedding dfonts: Although dfonts are Mac-only fonts—in fact, they're Mac OS X-only fonts—you can safely use them in a document that's going to be converted to a PDF. During the conversion, dfonts are embedded as regular TrueType fonts, so there's no problem with opening them on other computers (pre-OS X Macs or PCs).

As a PDF recipient, you can lessen the chances of PDF display problems by making sure you have the fonts a PDF might reasonably expect you to have available (because the PDF creator probably didn't embed those fonts). You may have problems if you've deleted:

♦ The folder `/Library/Application Support/Adobe/PDFL/7.0/Fonts` (or its `5.0` or `6.0` equivalent—whatever is your latest version), accessed by Acrobat Reader to render non-embedded fonts in PDFs

♦ Specific fonts from the `PDFL` folder

♦ System fonts that might substitute for the mistakenly trashed Adobe `PDFL` fonts, such as Courier.dfont and Times.dfont

◆ The Times or Helvetica MM fonts (Helvetica LT MM, HelveLTMM, Times LT MM, and TimesLTMM) from /System/Library/Fonts, which Preview uses to render non-embedded fonts in PDFs

Most common PDF problems originate on the creation end. I'm listing them here just so you'll know it's not *your* fault:

◆ **The PDF file size is humongous, yet it consists of only five pages with no graphics:** When the PDF creator chooses to embed an entire font instead of a subset (only the characters used in the original document), and the font is a rich OpenType with thousands of characters, it bloats the size of the PDF.

◆ **Text is spaced awkwardly, large letters look stretched:** The beginnings and ends of words and lines are critical in preserving the layout of a document. When fonts aren't embedded, they're simulated on your end; the substitute fonts are squeezed and stretched to fill the right amount of space on a line or to approximate the shape of an original drop cap.

◆ **Words that are supposed to be bold are plain but have multiple, over-printed copies:** Programs like Word that fake their way into bold text when there's no bold typeface available *do* overprint copies of plain-face text to bold it, and sometimes a PDF reflects that. (Fake, or "faux," styles are covered in Chapter 9.)

◆ **Text in special fonts looks fine, but text in basics like Helvetica, Times, Courier, and Zapf Dingbats is wonky:** The special fonts are embedded, so they display correctly. The others aren't embedded in Adobe-created PDFs because, since they (along with some others) are always installed with Acrobat or its Reader, they can always be found on the end-user's machine. That is, unless the user trashed one or more of the fonts or folders listed at the beginning of this section.

◆ **Most text looks fine except for *some* basic fonts, like Times and Helvetica:** Upgrades of Adobe Acrobat Reader since 5.0 have changed in regard to the fonts they installed, and therefore the ones that can be safely left unembedded; Acrobat 7.0, for instance, no longer includes Times, Helvetica, and Zapf Dingbats in its list of core "always available, don't bother embedding them" fonts. So, your Times and Helvetica system fonts, or other available versions on your computer, might be used when you open the PDF, but they may be different from the ones used when the PDF was created.

♦ **Everything looks fine but you can't edit the text in Adobe Acrobat:** When a subset of a font is embedded, only the characters that exist in the document are actually embedded, making it impossible to edit the text in that font.

Tip: The Unembeddables. No, that's not Disney/Pixar's latest movie—it's fonts that can't be embedded in PDFs (or anything else). A font designer gets to decide if her font is allowed to be embedded in a document, and that information is included in the font file. You don't have to wait for an embedding refusal from Adobe Acrobat; you can check ahead of time by using the System Profiler, which compiles an exhaustive list of information about installed fonts:

1. Choose About This Mac from the Apple menu.

2. Click More Info.

3. In the left column, expand the Software category, and click on Fonts.

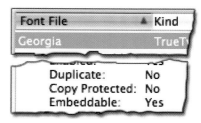

13 Prevent and Analyze Problems

Font problems are a fact of computer life. They shouldn't be, but they are.

Often the problems are very minor: *Why can't I type a √ with Option-V in this font?* Sometimes they're a little more pervasive: *Why isn't that font showing in the Font menu? Why can't I empty the Trash when this font is in it?* And other times they're dire: *Why does Font Book crash every time I open it? Why is every menu and dialog filled with garbled text?*

Solving a font-related problem is a simple two-step process: figure out what's causing the problem, and then fix it. Okay, maybe it's not that simple: symptoms can have many causes, and causes have many possible fixes. But with this and the next chapter, you can both narrow down symptoms to a probable cause and look up the cure most likely to work. Even better, you'll learn how to avoid some problems altogether.

◆ **If you're not in font trouble right now:** Read *Take Preventive Measures and Plan Ahead* (page 212) and implement its suggestions.

◆ **If you're unfamiliar with Mac troubleshooting methods:** Check **Table 18** (page 215), which rounds up the software utilities you'll need for some of the solutions described in this chapter—most of them are provided with Tiger. Review **Table 19** (page 221), which lists the testing and fix-it procedures that are described in *Learn Troubleshooting Procedures* (page 220).

♦ **If you're having a general problem:** If the problem is non-specific but you suspect it's a font problem, **Table 20** (page 239) will help you differentiate between general font problems and general system problems. If you're convinced it's a font problem, read *Tackle General Font Problems* (page 238) and use the troubleshooting flowchart on page 241.

♦ **If you're having a specific problem:** If your problem is easily pinpointed (you just put in a new font, then everything imploded; Character Palette won't open; Font Book's libraries are not listing their contents correctly), you should skip ahead to the next chapter, which describes specific problems and solutions. Many of the solutions referenced there, however, are covered in this chapter's *Learn Troubleshooting Procedures*.

Take Preventive Measures and Plan Ahead

I'm not sure how you'd measure an ounce of prevention or a pound of cure, but the philosophy holds: it takes less time and effort to prevent a problem than to fix it.

General Guidelines

Follow these simple guidelines to stay trouble-free, or at least make troubleshooting or fix-ups easier when a problem crops up:

♦ **Upgrade, upgrade, upgrade:** First, upgrade to Tiger: its general approach to fonts and native font-handling capabilities are miles ahead of its Mac OS X predecessors. (And, if Mac OS X 10.5 Leopard is out when you read this, chances are good that Leopard will do an even better job with font management, so when I say "upgrade to Tiger," I mean you should be working with Tiger—Mac OS X 10.4.x—at the very least.)

Next, keep upgrading Tiger versions. There's no excuse not to, since these minor updates are free. Font management has changed, sometimes significantly, with each 10.4.x version. In fact, the 10.4.4 upgrade actually provided new versions of Courier and Monaco dfonts to correct some glyph-display problems with CE and CY (Central European and Cyrillic) characters; the 10.4.7 Tiger provided a minor update to Font Book that took care of some problems in installing and removing fronts.

Finally, keep your applications updated with fixes as they become available, and upgrade to major revisions as soon as it's financially feasible. (A major, but nebulous, font problem that lasted for months for a friend in QuarkXPress 6, no matter what we did, disappeared when the documents were opened in the beta version of Quark 7; imagine what the released version does!)

♦ **Don't remove or disable system-critical fonts:** The core fonts, all in /System/Library/Fonts, are Keyboard.dfont, LastResort.dfont, Monaco.dfont, Geneva.dfont, LucidaGrande.dfont, Helvetica.dfont, and probably the two AquaKana fonts: AquaKana.otf and AquaKanaBold.otf. These are described in **Table 11** (page 91).

♦ **Don't add fonts to the System Fonts folder:** Put your fonts in ~/Library/Fonts, or in /Library/Fonts when you want multiple users to share them, or create user-defined libraries through Font Book (page 124). When you want to disable everything but the fonts in /System/Library/Fonts to mimic a "pure" system setup for trouble-shooting, you can't have extra fonts in it.

♦ **Close applications before installing, disabling, or removing fonts:** Adobe programs don't mind if you change fonts while they're open, but it can crash Microsoft applications.

Tip: Sneak Behind Word's Back with Font Changes. If you install or remove a font and then realize Word is open, or you switch into Word before you realize what you've done, just don't open the Font menu. Save and quit out of Word right away. Or, switch out of it right back in to Font Book and put the fonts back the way they were, at least temporarily—Word will never know that you changed things and then changed them back.

◆ **Validate new fonts:** Even if Font Book's validation process isn't top-of-the-line, it's all we've got (at least on a system level). Make sure you use it to validate fonts before, during, or after installation. (See *Validate Fonts,* page 75.)

◆ **Keep track of newly installed fonts until you're sure of them:** The new kid on the block is always the chief suspect when a new font-related problem crops up, so colorize (by using the Finder's File > Color Label command, as described in *Font-Tracking Techniques,* page 44), comment, rename, or use subfolders to sequester new and/or old fonts so you know which are which.

◆ **Make sure suitcases are packed correctly:** Unattached bitmapped fonts (without companion Type 1 printer files) can wreak havoc, and multiple-family suitcases can cause confusion. (See *Learn How to Pack a Suitcase for Mac OS X,* page 131, for details.

◆ **Use only one font manager:** Never have two font managers working at the same time—and Font Book counts as a font manager. The conflicting orders and information they give the operating system, and where they look for fonts, will cause grief; you'll have more font problems to deal with than if you had no manager at all. (Check *Prep for Changing Font Managers,* page 217, before you switch from Font Book!)

Know Your Tools

With a few exceptions, the troubleshooting and fix-it steps I describe throughout this book use software tools and procedures provided natively in Mac OS X; some third-party programs help in specific circumstances. **Table 18** rounds up both types of "tools,"; it shows whether the tool comes with Mac OS X, why you'd use it, and where you'll find it.

Mac OS	Other	Tool	☆ Why ★ Where
☑	☐	Disk Utility	☆ Repairing permissions ★ Applications > Utilities
☑	☐	Install discs	☆ Reinstalling the system or components ★ Where did you put them??
☑	☐	Font/DA Mover	☆ Repacking suitcases ★ www.takecontrolbooks.com/resources/0037/font-da-mover.html
☐	☑	Font Doctor	☆ Repairing corrupt fonts. ★ www.morrisonsoftdesign.com
☐	☑	Pacifist	☆ Extracting system components from install discs ★ www.charlessoft.com
☐	☑	Font Finagler	☆ Deleting system fonts caches ★ http://homepage.mac.com/mdouma46/fontfinagler/

Table 18: Font Troubleshooting and Maintenance Tools

Checkboxes: MS Gothic. Blank: U+2610, GID 1797. Checked: U+2611, GID 1798
Stars: Apple LiGothic. Hollow: U+2606, GID 317. Filled: U+2605, GID 318

Archive Your Fonts and Utilities

Font problems are a fact of computer life, so no matter how well you behave, you're bound to have some eventually. When you do, you'll wish you could just return to yesterday, or the day before, or last week—a time when your every move wasn't foiled by font problems.

Take a "snapshot" of your trouble-free font environment by creating archives of the most important (and most-likely-to-be-a-problem) font elements of your Mac, so you can return to yesterday. Use the Finder's File > Create Archive command to make a zipped copy of each element; it conveniently leaves the original in place so you can continue using it. You can store the archives right on your hard drive; they don't take much room, and they'll be at hand should you need them. Put them in their own folder; if you have no preferred method of storing these kinds of things,

I recommend that you use the top level of your "home" (user) directory—it's what you see if you click on the house in the default sidebar of a Finder window. Archive these items (using the Create Archive command for these and similar items is described in *Make Backup Archives,* page 41):

♦ **Fonts folders:** Ideally, you should archive your Fonts folders before you make any font changes at all—but it's probably too late for that. You might want to reconstruct the pure System and Library Fonts folders (`/System/Library/Fonts` and `/Library/Fonts`) using the list in Appendix B for archiving. At any point that your system's humming along nicely—and especially before you make any major font changes (additions, deletions, or reorganization)—you can archive all your Fonts folders, especially `~/Library/Fonts`, which holds the majority of your fonts.

♦ **Adobe Fonts folders:** If you use Adobe products, like Creative Suite or any of its components, you might want to archive the `/Library/Application Support/Adobe/Fonts` folder. But if you decide not to bother with that, do archive its subfolder, `../Adobe/Fonts/Reqrd/Base`. If you accidentally (or otherwise) erase this folder or its fonts, your CS applications won't run at all. (See *Creative Suite programs won't launch; they want "CMap files,"* page 284, for advice about this problem.)

♦ **Font Book:** Many users have been relieved to find that when nothing else worked, using a fresh copy of Font Book finally solved some vague but wicked font-related problem.

Sounds easy enough, doesn't it? But the problem is that there's no easy way to get a fresh copy of any system component, since the Installer doesn't let you pick the pieces you need. While the shareware utility Pacifist (described in the sidebar *Reinstall System Components with Pacifist,* page 234) lets you extract things from your install disc, the problem with that is that you may have updated your system since its original installation; Font Book has changed a bit with some of the Tiger updates.

So, the best approach is to create an archival backup each time you upgrade your system so you'll have a fresh updated copy of an item if you need it. You'll find Font Book in your Applications folder.

♦ **Character Palette and Keyboard Viewer:** Everything I said about Font Book applies here: sometimes a fresh copy of either of these items fixes an otherwise unfixable problem, the Installer doesn't let you reinstall them, and copies you extract using Pacifist may be older.

O Character Palette, where art thou? Neither Character Palette nor Keyboard Viewer exists as an application as we know it. The files you need to archive are CharacterPalette.component and KeyboardViewer.component, in /System/Library/Components.

Prep for Changing Font Managers

If you replace Font Book with a third-party font manager (see the sidebar *Font Book Replacements,* page 52), don't just jump in the deep end. Take some time to get things in order before you switch from Font Book—and again if you switch back.

If you're leaving Font Book:

1. **Archive your Fonts folders.** If you run into trouble with the new manager or switch back to Font Book for some other reason, you may want to restore the folders as they existed before the switch to the new manager (a font manager usually moves your fonts to different folders according to its own storage scheme). Use the Finder's Create Archive command to archive your Fonts folders separately or together. Here's where to find the folders:

   ♦ /System/Library/Fonts

   ♦ /Library/Fonts

   ♦ ~/Library/Fonts

   ♦ /System Folder/Fonts

2. **Archive Font Book.** If you switch back, you'll need it, but you can't have it hanging around in the meantime, arguing with the new manager. The zipped-up archive can't do anything but sit there.

3. **Delete Font Book.** Get rid of the non-archived copy.

If you're leaving the third-party manager:

If you decide your font manager isn't doing what you need and you want to switch to a new one or go back to Font Book, here's how to make a smooth transition:

1. **Turn off auto-start options in the font manager.** Change any options that set it to open at startup or in response to any specific activity (opening other applications, opening documents whose fonts are missing, and so on).

2. **Quit the font manager program and archive it.**

3. **Delete the font manager application.** You'll have the archived copy, so you can always unzip it if you want it back. This keeps it from launching unexpectedly, in case you haven't turned off all its components—which can be trickier than you think.

   If the program's installer offers an uninstaller, use it. A real uninstaller (and there ought to be a law requiring one for every program!) deletes any extraneous pieces scattered around your drive.

4. **Make sure the core system fonts are in** /System/Library/Fonts. Some managers may move the system fonts out of this folder, which is no problem while the manager is still telling the operating system where they are; but once you stop using the manager, the fonts won't be available to Mac OS X unless they're in one of the official Fonts folders. The core fonts are listed in the "Absolutely Necessary" section of Appendix C; find them and drag them back into the System Fonts folder if they're not in residence.

5. **Prevent the outgoing font manager from opening automatically.** Didn't I already address this? Yes, but if Step 1 is impossible because the program doesn't offer an obvious way to stop itself or its components from running, and you skipped Step 3 because it's so psychologically difficult to erase a program from your hard drive, you'll have to do your best to ensure that the manager doesn't pop up to "help" you after you've fired it. Check these three things:

   ♦ If the application's icon is in the Dock, uncheck Open at Login in its contextual menu (hold down the mouse button on the icon in the Dock to access the menu). Also, Remove it from the Dock since you're not going to be using it anymore.

♦ Go to the Accounts preference pane and, *with your account selected*, click the Login Items tab. Select any items related to the font manager and click the ⊟ button beneath the list to remove them. Unchecking the item is not sufficient; the checkboxes are for hiding or showing items, not adding or removing them (**Figure** 75).

Depending on the font manager and your page layout program, an extension or plug-in may have been added to your application. A beta version of Linotype Explorer X that I tested popped up a dialog when I opened an InDesign document that contained inactive fonts, many weeks after I thought I had gotten rid of the program entirely. I had forgotten to check for a leftover plug-in (InDesign > Configure Plug-ins), for a leftover plug-in.

Figure 75

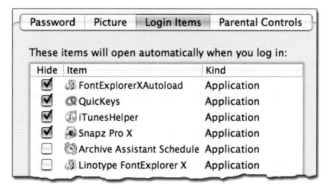

The Accounts preference pane shows two items, at the top and bottom of the list, that belong to Linotype's FontExplorer font manager; they open and run in the background—and open FontExplorer in the background—at your next startup, even if you've quit FontExplorer itself and it's not set to open at startup.

6. **Delete the system font caches**.

    This is described later in this chapter, in *Delete Caches and plists* (page 228).

7. **Restart**. If your font manager has been keeping your fonts in special folders, you may have a lot of file-dragging to do to put things back

for Font Book to manage. If you can't *find* the fonts that your manager managed, use Spotlight in the Finder to track them down, as described in *Find Misplaced Fonts* (page 96).

Learn Troubleshooting Procedures

You don't have to be an expert to perform tasks like a Safe Boot or setting up a new user account; all you need is the step-by-step instructions in this section. Some of the procedures described here help you figure out what the problem is, some of them actually fix problems, and some do both (as noted in **Table 19**). I've divided them into three groups:

♦ **General procedures:** This includes things like repairing permissions, setting up a new user account, and Safe Booting.

♦ **Delete caches and plists:** Mac OS X has font caches, but so do Microsoft and Adobe programs; and although Font Book's plist is practically famous, it's not the only plist that needs deleting.

♦ **Restore system components:** You can't reinstall "pieces" of the operating system with the Installer, but you can still get at them, whether you need to replace fonts or Font Book.

General Procedures

Many of these procedures are used for general (non-font-related) Mac problems, so you may already be familiar with some of them.

Warning! *A Safe Boot isn't all it's cracked up to be. Even if you're experienced enough to have started up in Safe Mode as a troubleshooting method, don't skip my instructions in* Start up in Safe Mode *(page 224). Contrary to popular belief, a Safe Boot doesn't trash all your font caches or necessarily limit you to only the fonts in* /System/Library/Fonts.

Restart your Mac

An oldie but a goodie: just save everything and restart. Sometimes glitches just go away, so it's worth a try!

Table 19: Testing and Fix-it Procedures			
Test	**Fix**	**Procedure**	**Comment**
	✘	Restart the Mac	Clears out mistakes in memory
	✘	Repair system permissions	A long shot, but easy to do
	✘	Repair font-file permissions	Not needed often
✘		Try a new user account	Narrows the scope of possible problems
✘	✘	Start up in Safe Mode	Ignores all but system-level items; performs housekeeping chores on things like font cache files and the disk directory
	✘	Delete caches and plists	Dumps possibly corrupted files
	✘	Restore system components	Replaces fonts, Font Book, Character Palette, and Keyboard Viewer
✘		Binary search for bad font	Tracks down a bad font
	✘	Archive and Install	Not usually needed for font problems
X's: MS PMincho: U+2117			

Repair permissions

If you spend some time on various user message boards, you'll find a lot of disagreement about whether repairing permissions across the board actually does any good more than once in a blue moon. But it's easy enough to do, doesn't take long, and has no downside, so it should be in your arsenal of troubleshooting weapons:

1. Open Disk Utility, in `/Applications/Utilities/`.

2. Click on your startup volume in the left panel.

3. Click the First Aid tab.

4. Click Repair Disk Permissions.

Reset font file permissions

The phrase "repairing permissions" always refers to the system permissions as just described. But when it comes to fonts, another kind of permission alteration is occasionally necessary:

1. Select the font file in the Finder and choose File > Get Info (Command-I).

2. Expand the Ownership & Permissions section.

3. Set the You Can pop-up menu to Read & Write.

You can do this only for items that you "own"; the default owner for most items is the Account owner. You can (sometimes) set the ownership back to yourself—assuming that's what went wrong—in the same Get Info window:

1. Expand the Details area.

2. Click the lock icon to unlock the Owner pop-up menu.

3. Choose your Account name from the pop-up menu.

4. Click the lock icon to lock the menu again (**Figure 76**).

Figure 76

The Get Info window provides a menu for setting the file permissions as well as for setting the owner—the one who's allowed to change the permissions.

Try a different user account

The majority of font-related problems are local to a specific user account. Setting up and switching to a new, clean account is one way to pin down where a problems lies—whether it's specific to your account or more pervasive. (Does account terminology seem like a foreign language—or a strange dialect—to you? See Appendix F for some background.) Setting up a second account is easy, although you need administrative privileges to do it:

1. Go to the Accounts preferences pane.

2. Click the lock icon at the bottom of the window to unlock it, providing your password when asked.

3. Click the ⊞ button beneath the Account list.

4. In the dialog that appears, fill in an account name, password, and so on (*Verify* means to type the password a second time), and check Allow User To Administer This Computer.

5. Click Create Account.

6. Use the Picture tab to assign a picture to this account if you're going to use *Fast User Switching*, described below.

7. Click the lock icon to close it and prevent changes.

Note: Font Book changes from one account to another. *You won't see "your" Font Book if you open it from within another account; collections, user-defined libraries, and the fonts in* `~/Library/Fonts` *are all specific to each user.*

Fast User Switching

If you keep a second account around for troubleshooting font problems, it's a real pain to log out of one account and log in to another, especially because you then have to log out of that account and log back in to yours, with the concomitant delays for starting up each time. But you can bypass the delays by activating Fast User Switching:

In the Accounts preference pane, for each account in the list:

1. Select the account name.
2. Click the lock icon at the bottom of the window to unlock it, providing your password when asked.
3. Click Login Options at the bottom of the accounts list.
4. Check the button Enable Fast User Switching.
5. Choose Icon from the View As menu.
6. Click the lock icon to lock the changes.

You'll get an Accounts menu in your menu bar (the generic-but-sure-looks-male-to-me silhouette icon); it lists the accounts on your computer, and you can choose one to switch from one account to another without logging out. And it does it with— as much as I promised myself 20 years ago I would *never* use "cool" to describe something in one of my books—the absolutely *coolest* visual effect around.

Start up in Safe Mode

Starting up in Safe Mode, also known as a *Safe Boot,* is a generic trouble-shooting procedure that has specific benefits for a system with font problems: it deletes some of the font caches for you, and puts you into a "Tiger-only" environment that ignores most of your fonts and all your third-party add-ons.

Every other description of Safe Mode startup you'll see starts with Step 3 here, but when you're diagnosing font problems, you need the preceding steps, too, as I explain a little further on. Here's how to start up in what I think of as "Even Safer Mode":

1. **Get rid of your user-defined libraries.** You can just "put them away" temporarily: go to `~/Library/FontCollections` and drag out the files whose names end in *.library*. These files track which fonts belong to the libraries, and where the fonts are located. You can put them back in the folder later, after you've used Safe Mode and solved your font problem. (There's more about this folder and its contents in *Collections or User Libraries Misbehave,* page 253.)

2. **Trash the folder `/Library/Caches/com.apple.ATS`.** A Safe Boot is supposed to delete all the system font caches, but it doesn't do a thorough job, so do it yourself.

3. **Restart in Safe Mode:** Restart normally, but as soon as you hear the startup sound (*not before*), hold down Shift.

4. **Release the Shift key when the gray Apple appears.** At this point you'll have to wait quite a bit—long enough to get worried, and perhaps even edge toward panic—as the progress wheel goes round and round and round and…. It can take several minutes before your login screen appears, so try not to freak out.

   If you don't see the words "Safe Boot" in red on your login screen, try starting up again, and get that Shift key down a little sooner.

In a Safe Mode startup, Mac OS X performs the following maintenance tasks, ignoring certain aspects of your operating environment:

- Checks and repairs the startup disk's directory; this is the same as using the Repair Disk command in Disk Utility.

- Loads only absolutely necessary extensions.

- Launches only system startup items.

- Disables login and startup items.

- Moves all *user* font caches to the Trash. (More about that "user" thing in a little bit.)

Here's the other thing it's *supposed* to do:

- Ignores all fonts except those in /System/Library/Fonts—if you open Font Book, you can't even see the fonts in other folders.

This last item is practically canonical, but it's **not true**, no matter what Apple says in its support documents. Safe Mode ignores the User, Computer, Classic, and Network Fonts folders, which would seem to leave only the system Fonts folder, but *user-defined libraries are still active*. Yours aren't, of course, because you followed the directions in Step 1.

Now, about "*user* font caches" being moved to the Trash: this is another problem I've not seen addressed elsewhere. As detailed in *Delete the system font caches* (page 228), /Library/Caches/com.apple.ATS contains subfolders for each user and one for the system, but Safe Mode deletes *only the user subfolders*. If you have endemic font problems, you need to dump the system cache subfolder, too (which you did in Step 2, right?).

So, once you're in Safe Mode, what do you do? Try to re-create your font problem—launch your word processor and type, for instance. If the problem's gone, you'll have narrowed down the possible causes to those items used in regular mode but not in Safe Mode (as described in Step 4 of the steps that comprise *Tackle General Font Problems,* page 238).

To start up again in regular mode, just restart the computer without the Shift key down; it can take several minutes for the first regular startup after a Safe Boot.

Use a Safe Login

This is a mini-version, or maybe a micro-version, of a Safe Boot: hold down Shift when you log in to an account, *after* you put in the password and hit Return. This prevents user-specific Login Items (listed in the Accounts preference pane) from loading.

Perform an Archive and Install

The last-ditch effort for ultra-serious Mac problems of any ilk is the Archive and Install option on your Mac OS X install disc. It puts a new, clean operating system on your Mac, shunting aside—but *saving*—the version you've been using, with all the additions and changes you've made. It's unlikely that a font problem will push you to this extreme. But if you find yourself *in extremis* and resort to it, the fonts you've installed won't be erased; you can use the Spotlight in the Finder to find them.

Find the Bad Font
out of a Hundred (or More)

When you suspect your font problems are due to a corrupted font rather than a system-wide problem, always assume it's the most recently installed one. When that piece of advice is useless because it could be any of a hundred or more fonts causing the problem, you don't have to take out and put back one font at a time.

The efficient approach is something left from previous Mac systems, where we'd try to find a recalcitrant extension among the many well-behaved ones: a binary search—which merely means you narrow the search by continually dividing your suspects into two groups. The procedure comes in two versions: a thorough one, and a short one for if you're feeling lucky. Here's the thorough version:

1. Quit your applications.

2. Working directly with the Fonts folder holding the suspected problem font, drag half of the possible culprits into a temporary folder on the Desktop.

This is much easier if you've tagged fonts with colors or names, or put them in subfolders, so you know which are the newly installed ones, as I recommended in *General Guidelines,* earlier in this chapter, and detailed in *Font-Tracking Techniques* (page 44).

3. Delete system font caches (page 228).

4. If Font Book has been having problems, Delete Font Book's plist (page 231).

5. Restart your Mac.

If there are no problems, the suspect font is in the off-loaded group, so put half of them back in service (colorize them first with the Finder's File > Color Label command, or keep them in a subfolder so it's easy to manipulate them as a group) and see if the problem resurfaces after the restart. If it does, the font is one of the recently returned fonts; if not, the problem is in the half that was left behind. And so on—keep dividing whatever group contains the bad font until you're down to only a few that can be added one at a time. Make sure you delete the font caches and restart after every shuffle, or any problems you encounter may be leftover from the last font arrangement you tried and not the current one.

Granted, you might have more than one bad font in the group, which means that at some point both halves of a group are going to cause problems—but that just makes the whole procedure that much more fun.

Here's the short version of the procedure:

1. Quit your applications.

2. Take out half of the fonts.

3. Restart your applications and see if the problem is gone.

This short procedure is only reliable if it has a positive result: the problem goes away when you move the fonts. If there's still a problem, it could be a corrupt font in the batch in use, or it could be information left in memory about the now-removed corrupt font; that's why the long version calls for deleting the font caches and restarting. You can continue the short-version binary-swap game and hope, or switch to the thorough version and try again.

Delete Caches and plists

A *cache file* stores data about what you've done recently; its usefulness is based on the assumption that you're likely to repeat your actions and it's faster to retrieve information from the cache file than to re-create it. A font cache stores information about recently used fonts, saving time that would otherwise be spent scrounging around your drive looking for the actual font file, opening it, interpreting the information… you get the idea. Since these files get heavy use, they're ripe for corruption, and once they're corrupted, all heck can break loose. Trashing font caches can fix many general font problems, and since they're re-created as necessary, you can trash away with abandon. Mac OS X has general font caches; Microsoft and Adobe also have their own font cache files.

A *plist* (pronounced "pea-list") is a *property list*, a file that stores a user's settings for a program or utility or a—well, for anything that can *have* settings. It serves basically the same function as a pre-Mac OS X preferences file and, in fact, you'll usually find plists in folders named Preferences. Not all plists get heavy use, but Font Book's does, so it's quite prone to corruption; Character Palette and Keyboard Viewer have plists, too.

When you get rid of a plist, you lose the special settings you've made for a program, so certain options and things like window positions return to their defaults; this is usually nothing more than a minor annoyance.

Delete system font caches

The general try-this-no-matter-what-the-symptoms-are approach to font problems is trashing the system font cache files. (That's font cache files that belong to the system, not cache files that belong to the system fonts!)

Tiger, unlike its Mac OS X predecessors, keeps all its font cache files in a single folder, so they're easy to delete:

1. Drag the folder `/Library/Caches/com.apple.ATS` to the Trash.

2. Restart your Mac.

Warning! Don't skip the restart! Cache-file information is continually swapped from memory to disk and back to memory. Deleting the cache files doesn't affect what's already in memory; if corrupted information is in memory, it gets written right back to the disk files.

On the restart—which you may find takes a little longer than usual—new font cache files are created so even if this doesn't solve your problem, it won't hurt anything, except that *all your disabled fonts in Font Book are enabled* (if that counts as hurting).

All the files in the com.Apple.ATS folder that you just trashed are referred to generally as "*system* font caches" to differentiate them from font caches created by specific applications. The folder has subfolders for each user account—the first user's is 501, the next 502, and so on—and one folder for caches shared by all the accounts, named System (**Figure 77**). They are all, however, considered *system* font caches.

Warning! *Starting up in Safe Mode, which is often credited with trashing all the font cache files,* does not delete all the system cache files, *but only the user-account folders inside com.apple.ATS. Get rid of the entire folder, or all the subfolders inside it, to completely delete the system font caches. Yes, I said this before, and I'll say it again before the end of this book; since it's contrary to the advice you'll get elsewhere, I want to hammer it home.*

Figure 77

This is an example of a com.apple.ATS folder's subfolders and files.

The 501 folder is the default folder for the first account created on an OS X Mac; 502 is for the second account, and so on.

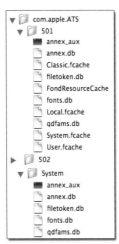

There are four types of cache files:

.fcache files hold internal information grabbed from font files.

Annex.aux, the largest file in these folders (over 200 times the size of the smaller ones) stores the character mappings for all the cached fonts.

.db files, the smallest caches, are basic lists of available fonts.

FondResourceCache holds information about OpenType fonts in use.

Some of the specific font-related problems that this all-purpose procedure can cure include:

♦ Garbled text in documents. (*Text is garbled in documents,* page 274, describes other reasons this happens.)

♦ Unexplained printing errors (with font substitutions, awkward spacing between words or lines).

- ◆ Problems with creating PDF files.

- ◆ Font menus that don't update when you install or remove fonts. (*A font doesn't appear in a Font menu*, page 271, suggests other possible causes and cures.)

- ◆ False font corruption warnings, particularly in Office applications—see *(Mostly false) reports of corrupt fonts* (page 282).

Third-Party Solutions: Font Finagler. With font cache files spread out all over the place in pre-Tiger Mac OS X, the $10 (or less) shareware utility Font Cache Cleaner, by Mark Douma, was handy because it did all the scurrying around for you. Now it's called Font Finagler, and it's less of a boon because all the cache files are in a single location now (although you don't have to remember where they are if you're using the Finagler). But if you're in a multi-Mac environment, Font Finagler provides an important special benefit: non-administrative users can clean out their font caches, a privilege usually denied to mere commoners (`http://homepage.mac.com/ mdouma46/fontfinagler/`).

Tip: Clear Out Old Font Caches. Mac OS X versions prior to Tiger stored font cache files all over the place; if you've been upgrading all along, you may have these useless files still sitting around. You can get rid of:

- ◆ From `~/Library/Caches`: Five files whose names begin with *com.apple:* FCacheClassicDomain; FCacheUserDomain; ATSServer.0050E4C50426. FODB_Classic; ATSServer.0050E4C50426.FODB_Local; and ATSServer. FODB_User. There may be additional files with similar names but with numbers inserted, like *ATS.system_257.fcache;* these can also be deleted.

- ◆ From `/System/Library/Caches`: three files whose names begin with *com.apple:* ATS.System.fcache, ATSServer.FODB_System, FCacheSystemDomain, and a fourth file, fontTablesAnnex.

- ◆ From `/Library/Caches`: com.apple.FCacheLocalDomain.

Delete the MS Office font cache

The Microsoft Office font cache is especially prone to corruption, per-haps because of all the fancy footwork Microsoft applications do to take care of fonts *their* way. For Office 2004, the file is `~/Library/Preferences/Microsoft/Office Font Cache (11)`. For Office X, the filename ends in `(10)`, but Office X has so many problems under Tiger that trashing the file isn't likely to solve them.

Delete Adobe font caches

Adobe creates private font cache files with names like AdobeFnt01.lst, AdobeFnt02.lst, and so on. Adobe has multiple Fonts folders for its use, and it spreads its cache files around, too. Close your Adobe applica-tions, and do a Finder Spotlight search for *adobefnt*. The search will turn up more than just the cache files, but delete all the cache files (the ones that end with a number and then *.lst)* that it does find.

Delete Font Book's plist

One of the easiest Font Book troubleshooting procedures—trashing its plist—also takes care of the majority of its problems:

1. Close Font Book.

2. Find and trash `~/Library/Preferences/com.apple.FontBook.plist`.

3. Reopen Font Book.

As with all plists, a new one is created as soon as you launch the applica-tion again, so you don't have to worry that you're getting rid of something that will keep a program from working. On the other hand, a preferences file is just that: it tracks your preferences within a certain application, so those items will be reset to their defaults. In Font Book's case, trashing the plist:

♦ Resets the default installation folder to User

♦ Returns the window to its default size and position

♦ Restores any settings you made regarding warning dialogs

Note that if the problem is not the plist, you might corrupt the newly created plist when you try working in Font Book and the other problem (whatever it is) rears its ugly head again. Repeated plist trashing is the order of the day when you're troubleshooting Font Book problems.

Deleting the plist *and* the system font caches probably cures 90 percent of general font problems.

No more plist/disabled worries: *Early versions of Tiger's Font Book also totally lost track of which fonts were disabled when you dumped the plist; version 2.0.2 resolved this issue.*

Delete Character Palette's plists

Character Palette has two plist files whose contents can get mangled rather easily; trash them both when you're having problems with Character Palette. Close Character Palette before you delete the files; there's no need to restart the Mac.

♦ `~/Library/Preferences/com.apple.CharPaletteServer.plist` stores information like Character Palette's last position on your screen and what's in its Favorites list, minor points that are lost when you trash the file.

♦ `~/Library/Caches/com.apple.CharPaletteCache.plist` helps speed along Character Palette's behavior.

Delete Keyboard Viewer's plist

Keyboard Viewer seems to be rock solid: I don't know of anyone who's had a problem with it yet, and I've been trolling message boards watching for an example. (Maybe nobody's using it?) That doesn't mean *you* won't have some problem sometime that can be cured by deleting its plist: `~/Library/Preference/com.apple.KeyboardViewerServer.plist`.

(The computer gods have mocked me in my hubris on behalf of Keyboard Viewer; between the time I wrote that paragraph and reviewed it during an editing pass, the Keyboard Viewer on my PowerBook, after years of quiet subservience, had taken to popping up to say hello at unpredictable intervals. *Character Palette crashes or generally misbehaves,* page 260, explains how to handle this if it happens to you.)

Restore System Components

The font-related system components you might have to restore at some point are:

- Fonts
- Character Palette
- Font Book
- Keyboard Viewer

You can't really "reinstall" system components because the Installer does only complete installation sweeps: you can't pick out a font, or Font Book, or any separate component. When you need a font-related system component restored, you have three-and-a-half options:

- **Use your archived copy:** Unzip the copy of the problem element that you made according to the suggestion in *Take Preventive Measures and Plan Ahead* section at the beginning of this chapter. You didn't plan ahead? Try the other options.

- **Get a replacement from a Mac friend:** You're a licensed user of the software, so it's not piracy or trespassing. Make sure it's the most recent version available (encourage your friend to update if she hasn't!).

- **Use Pacifist:** As described in *Reinstall System Components with Pacifist,* on the next page, this is a great shareware tool for extracting components from your install disc.

- **Update the operating system:** This is the half option, because it might not apply to you, or because it might not work. If you're behind a version or two in the free releases that Software Update can pull down, and if you're lucky, it will update the components giving you trouble. It won't replace fonts you've removed, but there have been occasional updates to individual fonts, and new versions of Font Book, Character Palette, and Keyboard Viewer could be included in the update.

Reinstall System Components with Pacifist

You'd like to reinstall all the system fonts in /System/Library/Fonts and /Library/Fonts because things have been a mess and you'd like to start from scratch. Or you want to use the Tiger foreign language fonts but didn't choose that option during installation. Or you need a fresh copy of Font Book or Character Palette because yours has imploded.

Unfortunately, Tiger doesn't let you do piecemeal installs. Fortunately, the $20 shareware program Pacifist does (www.charlessoft.com). You do have to be willing to get your hands dirty trolling through folders and files instead of simply checking options and clicking

Install, but it's worth the effort (besides, it's not as if you have a choice!).

Click Pacifist's Open Mac OS X Install Packages button when your Install disc is inserted, and it opens a window that shows a hierarchical list of the Install disc's contents; as you might imagine, that's a *long* list. Paths to items you want are labyrinthine (and depend on which system's on the Install disc); the system fonts, for example, are in Contents of OSInstall.mpkg/Contents of BaseSystem.pkg/System/Library/ Fonts on a G5 DVD. Luckily, the Pacifist search feature lets you get to things easily.

Pacifist can compare what's on

the install disc to what's on your hard drive, and it will even do an actual install of an element (with all its components also written to your drive), although you can just drag many items from the window onto your hard drive.

When you use Pacifist (and you will!), keep this in mind: many items have multiple versions available, so *make sure you select the one from the correct folder*. You'll find more than a dozen *Font Book.app* files, for instance, because there's one in every language package—but you'll need the one in the Essentials package. And, read Pacifist's brief but helpful documentation before you dive in.

Tip: Use Pacifist on an Update .dmg. You've upgraded Tiger religiously, watching that second-decimal-place number increment every few months, and now you're worried because the version of Font Book you want to extract from your install disc might be five versions behind the one that just died in your system.

Pacifist works with the virtual disks derived from disk images just as well as it does on real discs, so you can use it to extract the latest Font Book from a downloaded updater disk image. But not every system element is included in an update, so you won't always be able to find Font Book, or Character Palette, or whatever you need, in the most recent updater.

Restore or Add Tiger Fonts

Why can't you just download fresh fonts from Apple's Web site? Wrapping them in some sort of Mac OS X-flavored installer would keep them from being installed for any unauthorized use. Well, until they come to their senses about this, you at least have your archived Fonts folders to turn to, right? And there's always the find-a-friend option. But, depending on which fonts you're trying to install, you also have a few options with your Tiger install disc, even before you turn to Pacifist for its extraction capabilities.

Restore fonts to the System Fonts folder

You have two choices for restoring system fonts. One is incomplete, leaving out a few /System/Library/Fonts standards, but that may not matter to you, since they're foreign language fonts—it might be a good trade-off because it's so simple. The other method takes a little longer and requires your downloading the shareware Pacifist program, but it gets *all* the Tiger system fonts back on your drive.

♦ **Direct from the install disc:** Since your install disc has a system on it (that's why you can use it to start up your Mac), it has most of the system fonts in its own /System/Library/Fonts folder. Just navigate to the folder and grab the ones you need, dragging them to /System/Library/Fonts on your drive. Not all of the fonts are in the disc's Fonts folder; it's missing these files:

   ◇ Geeza Pro Bold.ttf   ◇ Hiragino Kaku Gothic Std W8.otf

   ◇ Geeza Pro.ttf   ◇ Hiragino Mincho Pro W3.otf

   ◇ Hei.dfont   ◇ Hiragino Mincho Pro W6.otf

   ◇ Osaka.dfont   ◇ Hiragino Maru Gothic Pro W4.otf

   ◇ OsakaMono.dfont

   If you don't need any of these foreign language fonts, you may not care that you're not restoring them.

♦ **Extracted with Pacifist:** To find all the fonts on your install disk with Pacifist, use its Find function to search for "Fonts" with Ignore Case unchecked so it finds fewer items but all the Fonts folders. The system fonts are in two different groups. One folder contains the fonts used on the Installer's system (the set missing the nine fonts listed in the last bullet); you'll find it in the path that includes `../Contents of BaseSystem.pkg/`. The other has the nine missing fonts; it's at `../Contents of Essentials.pkg/Library`.

Restore basic fonts to the Library Fonts folder

You can't get at these without using Pacifist, since they don't exist as separate files on the install disc. Search for "Fonts" and find the folder in `../Contents of Essentials.pkg/System/Library`.

Restore the Additional Fonts to the Library Fonts folder

These are the foreign language fonts that are optional during a system install. If you opted not to install them but now want to add them, you have two options:

- **Direct from the install disc:** You can access a separate installer from the Tiger disc for these fonts (note, however, that Pacifist lets you choose from among the fonts, while the Installer insists on your having all of them):

  1. On the install disc, double-click on the Optional Installs icon.

  2. Click your way through the standard starting screens for licensing agreements.

  3. On the Custom Install screen (see **Figure 78**), check Additional Fonts.

  4. Click Install.

- **Extracted with Pacifist:** You'll find the additional, foreign language fonts listed inside `/Contents of Additional Fonts.pkg`.

Figure 78

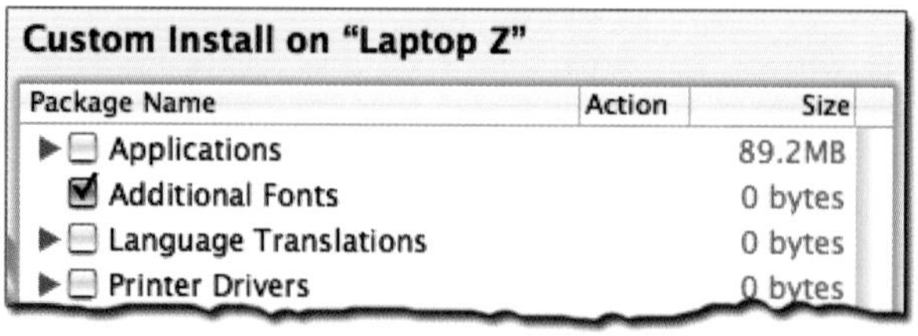

Using the Optional Installs program for additional fonts.

Custom Install on "Laptop Z"

Package Name	Action	Size
▶ ☐ Applications		89.2MB
☑ Additional Fonts		0 bytes
▶ ☐ Language Translations		0 bytes
▶ ☐ Printer Drivers		0 bytes

Restore Font Book

Restoring Font Book is a little more complicated than restoring fonts.

First, your fresh copy—archived, from a friend, or extracted with Pacifist—should be the most current version (because your operating system version is the most current one, right?). Font Book hasn't been changed with every minor update, but you don't want to miss any bug fixes. Will a slightly older Font Book version still run in a slightly newer system? Probably—and if you're behind on a bug fix or two, it's still better than no Font Book at all.

Next, there are a few steps necessary for a clean Font Book restoration—you can't just drag it onto your disk and go:

1. Delete your current Font Book from the Applications folder.

2. Delete Font Book's plist (page 231).

3. Delete the folder ~/Library/FontCollections.

   This isn't absolutely necessary unless your problems are collection- and library-based, in which case you may have already trashed the files in this folder, as suggested in *Collections or user libraries misbehave* (page 253).

4. Delete system font caches (page 228).

5. Put your fresh copy of Font Book in the Applications folder.

   If you're using Pacifist to extract Font Book from your install disc, use its search function to look for "Font Book.app"; of the 15 or so hits you'll get—one for every language package—work with the one that is in the path ../Contents of Essentials.pkg/Applications.

6. Restart.

Restore Character Palette or Keyboard Viewer

As with restoring Font Book, when you restore Character Palette or Keyboard Viewer, you should get the most recent version as a replacement. Then:

1. In the Input Menu tab of the International preference pane, turn off Character Palette or Keyboard Viewer by unchecking it in the list.

2. Delete Character Palette's plists (page 232) or delete Keyboard Viewer's plist (page 232).

3. Delete the current version of the utility from /System/Library /Components (the files are ChazracterPalette.component and Keyboard Viewer.component) and replace it with the fresh copy.

    If you're using Pacifist to extract Character Palette or Keyboard Viewer from your install disc (search for those .component files), make sure you get the version that's in the ../Contents of Essentials.pkg/.. path, and not one of the foreign language versions included on the disc.

4. Turn Character Palette or Keyboard Viewer back on by checking it in the International preference pane's Input Menu tab.

If you have any immediate problem with Character Palette's or Keyboard Viewer's behavior in the Input menu (the icon isn't next to the name, choosing it doesn't do anything), proceed to the methods described in *The Input menu misbehaves* (page 256); the simpler suggestions there should be sufficient to get the fresh version to do your bidding.

Tackle General Font Problems

Some problems are obviously font-related: you put in a new font and it doesn't show up in a menu or everything starts crashing. And when you have what's obviously a font-related problem, sometimes it's an easily identified symptom: Font Book doesn't list all your user-defined libraries, for example.

But in many situations, it's not all that clear. Is the crashing from a system-wide problem totally unrelated to fonts? Is it a problem with a system component related to fonts (like Character Palette) but not actually a *font* problem? And if it seems to be a font problem—is it a font, or is it Font Book? And how do you approach fixing a problem whose symptoms are nonspecific? Take a deep, cleansing breath and follow these steps:

1. **Decide the probable cause:** Use the guidelines in **Table 20** to assign the blame to font files, Font Book, or a more general problem. You'll find

Table 20: Laying the Blame

Font	Font Book	Other Mac OS X element	Comment
⊙		●	No startup: stuck on blue screen
◐		●	Random crashes and freezes; no apparent font-related problem
◐		●	Applications crash on launch
●	◕	◐	Microsoft applications crash on launch
◕	●	◕	Font Book crashes or otherwise misbehaves
◕		●	Character Palette crashes or otherwise misbehaves
		●	Keyboard Viewer crashes or otherwise misbehaves
		●	Input menu misbehaves: doesn't list items, doesn't respond
●	◕		Applications crash when you select fonts (any or specific)
●	◕		Menus or dialogs appear in foreign language text
◐		◐	Applications crash when you print
◐			Fonts are substituted or spaced oddly when you print
●			Garbled menus or dialogs
●		◕	Text is garbled in documents
●	◐		Installed fonts missing from font menus
●	◕		Documents default to foreign language text despite proper settings
	●	◕	Collection or user-library information in Font Book or Font panel acts up

Font
Font Book
Other Mac OS X element

● Most likely the problem
◐ A good chance it's the problem
◕ Possibly the problem
⊙ This font-related startup problem fixed in Mac OS 10.3

Circles: Apple Symbols. Whole: U+25CF, GID 222; Half, U+25D1, GID 224; Quarter U+25D4, GID 227
Bulls eye: U+2609, GID 298.

some overlap: Character Palette issues, for instance, could be blamed on Character Palette itself (a system component), but since Character Palette is somewhat sensitive to corrupt fonts, the problem might be a bad font.

2. **Try a quick fix:** If you can identify a font-related problem in addition to general symptoms (you may be crashing a lot randomly, but you've noticed Character Palette doesn't always open the first time you choose it from the Input menu), look through *Learn Troubleshooting Procedures* (page 220) for related actions—deleting Character Palette's plist, for instance. This can take less time—even if you try two or three procedures—than a full-blown analysis to narrow down the problem.

3. **Analyze the problem further:** The flowchart in **Figure 79** shows you how to use various troubleshooting procedures to zero in on your problem. In many cases, one of the steps in the chart will also fix the problem you're having.

   ♦ If your path takes you to the "Unlikely a font problem" box, you should consult a general Mac troubleshooting reference; you may have no option other than to *Perform an Archive and Install* (page 226), as noted in the chart.

   ♦ If you wind up in either of the red boxes, proceed to Step 4.

4. **Tackle items in the area indicated on the flowchart:** When you've followed all the flowchart steps and you still have problems, you'll at least know where to concentrate your efforts, as described in *User-specific items* (page 242) and *All-user items* (page 243).

Figure 79   ## Analyze and Solve Nonspecific Font Problems
(You're using the most recent Tiger update • No recently installed fonts)

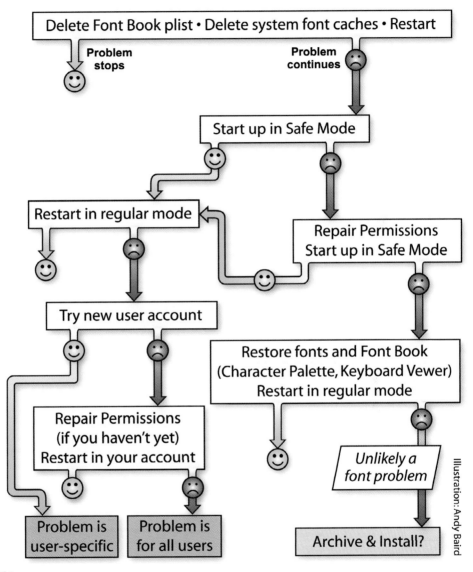

Faces: MS PGothic.
Smile: U+263A, GID 17872
Frown: U+2639, GID 17871

Use this flowchart to isolate the cause of your problem and solve it. The procedures referred to in the yellow boxes, and the gray one, are in the Learn Troubleshooting Procedures *section of this chapter (page 220). If you wind up in one of the reddish boxes at the bottom left, check the suggestions on the previous and next pages. (A copy of this flowchart is at the very back of the book.)*

User-specific items:

When problems occur in your account and no other, these are your suspects:

- Fonts in `~/Library/Fonts`.

- Fonts in user-defined libraries. (These are also accessed in Safe Mode if you don't deactivate them before going into Safe Mode.)

- Font Book's plist.

- Font Book files in `~/Library/FontCollections`, described in *Collections or user libraries misbehave* (page 253).

- Character Palette plists.

- Keyboard Viewer plist.

- Font cache files in the `/Library/Caches/com.apple.ATS/501` folder. The 501 folder is for the main account; there's a 502 folder for the second user account, and so on.

- Microsoft Office font cache files.

- Adobe font caches.

- Login items specific to your account. You can *Use a Safe Login* (page 226) to filter out this possibility.

- Any utility running in the background *or* foreground that isn't used in other accounts. (Watch out for third-party font managers clashing with Font Book!)

All-users items:

When problems occur in other user accounts as well as your own, but they don't occur in Safe Mode, check:

♦ Fonts in /Library/Fonts.

♦ Font cache files in /Library/Caches/com.apple.ATS/System.

♦ Login items used by more than one account. You can *Use a Safe Login* (page 226) on each account to test this possibility.

♦ Any utility that runs in the background *or* foreground in all accounts. (Watch out for third-party font managers!)

♦ Safe Mode items: These are the font-related items that are common to all users *and* are used in Safe Mode. You can rule them in or out as suspects depending on how your Mac behaves in Safe Mode:

◊ Fonts in **/System/Library/Fonts**. Safe Mode isn't smart enough to pick system-installed fonts; if you've put fonts in this folder, they're used in Safe Mode.

◊ Fonts in active user-defined libraries. I describe the "only /System/Library/Fonts" fallacy in *Start up in Safe Mode* (page 224); make sure your user libraries are deactivated.

◊ Font Book. Only its plist and its related files in ~/Library /FontCollections are user-specific.

◊ Character Palette. Only its plists are user-specific.

◊ Keyboard Viewer. Only its plist is user-specific.

Solve Specific Problems

If you've suffered through general font problems that seemed impossible to pinpoint, it's almost a relief to have a problem that's more specific in nature: Font Book is misbehaving, an icon changes, a font file can't be erased, character formatting doesn't seem to "take"... all sorts of annoying but identifiable things. The problems and solutions in this chapter fall into these categories, with each section beginning on the page specified:

Font Book Problems

It's not always easy to differentiate general font problems from those caused by Font Book (see **Table 20**, page 239, for help with that)—which means it's not all that clear what you should do about them, either. If you're convinced that you have a Font Book problem but can't pinpoint it, start with the first entry here, about non-specific problems. If you can pinpoint the problem a little—it seems connected to user-defined libraries, say, or the dots that mark duplicate fonts don't seem to make sense—scan the rest of the entries in this section to find something that matches your problem.

Nonspecific problems or Font Book crashes on opening

Many things can cause or contribute to general Font Book problems or an on-launch Font Book crash, but let's assume it's not a system-wide problem (and, if Font Book's crashing, it's the *only* thing that's crashing on opening).

Here's the drill (feel free to combine steps like deleting groups of files, and stop at any point your problem's solved!):

♦ **Delete Font Book's plist:** This step alone, described on page 231, has a high success rate; no restart necessary.

♦ **Delete Font Book's plist, delete system font caches, and restart:** Even if you tried deleting the plist already, do it again in this step because the unsolved problem may have corrupted the newly created replacement plist. (See *Delete system font caches,* page 228, if you need help with that procedure.)

Lather. Rinse. Repeat. Those simple instructions sold twice as much shampoo as anyone really needed, but you should repeat this "delete the plist, delete the font caches, restart" trilogy after each step below because using Font Book while things are still going wrong can (re)corrupt its plist, and doing anything while fonts are naughty can ruin the new system font caches.

♦ **Check for corrupt fonts and suitcases:** As usual, it's a last-in, most-suspect situation. Take out the suspects; sequester the whole ~/Library/Fonts folder as a quick test.

◆ **Delete collection and library fcaches:** Nothing happens to the collections or libraries themselves, as described in *Collections or user libraries misbehave* (page 253).

◆ **Delete collection and library files:** If you have extensive collections and user libraries and don't want to rebuild them, you can move them out of ~/Library/FontCollections temporarily to see if their absence improves things. The files are described in *Collections or user libraries misbehave* (page 253).

◆ **Delete files used in common with Font panel:** These files, com.apple. Favorites.collection and com.apple.Recents.collection are also in ~/Library/FontCollections.

◆ **Follow the flowchart:** If nothing has worked so far, jump into the flowchart in **Figure 79** (page 241) with the step *Start Up in Safe Mode* and continue from there.

A font isn't in the expected folder or library after you install it

This is almost always (okay, *always*, no *almost*) a user error—or at least a misunderstanding, usually caused by one of Font Book's potentially confusing Default Installation Location pop-up menu or its less-than-crystal-clear Collection list:

◆ **The Default Installation pop-up menu:** Check *Set Font Book's Preferences* (page 51), especially for its explanation of what the Computer choice in the menu represents.

◆ **The Collection list:** Table 9 (page 68) describes where a font winds up when you drop it on an item in the Collection list.

Font Book can't see a font in a Fonts folder

You know the font is in the folder because you looked, and there it is. And you looked in a *Tiger* Fonts folder, not an application's Fonts folder. Assuming the font is a supported type and there's nothing wrong with the font file itself, consider the following situations and solutions:

- **You previously deleted the font from within Font Book:** The file itself may not have been removed, but Font Book isn't listing it because you told it to remove the font—so it removed the font from the *list* but not from the folder. This happens with /System/Library/Fonts, and with /Library/Fonts if you don't have administrative privileges. You have to manually remove the file from the folder and install the font again, as described in *Remove or Replace System Fonts* (page 87).

- **It has nothing to do with a Font Book-deleted file:** The most likely fix is to delete Font Book's plist (page 231); if that doesn't work, delete system font caches (page 228).

- **The font is part of a collection or library:** See if there's a related cache file and get rid of it; *Collections or user libraries misbehave,* page 253, explains what to look for.

- **The font is a Type 1 font:** You might not have the proper bitmapped font companions (don't trust just the name of the suitcase) or it might be an older file that Mac OS X doesn't support (see *A PostScript Type 1 font won't install,* page 269).

A font is listed in the User library but not in All Fonts

This is, of course, logically impossible, but that doesn't mean it doesn't happen; delete Font Book's plist (page 231).

Tip: Whoops! When You Drop a Font in the Wrong Place... If you drag a font file into Font Book and drop it on the wrong spot, you don't have to go back to the Desktop and grab it again. You can drag it, using the Font list, from one spot to another. This picture shows Optima already in the Computer library (note Computer is selected in the Collection list), and being dragged into the User library. As with any Font Book font installation, a *copy* of the font is placed in the new location, so after you drop it where you really want it, select it from the "wrong" place and delete it.

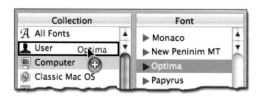

The Font list shows a double listing for the same font

This is not the same as a duplicate font; this is when Font Book lists exactly the same font (you can check the file location in Info view) more than once. If simply closing and reopening Font Book doesn't fix it, delete Font Book's plist (page 231).

The preview area displays the wrong font

Sometimes this is just a window refresh problem, and a previously selected font remains in the preview area: just click another font and then come back to the one you really want to see. If the problem, illustrated in **Figure 80**, persists, delete Font Book's plist (page 231).

Figure 80

```
PostScript name  LucidaHandwriting-Italic
     Full name  Lucida Handwriting Italic
        Family  Lucida Handwriting
         Style  Regular
          Kind  TrueType
      Language  English
       Version  Version 1.67
      Location  /Users/Sharon/Library/Fonts/Gloucester MT Extra Condensed
```

When a Sample view doesn't match the font you've selected in the Font list, Font Book is very confused. This screenshot shows part of the Info view in this situation: the font is identified as Lucida Handwriting Italic (which was selected in the Font list), but the full path in Location *shows the file being accessed is Gloucester MT Extra Condensed, the font that was showing in the Sample view.*

The preview area shows nothing in Sample view, and you can't type in Custom view

Since the Sample view shows the basic Roman alphanumerics, it displays nothing when you select a font without these Roman characters. Unless you switch to an appropriate input keyboard for a non-Roman font, you're typing nonexistent Roman characters in Custom view. So, nothing is actually wrong—this is the way it's *supposed* to work.

The Classic library isn't listed

If Classic is installed on your Mac but there's no Classic library in Font Book's Collection list:

1. Quit Font Book.

2. Go to the Start/Stop tab of the Classic preference pane.

3. Click the Start button.

4. Close Preferences.

5. Relaunch Font Book.

There's no Removal confirm dialog

If you use a Remove command or hit Delete, and fonts, collections, or libraries disappear without your Mac double-checking with you, then the remove warning has been turned off. You turn it off by checking Do Not Ask Me Again in the confirm dialog when you remove a font; then, of course, you can't uncheck it because the dialog never shows up again. The fix is to delete Font Book's plist (page 231).

Your disabled fonts are re-enabled

If you open Font Book and find all your disabled fonts have become en-abled again, it's not necessarily a problem with Font Book—it could be a feature. Two standard troubleshooting routines result in all fonts being re-enabled:

♦ Start up in Safe Mode (page 224).

♦ Delete the system font caches (page 228).

Both procedures erase your user account's font caches. As a result, Font Book no longer knows which fonts were disabled, and on your next startup, which should follow immediately after each of these procedures, every-thing's enabled. (In initial versions of Tiger's Font Book, deleting Font Book's plist also re-enabled all disabled fonts.)

You can't prevent this, but you can make it easier on yourself if you create a Font Book collection that holds all the fonts that you usually keep disabled, so you can turn them all back on in one fell swoop.

A TrueType font is marked as disabled in Font Book but shows in Font menus

This happens with older TrueType fonts that are in "multi-family" suitcases: font files with more than font family inside. The fonts in these mixed suitcases can't be disabled reliably. See *Learn How to Pack a Suitcase for Mac OS X* (page 131) for information about organizing suitcases properly.

Duplicate-dot dilemmas in the Font list

Sometimes the dot-marked duplicates in Font Book don't seem to make sense but, in fact, are working perfectly. (Font Book doesn't mark every copy of a duplicate font as a duplicate: it considers the one it's using as the original, and any additional copy is a duplicate.) **Figures 81-83** describe three common confusing displays.

Figure 81

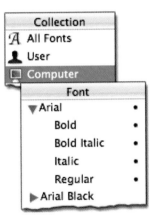

When a family or faces are marked as duplicates but only one copy is listed, you are likely looking at a subset of your font collection. In this picture, Computer is the selected library so the duplicates in the User library aren't shown in the Font list.

Figure 82

This listing, with All Fonts selected, presents a puzzle: two different typefaces (Bold and Regular) are showing, yet one is marked as a duplicate. This is a result of some misnaming in older font files. Note the font name is Arial Rounded Bold, which means the base font face is already bold. The older file's embedded information identifies the face as Bold, while the newer file correctly identifies it as Regular. Despite the differing naming conventions, the fonts are the same, so one is correctly identified as a duplicate.

Figure 83

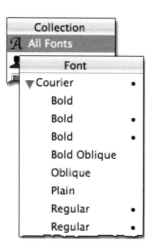

This triple Courier listing is confusing for two reasons: one font file has more typefaces than the other, and it also identifies its base font by a different name. Two of these three Courier copies have only Regular and Bold faces; these happen to be the ones marked as duplicates. The active font has two additional faces— Bold Oblique and Oblique—and identifies its base font as Plain rather than Regular.

Resolving duplicates disables every copy of a font

If you use Font Book's Edit > Resolve Duplicates command with a font family name selected, it correctly disables all but the copies uppermost in the font-use hierarchy (described in *The Font Access Order,* page 15). But the command acts on *all selected typefaces* in a family, so if the family name is expanded and you select all the typeface copies, or if you've used Select All in the Font list and some (or all) of the families are expanded, you'll wind up with *all* copies of a font disabled.

Multiple fonts or typefaces disappear when one is removed

Two similar situations trigger this seeming bug (but it's a feature, really):

♦ You had a typeface selected, but it was part of a file (usually a Mac TrueType) that included several other typefaces.

◆ You deleted a PostScript Type 1 file whose bitmapped suitcase companion (deleted along with it) had more than one font family in it.

In both cases, removing the one font you selected in the Font list moved the entire file and all its contents to the Trash.

A font doesn't show up in Font Book (or menus) after you've added it to a folder that you've defined as a user library

The issue here is that you can't define a folder as a user library—you can only define *fonts* as part of a user library. If you dragged a folder from the Finder into Font Book to either create a library or add fonts to an existing one, it's only the *fonts* that count, not the *folder*. So, adding a font file to that folder does nothing as far as Font Book is concerned.

Drag the font file directly to the User library in Font Book's Collection list to add it to the library. You can do this before or after you put it in the folder, since Font Book keeps track of user-library font files if you move them.

Library contents disappear when the library is renamed

This one's not a feature, it's a bug. The library contents are not lost, however; closing and reopening Font Book displays them again.

Collections or user libraries misbehave

Font Book stores library and collection information in ~/Library/ FontCollections. (Remember, that tilde in front of the pathname stands for "user," and it means you should start looking in your User directory, represented by the Home icon in the sidebar of a default Finder window.) **Figure 84** shows a typical FontCollections folder: there's a *.library* file for every user-defined library, and a *.collection* file for each collection. In addition, there's a *.fcache* file for any library or collection that's frequently changed. Any of these files can get corrupted and cause all sorts of problems. These files affect *only* Font Book organization; deleting them *does not affect your fonts* in any way.

Figure 84

The FontCollections folder stores information about Font Book's collections and user-defined libraries.

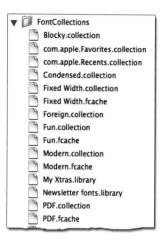

▼ 📁 FontCollections
   📄 Blocky.collection
   📄 com.apple.Favorites.collection
   📄 com.apple.Recents.collection
   📄 Condensed.collection
   📄 Fixed Width.collection
   📄 Fixed Width.fcache
   📄 Foreign.collection
   📄 Fun.collection
   📄 Fun.fcache
   📄 Modern.collection
   📄 Modern.fcache
   📄 My Xtras.library
   📄 Newsletter fonts.library
   📄 PDF.collection
   📄 PDF.fcache

If a collection or library name disappears from the Collection list:

Whether it's intermittent or permanent, if this is the only problem, it could due to incorrect privilege settings for the FontCollections folder, so try this first:

1. In the Finder, select the folder `~/Library/FontCollections`.

2. Chose File > Get Info (Command-I).

3. Under Ownership and Permissions, make sure Read and Write is selected.

If your permissions were not already set to this privilege, your Collection list should behave properly after this. If that doesn't work, try the solution described next.

If you have other problems with collections or libraries:

Collection and user-defined library problems vary widely; they may be limited to a single collection or library, or affect many of them. Collections are more prone to problems because they're altered more often.

Problems include:

♦ The collection/library doesn't display newly added fonts.

♦ The Font list for the collection/library changes even though you haven't added or deleted anything.

♦ A collection/library name disappears from the Collection list.

♦ Selecting a collection/library displays the fonts from a different collection/library.

♦ Clicking on an item in the Collection list makes Font Book quit.

If you delete Font Book's plist (page 231) the problems might clear up, but it's likely you need a more targeted fix.

The (almost) sure cure is to trash the entire FontCollections folder—a new one is created as soon as you open Font Book again—but you may not want to lose all your Font Book organization if it's not necessary. In that case, you can try to solve the problem in a tiered fashion:

1. Quit Font Book.

2. Remove all the .fcache files from the FontCollections folder, and test Font Book again. If it works, you're done. Otherwise continue with:

3. Remove the .collection or .library files from the FontCollections folder that are related to the specific collection or user library that's giving you trouble. If that works, you're done. But, if the problems persist:

4. Bite the bullet and get rid of the FontCollections folder, but if you use the Font panel in Apple applications and want to preserve its Favorites and Recently Used lists, leave the folder in place and instead delete all the files inside of it except *com.apple.Favorites.collection* and *com. apple.Recents.collection*.

Note: Odd icons in FontCollections folder. The icons in `~/Library/FontCollections` are supposed to be unadorned, generic, corner-folded-down document icons. Installing Adobe Creative Suite 2 changed all my *.collection* icons in the FontCollections folder to this attractive but misleading icon. There's no effect on how the files function, so if you see something like this, be annoyed but don't be worried.

Black.collection

Input Menu Problems

Sometimes the Input menu, whose "name" is a little flag on the right side of the menu bar, takes on a mind of its own. (As for foreign language input keyboards, the main problem I have with them is that they don't seem to increase my fluency at all; if you have the same problem, you won't find that solution here.)

You have no Input menu

There's no Input menu in Mac OS X unless you give it a reason to exist by turning on something for it to hold: Character Palette, Keyboard Viewer, or input keyboards. They're all turned on through the International preference pane's Input Menu tab.

The Input menu misbehaves

You've set up the Input menu and its contents through the International preference pane but the menu doesn't show up in the menu bar, or it does but not all the items you checked are listed, or there's some other wonkiness: you can't select items, their icons are missing (**Figure 85**), they appear and disappear from the menu. You've addressed specific issues like dealing with Character Palette's and Keyboard Viewer's plists, so you think it's a more general problem with the Input menu itself.

Figure 85

The missing icon in front of the Hide Character Palette command can indicate a problem with the Input menu.

Here are four possible fixes, in order of simplicity—if one doesn't work, move on to the next:

♦ **Restart.** Always worth a shot.

♦ **Remove and then replace the Input menu.** In the Input Menu tab of the International preference pane:

1. Uncheck Show Input Menu In Menu Bar.

2. Close the Preferences window.

3. Reopen the International preference pane and recheck Show Input Menu in Menu Bar.

- ◆ *Really* **remove and then replace the Input menu.** This is a more forceful way of doing the same thing I just described, but it works sometimes when the "gentle" method doesn't. With the preference pane *closed:*

   1. Remove the Input menu by Command-dragging it off the menu bar.

   2. Reactivate the Input menu by checking Show Input Menu in Menu Bar, in the International preference pane's Input Menu tab.

- ◆ **Remove and then** *really* **replace the Input menu.** If the previous methods don't work, it's time to change how you reactivate the Input menu:

   1. In the International preference pane's Input Menu tab, uncheck Show Input Menu in Menu Bar.

   2. Close the Preferences window.

   3. Navigate to /System/Library/CoreServices/Menu Extras.

   4. Find the *Textinput.menu* icon and drag it into the menu bar.

      Yes, you heard me—drag the file into the menu bar where you want the Input menu to be. And there it is!

Character Palette Problems

While Character Palette isn't a shining example of an obvious interface, it's extremely useful—and sometimes your only option for inputting off-the-keyboard characters. The more you use it, the more you'll like it. And the more you'll increase your chances of running into problems with it.

Character Palette problems that aren't problems

Items that may seem like problems but are actually features (no, really—I didn't mean that sarcastically) include:

♦ Some installed fonts aren't in the pop-up menu in Glyph view. The menu doesn't show disabled fonts or fonts in application Fonts folders— a font must be viewable in Font Book to be seen in Character Palette.

♦ The Insert or Insert With Font button is always dimmed. Always? This button is dimmed more often than not; if you're in a program that can't display non-Unicode glyphs and you've picked one of those for insertion, you're out of luck (see *The World According to Glyphs,* page 149). The button also remains dimmed if you're using a program that doesn't work with Unicode at all, like Word X.

♦ Nothing ever shows in the Glyph Variants section. Nothing? *Ever?* Try selecting the glyph for the numeral one and then select the Zapfino sample in the Collections area. It just seems like nothing ever shows up because so few standard fonts have glyph variants defined.

Scrollbars are missing on any Character Palette section

This is a simple matter of resizing Character Palette vertically, since at some point there's not enough room for Character Palette to include the scrollbars in some or all of its sections. You can resize the entire Palette, or use one of its internal resize controls (see **Figure 86**) to reapportion the relative sizes of its segments.

Figure 86

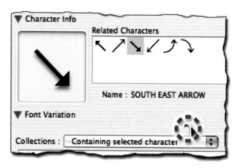

Circle: InaiMathi
U+25CC GID 277

Drag the Character Info area up and down (grab the little dot circled in this picture—or anywhere to its left or right) to resize the areas above and below it.

Character Palette opens off-screen
or gets stuck behind the menu bar

Why in the world this happens is beyond me, but, coincidentally enough, even as I was writing about Character Palette, I opened it and its entire upper area and left edge were off my screen; with no access to the title bar I couldn't move it. (*Why* don't we have grab-any-edge-of-the-window-to-drag-it capability in Mac OS X?) Some users find that Character Palette sometimes gets stuck *under* the menu bar! Here are two possible fixes:

♦ If you can get at the lower left of the Character Palette window, use the Action menu's Minimize Palette on Application Switch command, and then switch to another application to get the little Character Palette window. Move it anywhere and then zoom it back to normal size; it should open fully accessible.

♦ Close Character Palette (using the Input menu's Hide Character Palette command, since you can't reach its close button) and delete Character Palette's plists (page 232).

The Insert/Insert With Font button is active but doesn't work

Try setting the document font to match the font you've selected in Character Palette. (And check whether Character Palette's search field is active, because if it is, the character you're clicking on is entered in the search field instead of your document.)

The Insert With Font button
inserts a character without the font

Set the font in the document to match the one chosen in Character Palette; or, just reformat the character to the correct font after it's inserted in your document.

Dragging a character directly from the Font Variation section retains the font information more reliably than clicking the button, double-clicking from any other area, or dragging it from the character well.

Character Palette crashes or generally misbehaves

Character Palette sometimes presents with odd symptoms that can come and go, or stay and get worse, such as:

♦ Its pop-up menus are useless because they flash open and quickly disappear.

♦ It doesn't appear when you choose Show Character Palette from the Input menu.

♦ It crashes on opening or when you click in its window.

♦ It stops responding: you can't use its pop-up menus or scroll anything.

♦ It opens when you don't want it to.

All these symptoms, and more, are almost always cured when you delete Character Palette's plists (page 232).

Tip: Tuck away a rebel Character Palette or Keyboard Viewer. When you don't have time to stop and deal with an out-of-control Character Palette or Keyboard Viewer that just pops at will and won't leave you alone, you can get either one out of your way quickly: send it to the Dock with the minimize button. It will sit there quietly, and happily, knowing that it's still open whether or not you want it to be.

Keyboard Viewer Problems

Keyboard Viewer is a barely updated version of the Key Caps utility that has been around for nearly two decades. Still, it serves its purpose and almost never acts up. Except sometimes.

Keyboard Viewer doesn't update its view when you choose a new keyboard layout from the Input menu

If Keyboard Viewer is open when you choose a new keyboard from the Input menu, it might not register the change. Choosing the same item again from the Input menu usually makes Keyboard Viewer pay attention; if not, close it and then reopen it.

The font you choose in Keyboard Viewer is not being used in your document

This is in the "feature, not a bug" category. The font you choose from Keyboard Viewer's pop-up menu is independent of whatever you're doing in your document; even if you click on Keyboard Viewer to enter characters in your document, the document's font formatting is in charge.

Keyboard commands like Command-Q don't work when you switch keyboards

Keyboard layouts that move the Roman letters around require that you rewire your brain a little to use standard Command-key combinations. The French layout, for instance, uses an AZERTY arrangement instead of the English QWERTY. Pressing what you *think* is Command-Q for Quit actually generates a Command-A for Select All. (See *Watch Out for Keyboard Commands on Foreign Keyboards,* page 196).

In addition, input keyboards can redefine combinations with modifiers like Command and Control as easily as they redefine what's produced with Shift or Option. Although I haven't found it true on any Tiger-supplied keyboards, it's possible for a keyboard to have *nothing* defined for the Command-key combinations, so that pressing Command-anything does nothing!

Use Keyboard Viewer to see what keystrokes and combinations are available in your chosen input keyboard.

Keyboard Viewer crashes or generally misbehaves

Keyboard Viewer is not as temperamental as Character Palette, but it's not perfect, either. To solve general problems, like crashing or refusing to open in the position where it's supposed to, delete Keyboard Viewer's plist (page 232).

Input Keyboard Problems

Some foreign language keyboards are missing from the International pane's list

Some foreign language keyboards won't be listed if there's no appropriate font installed.

You logged out with a foreign keyboard active and now you can't log in

Log out with a foreign keyboard active, and you might not be able to enter your password when you log back in: the alternate keyboard remains active and your password characters might not be available from it. Here are some things that can help you avoid this snag:

♦ **Change the keyboard trigger for keyboard switching:** The default Command-Spacebar is easy to type accidentally and can switch you to a foreign keyboard as you log out; it's also the default trigger for a Spotlight search. (I'm only the messenger!) See *Clash of the Keyboard Shortcuts* (page 195).

♦ **Select your password carefully:** Make sure the characters you need are available on your foreign language keyboard (numbers are pretty ubiquitous), and know which keys produce them.

♦ **Put keyboard choices on the login screen:**

1. Open the Accounts preference pane.

2. Select your Account in the list.

3. Click the lock icon at the bottom of the window to unlock it, providing your password when asked.

4. Click Login Options at the bottom of the Account list.

5. Check Show Input Menu in Login Window.

6. Click the lock icon to lock the changes.

On subsequent startups, you'll get a keyboard menu in your login dialog so you can switch keyboards.

♦ **Forgo the password:** If you're the sole user of your Mac and security is not an issue, set up an automatic login so you never have to type your password (unless you're using Safe Mode, which still requires it). Use the steps just described for changing login options, substituting:

5. Check Automatically Log In As.

When it's just not your day, and you lock yourself out of a login because of a foreign keyboard, there's a simple workaround that *might* work, and a more elaborate one that's a sure thing:

♦ **Use a different account:** If you're lucky enough to have another account with administrative privileges already set up, you can log in to it and change the password for your locked-out account to something that you can type from the foreign keyboard. While you're in the other account, switch to the keyboard in question and figure out a new password that's typeable.

♦ **Do the you-don't-need-a-password end run:** If there's no other account you can use, or you can't enter your password characters from the foreign keyboard, all is not lost:

1. Start up with the Tiger install DVD.

2. Ignore the Installer screen; choose Utilities > Reset Password.

3. Select your Mac's volume.

4. Select the user name of the original administrator account.

   Don't select *System Administrator (root)*; that's a whole 'nother world.

5. Enter a new password.

   You have to stick to something safe, like numbers, that will be usable with the foreign keyboard still active; something like 123 will work with almost any keyboard, and you can change it later, after you log in.

6. Click Save.

7. Restart.

Font File and Icon Problems

You can guess what might go wrong with a font *file*—from not being able to copy it to its refusing to be thrown out with the Trash—but you'd be amazed what can go wrong with the icons themselves!

A font file can't be moved or copied

Some old font files put up a fuss when you try to copy them or move them from one folder to another. Reset font file permissions (page 222) to make them behave.

If you're working with fonts in /System/Library/Fonts (or /Library/Fonts when you don't have administrative privileges), it's normal for a font file to refuse to *move* out of the folder, and simply make a copy of itself in the target location; see *Remove or Replace System Fonts* (page 87) for details.

A font refuses to go out with the Trash

There are several reasons a font might not go gentle into that good Trash, and several solutions to try:

♦ **If the font was dragged to the Trash directly from a Fonts folder or user-defined library:** It's likely Tiger thinks it's still using the font (even if you replaced it with a file of the same name to get a better version). Delete the system font caches (page 228), and don't forget that a restart is part of the procedure.

♦ **Otherwise:** Try these solutions, which I list in the special order used so often in troubleshooting—instead of "most likely to work," it's more like "not necessarily very likely, but easy to do, so might as well do it before the more time-consuming stuff":

  ♦ If the font's icon has a lock on it, unlock it: Select the file and choose File > Get Info (Command-I). Uncheck the Locked checkbox in the General area.

  ♦ In the file's Info window, verify that you have Read & Write access to the file; if you don't, give yourself access as described in *Reset font file permissions* (page 222).

- Close all your applications, drag the font file out of the Trash and put it back in (let go of it in-between—drop it on the Desktop for a moment).

- Restart.

- Delete system font caches (page 228).

Font files have strange icons

Font icons other than the standard ones show up under three general circumstances:

- **The icon is correct, but for a font file format that Mac OS X doesn't support:** There's nothing you can or should do about this—there's nothing wrong!

   This graceful icon signifies a loose (non-suitcased) TrueType or bitmapped font, a file format used prior to Mac OS X; its Finder Kind is Font.mdimporter. This is not a problem in and of itself, but you can't use this file type because Mac OS X doesn't support it.

- **The icon *used* to be correct, but changed somewhere along the way:** This usually results from using a third-party font manager or other font utility. It's almost always just a cosmetic problem that doesn't affect a font's performance; getting rid of the triggering application and restarting usually resets the icons to their Mac OS X norm. "Getting rid of" sometimes means you must not only make sure it's not running (in the background or foreground), but also take it off your drive. If you want to keep it for future use, you can use the Finder's File > Archive command to zip it, and trash the original; an application isn't "seen" when it's in a zipped file. Here are some typical examples:

   Prior to 10.4.3, this retro-design (circa System 7) suitcase icon showed up on suitcase font files if you had the venerable Font/DA Mover application around, as described in *The Font/DA Mover effect* (page 133).

My font files started switching to generic blanks whenever I moved them out of their Fonts folders. The culprit turned out to be a shareware font utility I was testing; getting rid of the application solved the problem.

 My font icons took on this cheery look (love that red on the turned-down corner!) when I used Linotype FontExplorer; they changed back to normal when I stopped using it and reactivated Font Book.

 This Adobe OpenType icon suddenly showed up on more than 30 .otf files in my Adobe Fonts folder after I installed ATM (Adobe Type Manager) in my Classic environment. Their Open With properties needed adjusting; I describe how to do this in *OpenType icon changes to an "O"*, next.

♦ **The icon was odd from the beginning:** Some font icons are just different from the get-go, especially if they're older fonts.

 This icon showed up on an old font, but only on one of the two machines I was using; Font Book said it was corrupted until I fixed the Open With property (for more details, see *A faux corruption,* next page). (The icon belongs to GraphicConverter, a utility included with some Macs.)

 This icon graced *ITCKabel*, a bitmapped Type 1 companion. The font wouldn't install because it was an old version, but the icon puzzled me for longer than I would like to admit (my story, and I'm sticking to it, is that I was misled by the font's being a problem to start with). It was merely a custom icon pasted over the regular one in the Get Info window. You can restore an original icon in this situation by selecting the icon in the Get Info window and pressing Delete.

OpenType icon changes to an "O"

If you install ATM in the Classic environment (which you must to get smooth font rendering, as described in *PostScript Type 1 fonts in Classic documents have "the jaggies"* (page 285), OpenType font icons may change—which is extra-strange since Classic doesn't use OpenType fonts. The Adobe OpenType icon showed up on more than 30 of my .otf fonts in the /Library/Application Support/Adobe/Fonts folder. Why that folder, which neither Classic nor standard Mac OS X accesses? I don't know. Why not *all* the .otf fonts? I don't know.

But I do know the cure. These files were having an identity crisis and wanted to be opened by ATM. Change an icon's Open With property to get it back to normal:

1. Select the icon in the Finder.

2. Choose File > Get Info.

3. In the Info window, expand the Open With section, if necessary, and choose Font Book from the pop-up menu.

Tip: Make multiple "Open With" changes. If you have lots of font files that are confused as to their parentage, you don't have to change their Open With properties one at a time. Select the files in the Finder, and hold Option as you choose File > Get Info, or press Command-Option-I. A single Info window opens for all the items, and changing the Open With property in the window changes it for every file.

A faux corruption

This particular bug was so incredibly strange, it's possible not one reader of this book will encounter it. However, the method that fixed the problem may come in handy for other, similar, problems.

I had an old PostScript Type 1 font, Princetown, that Font Book tagged as seriously damaged when I tried to install it on my PowerBook. I moved the files to my desk Mac and the theretofore normal suitcase icon changed to something I couldn't identify, and its Finder Kind changed to *Paintbrush document.* I moved the files back and forth between the machines, and every time it showed as a font icon on the PowerBook and the changed icon on the desk machine.

Removing the file's .scr extension didn't change anything; in fact, in Get Info (on the desk machine with the weird-icon file), the name came up with the extension still on it, and the file defaulted to an Open With of GraphicConverter.

The fix was both simple and absurd: in the Get Info window, I chose Font Book from the Open With pop-up menu (**Figure 87**). The icon changed to a font icon, the kind changed to Font suitcase, and it installed flawlessly. Copied back to the PowerBook, it installed there, too, with no corruption reported. Go figure.

Figure 87

Selecting Font Book as the Open With option in a Get Info window can solve the problem of a "confused" font file.

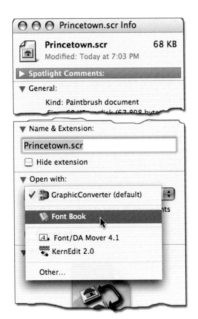

A font icon changes when you move it to a different folder

Right, it makes no sense. But I watched it happen many times, to Apple-supplied fonts going from one Fonts folder to another. It didn't seem to affect the font's performance in any way, but it bothered *me* a lot. I found a fix:

1. Select the icon in the Finder.

2. Choose File > Get Info.

3. In the Info window, expand the Open With section if necessary and choose something *besides* Font Book in the pop-up menu.

   If there's no other application listed in the menu, choose Other, and select *any* application in the Open dialog, navigating around until you find one; TextEdit is a safe bet.

4. Choose Font Book in the menu again.

I've never even found it necessary to close the Get Info window and reopen it between the two menu selections.

PostScript Font Problems

The near future has PostScript fonts replaced by OpenType, which can only be a good thing, because the majority of problems you'll run into with Type 1 fonts is due to the double-file suitcase/printer font approach.

Helvetica Fractious

If you use the Type 1 font Helvetica Fractions, don't. It is decidedly Mac OS X-unfriendly and causes all sorts of general mayhem. It has particularly nasty effects in Address Book and iChat, where it displays overlapping numbers and characters—even though you're not actually *using* it (on purpose); Safari is not very fond of it either. So, if you've installed this font, you should uninstall it right away.

Times Phrenetic

Everything I just said about Helvetica Fractions is also true for Times Phonetic.

A PostScript Type 1 font won't install

Problems installing PostScript Type 1 problems have several variations:

◆ You double-click on one of the components and nothing happens, or Font Book opens but a Preview window for the font does not.

Occasionally one or both of the companion files in question are copied to the correct Fonts folder, but you wouldn't know it by looking at Font Book, because they don't appear in the Font list.

- The font *seems* to install in Font Book (you get a Preview window with an Install button) but the font never appears in the Font list or, if it does, the Preview pane is blank.

- The font seems to be installed (according to Font Book's list) and you even see the files in the target Fonts folder, but the fonts are not in any menus.

- You drag the files directly into a Fonts folder but the font never appears in Font Book.

Any of these problems can occur for any one (or more) of these reasons:

- You're missing either the suitcase file or the printer file for the font. Find the missing component!

- The companion to the printer font is a loose, non-suitcased bitmapped font (a file format in use from System 7 through Mac OS 9), which Mac OS X can't handle.

- The suitcase file that you think is the printer file's companion is not: it doesn't have the right bitmapped font in it, despite its name. (Or, it's actually empty—yes, I've seen that happen!) This isn't all that easy to determine because there's no way to open a suitcase file in Mac OS X—read *Work with Suitcases in Mac OS 9* (page 131) and *Use Font/DA Mover* (page 133) for some tricks in that regard.

- The suitcase for the font you're installing has the same name as a suitcase already in use for a different printer file. If you've renamed and/or repacked your suitcases over the years, and especially if you've used font managers in your Mac OS 9 years (they didn't care if suitcases had the same name) this problem can creep up on you. When you tell Font Book to install the new Type 1, it copies the printer file to the Fonts folder; it prepares to copy the suitcase into the folder but sees one by that name already there, so it doesn't copy the new one.

- It's an Adobe pre-1992 font, some of which are missing the FOND (family information) resource that became necessary when Apple redefined internal font format requirements for the PowerPC. The real problem is in figuring out if this is the problem: the creation and modified dates that you can access are not necessarily the genuine ones. Just keep in mind that if you've had the fonts longer than your favorite pair of socks, it might have this internal problem. (Adobe offers reasonably priced upgrades for old fonts; you kept your original disks and receipts, right?)

If Font Book won't install the font but you *really* need to use it, sometimes dragging the font components directly into one of the Fonts folders is enough to make it work (and even show up in Font Book next time you open it).

You should also make sure that the inability to install some fonts isn't Font Book's problem—can you install other fonts? Is everything else working smoothly? Delete Font Book's plist (page 231), and then see if Font Book agrees to install the font.

Font Menu and Font Panel Problems

By "Font menus," I mean, generally, any place that lists fonts: actual Font menus in the menu bar, submenus, pop-up menus, the Font panel's Family list, and so on.

A font doesn't appear in a Font menu

A missing font can be the result of anything from its being in the wrong place to its being corrupted, and many things in-between.

If you've installed the font through Font Book, consider:

♦   Look again! Fonts are not always listed alphabetically or the same way from one application to the next.

♦   Fonts in a user's Fonts folder are available to only that user.

♦   Disabled fonts don't appear in menus. (You'll probably be embarrassed if this turns out to be the "problem.")

♦   Fonts stored in the Mac OS 9 folder sometimes don't show up in Tiger Font menus until you force the issue; see *Fonts in the Classic Fonts folder don't show up in Tiger Font menus* (page 285).

+ Microsoft applications don't list *RTL* fonts (right-to-left scripts like Hebrew and Arabic). See *Some foreign language fonts don't show up in Microsoft menus* (page 281).

If you've put the font file directly into a Fonts folder:

+ Does the font show up in Font Book?

    ◊ **If it's in the Font list:** Use Font Book's Validate Font command on it to see if it's corrupted; if it is, replace it with a fresh version.

    ◊ **If it's not in the Font list:** It's likely corrupted, an unsupported font type, or a Type 1 missing one of its files. Use Font Book's Validate File command to check it for corruption.

+ Check that Mac OS X supports this font type (see *Supported Font Types,* page 2). While Font Book lets you install only "legal" fonts, there's nothing to stop you from dragging any old font directly into a Fonts folder.

+ Make sure you've put in all the components of a Type 1 font: the bitmapped suitcase and all the printer fonts. Font Book takes care of this for you, but you may have missed a file during the manual installation.

+ Fonts in an application Fonts folder (like Adobe's) appear only in specific applications.

+ Fonts in Microsoft's Fonts folder (`/Applications/Microsoft Office 2004/Office/Fonts`) are not installed at all; the folder is merely a holding area (see *The fonts in the Microsoft Fonts folder aren't in Font menus,* page 280).

You've noticed fonts in Fonts folders that aren't in menus:

+ The operating system uses some fonts that aren't meant for mere mortals: Keyboard, LastResort, AquaKana, and Helvetica and Times MMs (Multiple Masters). These fonts are meant for the operating system's use and aren't supposed to appear in menus.

+ Adobe applications use Adobe Sans MMs and Adobe Serif MMs, but you can't.

If none of the above situations apply:

♦ Make sure you're using the latest version of the font.

♦ Remove and reinstall the problematic font.

♦ Delete Font Book's plist (page 231).

♦ Delete system font caches (page 228).

♦ If fonts are missing from only Adobe applications, delete Adobe font caches (page 231).

The collections in Font panel are not coordinated with those in Font Book

There's likely a problem with specific *.collection* files or their related cache files, which Font Book and Font panel share; *Collections or user libraries misbehave* (page 253) describes these files. Try deleting just the caches first; if that doesn't work, you'll have to get rid of the .collection files and lose your collection information. *You don't lose your fonts*, just the collection-based organization you had.

Font panel loses track of your Favorites or Recently Used fonts

The files com.*apple.Favorites.collection* and *com.apple.Recents. collection* in ~/Library/FontCollections track these lists. Getting rid of them will empty the two lists in Font panel, and let you start new, well-behaved lists.

Font and Character Formatting Problems

Font changes, character substitutions, formatting weirdness... most of these can be laid at the Unicode door, but a few other factors can come into play.

Text is totally garbled

You open a document and not just a *few* characters are wrong—they're *all* wrong. The basic possibilities are:

♦ You've disabled or removed a core system font. Activate or replace the font *immediately* because you may find your menus and dialogs biting the dust next. (Core system fonts are listed under "Absolutely Necessary" in Appendix C.)

♦ You have Helvetica Fractions installed, which notoriously messes up font display in several Apple applications. Times Phonetic has also been implicated in this situation. Delete them.

♦ This one has nothing to do with fonts: You've opened a document in an application other than the one that created it. Force-opening "strange" documents in, say, TextEdit results in what looks like garbage characters (**Figure 88**)—but garbage is in the eyes of the beholder, and those characters are actually information about the document that the parent application knows how to interpret.

Figure 88

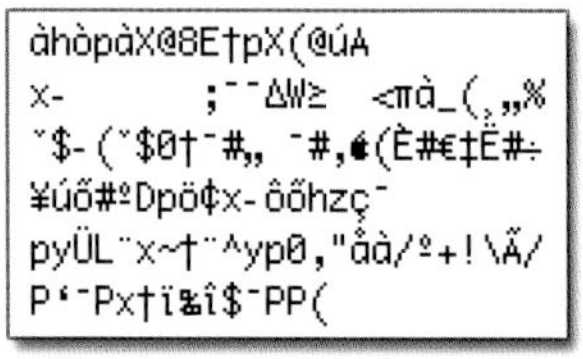

àhòpàX@8E†pX(@úA
x-   ;¯¯ΔW≥ <πà_(¸„%
˘$-(˘$0†¯#„ ¯#,¢(È#¢‡È#÷
¥úõ#º Dpö¢x- õõhzç¯
pyÜL¨x~†¨^ypθ,"åà/º+!\Ã/
P˘¯Px†ï&î$¯PP(

Garbage characters like this in a document can be a simple matter of your having opened it in the wrong application.

♦ There's no obvious explanation for the behavior. Delete system font caches (page 228).

Text is garbled in menus and dialogs

The Helvetica font is so important to Mac OS X that your menus and dialogs can explode if you don't keep a copy of it around. It doesn't have to be the Helvetica.dfont that's installed by default in /Library/Fonts; any copy of Helvetica, of any font type, in any Tiger Fonts folder (not an application Fonts folder) will keep things from looking like **Figure 89**. (Disabling all your Helveticas has the same result as removing them.)

Figure 89

A Dock item's pop-up menu can look like this if Tiger can't find a copy of Helvetica.

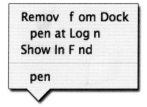

Remov f om Dock
pen at Log n
Show In F nd

pen

Boxes or incorrect characters are substituted

Occasional boxes or substituted characters are due to the differences between the font originally used for the document and the one being used to open it later. (To add insult to injury, sometimes the document in question was created on your own, pre-OS X Mac.) Sometimes the font difference is obvious, and other times more subtle:

♦ You don't have the original font and your substitute font doesn't have all the characters needed. Get the correct font, or try changing the font in the document to one that has the correct characters.

♦ You *seem* to have the correct font—it has the same name—but in fact either yours or the originator's is an older, perhaps non-Unicode compliant, version. Match the fonts, or reformat the text.

♦ The document was created in an application that can handle glyphs beyond the Unicode-defined ones, and you're viewing it in a program that can't display those glyphs. (See *The World According to Glyphs*, page 149.) The best you can do here is ask the originator for a PDF of the file so you can see it correctly.

♦ The document was created on "the other" platform with older fonts whose character IDs don't match *your* font character IDs. (We inherited this mess from earlier years, when Macs and PCs went their own ways in regard to how they handled character references.) If you know what characters are substituted (say, the Ó for a curly apostrophe), it's possible to perform search-and-replace operations to make the document readable on your end.

Standard Option-key combos
like Option-V enter the wrong characters

Option-V gives you a checkmark ($\sqrt{}$—okay, it's really a square root symbol in most fonts, but you know what I mean), and Option-8 provides the beautifully useful bullet (•). When these, and other standard Option combinations stop working, it's due to one of three problems:

♦ You've chosen a non-standard keyboard layout from the Input menu (after having turned on the layout from the International preference pane's Input Menu tab).

♦ You're using the U.S. Extended keyboard layout, which, because it provides so many "dead-key" Option combinations for accents, has to sacrifice the input of many standard Option characters.

♦ You're using a font that is not conforming to either the old Mac encoding scheme (what characters are generated by what keys) or the new Unicode one. The biggest sinner in this area is the Adobe PostScript Type 1 font Symbol, which clings to its always-been-different key layout. I originally saved as special slap on the wrist for Apple for including a mixed-up Handwriting-Dakota font with iLife, but the iWeb 1.1 update installs a new version of the font that's mapped correctly. (That only goes to show that I was right when I said "Upgrade, upgrade, upgrade" back on page 212.)

In the first two cases, just switch to a different keyboard layout to enter the character you need, and then switch right back to the keyboard you're using. If Adobe's Symbol font or the older Handwriting-Dakota is the issue and you want to use it instead of changing fonts, use Keyboard Viewer to find the characters you need.

The letter O followed by a slash turns into a slashed Ø

If you type the letter O followed by a slash and it turns into a slashed O, you must be using Palatino, Hoefler, Chicago, or New York in a program like TextEdit, Pages, or FileMaker.

Palatinø

In a case of "when smart fonts do stupid things," the helpful technology that substitutes a single ligatured character for the letters *fi*, or sticks in swashy-tailed lowercase *g*'s when you type two in a row, is "helpfully" substituting a single, different character when you type an O (upper or lowercase) followed by a slash. (You think an O isn't often followed by a slash? You forget that Web URLs and Mac OS X pathnames both use slashes to separate names!)

If you're in an application that uses the Font panel, you can turn off this feature:

1. Open the Font panel (Command-T).

2. From the Action menu (the gear icon in the lower left of the Font panel), choose Typography.

3. In the Typography panel, expand the Diacritics section (if you don't have a Diacritics section, select a font—such as Palatino—that offers diacritics).

4. Select Don't Compose Diacritics.

   This turns off the Compose Diacritics button. (A diacritic is a mark, like an accent, that's placed above, below, or—as in this case—right through a Roman alphabetic character.)

In some programs, like Word, this never happens. In others, like FileMaker, it happens but there's no Typography panel or equivalent to control it; your only recourse there is to avoid using certain fonts.

Extra blank lines appear between lines of text

They're not exactly blank lines, because you can't remove them; it's more like the line spacing changes to quadruple while it's still officially set to single. This is one of the many things that can be fixed when you delete system font caches (page 228).

Lucida Grande keeps getting applied to your text

If you use an alternate keyboard (see *Understand Alternate Keyboards,* page 189) and try to type characters not included in your current font, Lucida Grande jumps in to save the day, providing those missing characters.

Text refuses to change to a new font

If the text includes special characters that aren't included in the new font, Mac OS X may overrule the font change, leaving the text in a font that contains the characters you've typed.

The font changes when text is pasted between applications, or is imported

The font may not be available in the second application (Adobe applications have a ton more fonts available to them).

But don't overlook something else that's not a font problem at all: you might have different style definitions in each place. If your Body style is defined as 12-point Verdana in the first document, and the receiving document or application defines Body as 14-point Baskerville, the font is *supposed* to change.

Character styles change when text is pasted or imported

This is most often seen with bold and italic styling, but it's not limited to those two. The changes all boil down to what typefaces are available on the originating and receiving ends:

- The font is not available in the receiving application, and the font that's substituted does not have the same variety of typefaces.

- The font *versions* differ on each end, and one version has more typefaces than the other.

- The same font is used on both ends, and it doesn't have the typeface in question—but one of the applications faked the style. Microsoft applications, for instance, create fake bold versions of a bold-less font by "overprinting" the text horizontally, with each copy offset by a pixel or two (or three).

- Special formatting options are available in one application, but not the other. Word's strikethrough style, for instance, doesn't carry over to InDesign; the Font panel shadowing options work in few places besides Apple programs.

iTunes switches to Hebrew: In the oddest-of-all category, if Hebrew appears in place of English in iTunes, it's almost always because of an extra copy of Lucida Grande in /Library/Fonts or ~/Library/Fonts. A single copy belongs in /System/Library/Fonts.

Safari Font Problems

Some of the items in this section might apply to browsers other than Safari, although the specific solutions (like how to set preferences) would differ.

Special characters, like accented letters, turn into other characters or question marks in diamonds

This is caused by encoding mismatches between what was specified for the Web page and what you're browser is using. *Refine Your Web Page Reception* (page 205) explains the problem and how to deal with it.

Some pages on a site are fine, others present font gibberish

If the "fine" pages contain the same *kinds* of characters as the "gibberish" pages—curly quotes and accented letters, say—the problem is unlikely to be from mismatched encodings or missing fonts. Try any of these solutions (the second one is the most likely to work in this situation):

◆ Quit and restart Safari.

◆ Reset Safari's cache: Choose Safari > Empty Cache and then click Empty in the dialog that appears. This deletes the file that stores information about the pages you've visited recently so they reload quickly.

◆ Delete the system font caches (page 228).

Web page text is rendered as fractions

This is caused by the PostScript font Helvetica Fractions. There's no "fix" for this other than removing the font.

Arabic-language pages don't display correctly

The Arial and Times New Roman fonts Microsoft supplies—generally superior to the Tiger versions because they have so many more characters (see **Table 13**, page 109)—interfere with Arabic text rendering. Deactivate them with Font Book or remove them from ~/Library/Fonts.

Other Windows TrueType fonts that interfere with Arabic pages are Tahoma, Arabic Transparent, and Traditional Arabic.

Microsoft Office Font Problems

Microsoft applications have always had their own rules, and they have their own problems, too. Most of them, however, are easily dealt with.

The fonts in the Microsoft Fonts folder aren't in Font menus

The folder /Applications/Microsoft Office 2004/Office/Fonts is a mere holding area for Office's use; it's not an "Application Fonts folder" as Mac OS X defines it (see *Application Fonts Folders,* page 12). When you run an Office application for the first time in any user account, it installs the fonts from its folder into your User Fonts folder (~/Library/Fonts). If you remove the fonts from the User Fonts folder, they won't be in Font menus; their continued existence in the Microsoft folder makes no difference to Font menus.

You deleted the Microsoft fonts from your User Fonts folder

You may not view this as a problem, until you realize that of the twelve fonts that both Tiger and Microsoft provide, seven of the Microsoft fonts are later, better versions (as detailed in **Table 13,** page 109).

Microsoft keeps all its Office fonts in reserve, in /Applications/Microsoft Office 2004/Office/Fonts, so you can easily reinstall the ones you removed: Option-drag the missing fonts from the Microsoft folder to your User Fonts folder. (Option-dragging makes a copy of what you're dragging, so the originals stay in the Microsoft folder.)

Office applications take
a long time to "optimize font menus"

Microsoft applications build their Font menus each time you launch them. After you delete the Microsoft Office font caches (page 231) or change your font lineup by adding, deleting, disabling, or enabling fonts since the last time you launched an Office application, the program takes longer to start up. There's nothing wrong here, and the next startup (if you haven't changed fonts) will be quicker.

Some foreign language fonts
don't show up in Microsoft menus

Microsoft doesn't support RTL (right-to-left) languages like Hebrew and Arabic, so those system-supplied fonts (like New Peninim) won't show in Microsoft products. Other complex language scripts, like Hindi, and fonts like Devanagari MT, aren't supported, either.

But the foreign language keyboards let you type right-
to-left in Word and you even get the correct language script

Yes, but…

Select a Hebrew keyboard and start typing, and Word jumps into Lucida Grande or Times New Roman and you get characters typed right to left, even if the insertion point doesn't move correctly. That's the "yes" part.

Here's the "but" part: copy those characters and paste them into another program and they lose their right-to-leftness. Say you want to type the word *shalom*, whose Hebrew-spelled equivalent is *SLOM;* they have to appear as *MOLS*, since they're read right-to-left. With a U.S. keyboard and a Hebrew font, you have to type the letters in reverse order to get things to look right in the end after you paste; can you imagine typing English words sdrawkcab all the time? Switching to a Hebrew keyboard with Word active lets you type the letters S-L-O-M in that order and have them appear correctly, as MLOS. But pasted or imported to InDesign, the letters revert to their typed order: SLOM.

Permanent RTL: If you're working in an application designed for RTL (right-to-left) or other complex input, you won't have these problems. Unless, perhaps, you try to intersperse your RTL standard text with some English or other Roman-based left-to-right text.

(Mostly false) reports of corrupt fonts

This is the biggest Microsoft/Mac OS X headache: launch an Office application and get a report of a corrupt font. And another one. And another. Once Office thinks a font is a problem, it tends to report every single font afterward (in Font menu order) as corrupt, too.

Sometimes this is triggered by an actual corrupt font; more often Word (or the application in question) just gets it into its head that there's a problem, when there really isn't.

The first thing to know is that you don't have to click your way through all the corrupt-font warnings (there could be a hundred!) once they start: press Command-Option-Esc to force quit your way out of that trap. Then try some of these fixes:

♦ **Restart Word and see if the same thing happens:** If the initial corruption report was for a font toward the end of the alphabet, it's possible that the next startup won't be a problem.

♦ **Delete the MS Office font cache:** This almost universal fix for Office font problems, described on page 231, probably works 90 percent of the time for solving the corrupt-font reporting problem.

As you try other fixes, you should always *trash this file after every "corrupt font" startup* because while another fix may take care of an underlying problem, this cache remembers what things were like the last time you tried to start Word.

♦ **Delete the system font caches:** The combination of trashing Office's font cache and the system font caches (see page 228) does the trick 98 percent of the time (according to my official survey).

♦ **Resolve duplicates:** Use the Resolve Duplicates command in Font Book (page 113) and try again.

Keep duplicates disabled: Microsoft products, particularly Word, seem to work more reliably if you keep all your duplicates disabled. If you're constantly running into font-related problems with Microsoft applications, keep your duplicates resolved in Font Book.

Adobe Application Font Problems

For applications that provide the most fonts and the best font management around, Adobe programs have surprisingly few font problems of their own.

A font name is bracketed in InDesign's font list

A font in brackets in InDesign's toolbar font list means that InDesign sees a bitmapped suitcase font without its PostScript printer file. The font could be in any of the Mac OS X Fonts folders (where it's ignored by other applications) or in the Adobe Fonts folder—/Library/Application Support/Adobe/Fonts.

Even though you may not care about the inability to use the font (**Figure 90**), you should fix the problem—a mix-up with a font of the same name, or crashes and cache corruption are probably not far away. Your challenge, however, is to find that bitmapped font—it might have slipped through inside a suitcase of other companion fonts. See *Find Misplaced Fonts* (page 96) for details about using the Finder's search capabilities to look inside suitcases.

Figure 90

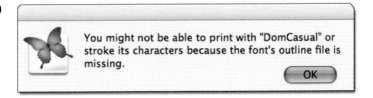

A bracketed font name in InDesign's menu means there's an "orphan" bitmapped suitcase font—one without its printer (outline) companion. Selecting the font results in this warning.

Creative Suite programs won't launch; they want "CMap files"

Adobe programs don't just provide *you* with a wide variety of fonts, they also provide *themselves* with a few necessities. Inside the Adobe Fonts folder (`/Library/Application Support/Adobe/Fonts`), which holds all the lovely fonts you're using, is a folder named Fonts Reqrd. This folder has two subfolders, .Base and .CMaps: the first holds the fonts Adobe applications need for their windows and palettes; the second holds files that track special character-ID mapping that some Adobe fonts use. Without both these folders, Creative Suite applications can screech to a standstill.

Unless you've archived these folders as suggested in *Archive Your Fonts and Utilities* (page 215), you'll have to reinstall the Suite to get these folders back.

Find a friend: *My real recommendation is to find someone to take pity on you—someone who also has Creative Suite—and get a copy of the Reqrd folder from her. As long as you're a legitimate user of the software, who cares if you get a copy of the required fonts from someone else?*

Put the folder in the correct spot or the Adobe applications won't see it; if necessary, create the Fonts folder, and even the Adobe folder, so you have the correct enclosing folders (`/Library/Application Support/Adobe/Fonts`) for the Reqrd folder.

InDesign doesn't show some of a font's faces in its menus

When you're absolutely, positively sure you have all the correct files for the typeface that's missing (it's installed, and active, in Font Book or in your other font manager), check for a second version of the font.

In laying out this book (which I can write about because we're laying out the early chapters as we edit the later ones), everyone involved ran into a similar font problem: certain styles of the Optima PostScript Type 1 font used for the headings and sidebars were reported as unavailable, despite their being installed properly. The problem turned out to be that each person also had the Optima dfont installed, and deactivating that cured the "missing" typeface problem.

I tracked down this problem just in time, because a day after pinpointing it, a friend called with a similar problem: he couldn't access certain Helvetica (PostScript) typefaces in InDesign. When he turned off his Helvetica dfont, the problem cleared up.

Classic Environment Font Problems

If you wait a little longer, all these problems will go away... because the Classic environment will have gone away.

PostScript Type 1 fonts in
Classic documents have "the jaggies"

Mac OS X renders TrueType fonts in Classic smoothly, but it doesn't take care of the bitmapped fonts used as PostScript companions. For that, you need ATM Light 4.6.2 or later, which you can get at www.adobe.com/products/atmlight/main.html.

Fonts are unpredictably substituted in documents

If a document uses a font stored in the Classic Fonts folder and you wind up with unexpected font substitutions when you use it in either Classic or Tiger, it could be because:

♦ It's a bitmapped font without a PostScript printer file companion.

♦ You have more than one Mac OS 9 System Folder available to your Mac—that is, either on multiple volumes of your internal drive or on attached drives.

♦ Your Mac OS 9 System Folder and Mac OS X system are on different volumes.

Fonts in the Classic Fonts folder
don't show up in Tiger Font menus

Sometimes you have to "poke" Classic before its fonts are available to Tiger: in the Start/Stop tab of the Classic preference pane, click on the System Folder under your drive's name. If that doesn't work, then start up the Classic environment, either with the Start button in the same preference pane or by opening any Classic application. You can quit out of Classic right away, and you should have to do this only once to get Tiger to see the fonts.

Appendixes

Appendix A: Font Specs

Table 21: Font Specs

	Name or Extension	Description	Finder Kind	Font Book Kind	Comment
Supported in Mac OS X					
Bitmapped suitcase					
FFIL	.bmap or .scr (optional)	Original Mac screen font; companion to PostScript Type 1	Font Suitcase	(Companion file shows as PostScript Type 1)	Supported only as PostScript Type 1 companion font
PostScript printer font (Type 1)					
LWFN	5-letter family name plus 3 letters for each style	Outline font; needs bitmap FFIL companion	PostScript Type 1 outline font	PostScript Type 1	Needs companion bitmap file
TrueType (Mac)					
FFIL	Font family name	Single or multiple TrueType fonts in a suitcase file	Font Suitcase	TrueType	
TrueType (Windows)					
TTF	Font family name .ttf or .ttc extension	Cross-platform	Windows TrueType font	TrueType	
Multiple Master instance					
LWFN FFIL	Same as PostScript printer font and suitcase, plus "MM"	A special Post-Script Type 1 font, editable in previous systems	PostScript Type 1 outline font	PostScript Type 1	Basically a Type 1 font; its companion suitcase file also has MM in its name
					(continues)

Table 21: Font Specs (continued)

	Name or Extension	Description	Finder Kind	Font Book Kind	Comment
Supported in Mac OS X					
OTF	**OpenType**				
	Font family name .otf extension	Outline fonts for screen and printers; cross-platform; Unicode	OpenType font	OpenType PostScript	Replacing PostScript Type 1 fonts
DFONT	**dfont**				
	.dfont	Mac-only format	Datafork TrueType font	TrueType	No separate resource fork, all info in data fork
Not supported in Mac OS X					
A	**Non-suitcased TrueType or bitmapped**				
	Family or face; bitmapped often includes point size	TrueType or bitmapped font left from previous OS	Font.mdimporter	n/a	Use it in a pinch, but suitcase it as soon as possible
	Windows-platform PostScript Type 1				
	Family or face; usually partial name .pfb extension	Windows PostScript Type 1	Document	n/a	Cannot be used on a Mac

Appendix B: Tiger Fonts

The three tables in this appendix list the fonts Mac OS X (Tiger version, 10.4.x) installs in your Fonts folders:

♦ **System Fonts folder:**
   Fonts always installed in /System/Library/Fonts, **Table 22**

♦ **Library Fonts folder:**
   Basic fonts always installed in /Library/Fonts, **Table 23**

♦ **Library Fonts folder:**
   Additional fonts installed as an option in /Library/Fonts, **Table 24**

Table 22: Basic Tiger Fonts in the System Fonts Folder

Font File	Language/ Script	Font File	Language/ Script
AppleGothic.dfont	Korean	Hiragino Mincho Pro W6.otf	Japanese
AquaKanaBold.otf	Japanese	Keyboard.dfont	
AquaKanaRegular.otf	Japanese	LastResort.dfont	
Courier.dfont		LiHei Pro.ttf	Chinese
Geeza Pro Bold.ttf	Arabic	LucidaGrande.dfont	
Geeza Pro.ttf	Arabic	Monaco.dfont	
Geneva.dfont		Osaka.dfont	Japanese
Hei.dfont	Chinese	OsakaMono.dfont	Japanese
HelveLTMM		STHeiti Light.ttf	Chinese
Helvetica LT MM		STHeiti Regular.ttf	Chinese
Helvetica.dfont		Symbol.dfont	
Hiragino Kaku Gothic Pro W3.otf	Japanese	Times LT MM	
Hiragino Kaku Gothic Pro W6.otf	Japanese	Times.dfont	
Hiragino Kaku Gothic Std W8.otf	Japanese	TimesLTMM	
Hiragino Maru Gothic Pro W4.otf	Japanese	ZapfDingbats.dfont	

Table 23: Basic Tiger Fonts in the Library Fonts Folder

Font File	Language/Script	Font File	Language/Script
AmericanTypewriter.dfont		Futura.dfont	
Andale Mono		Georgia	
Apple Chancery.dfont		GillSans.dfont	
Apple Symbols.ttf		HelveticaNeue.dfont	
Arial		Herculanum.dfont	
Arial Black		Hoefler Text.dfont	
Arial Narrow		Impact	
Arial Rounded Bold		Kai.dfont	Chinese
Baskerville.dfont		MarkerFelt.dfont	
BigCaslon.dfont		Optima.dfont	
Brush Script		Papyrus.dfont	
Chalkboard.ttf		Skia.dfont	
ChalkboardBold.ttf		Times New Roman	
Cochin.dfont		Trebuchet MS	
Comic Sans MS		Verdana	
Copperplate.dfont		Webdings	
Courier New		Zapfino.dfont	
Didot.dfont			

Table 24: Additional Tiger Fonts in the Library Fonts Folder

Font File	Language/ Script	Font File	Language/ Script
#Gungseouche.dfont	Korean	Gurmukhi.ttf	Indic
#HeadlineA.dfont	Korean	HelveticaCY.dfont	Cyrillic
#PCmyoungjo.dfont	Korean	InaiMathi.ttf	Tamil
#Pilgiche.dfont	Korean	Krungthep.ttf	Thai
AlBayan.ttf	Arabic	KufiStandarGK.ttf	Arabic
AlBayanBold.ttf	Arabic	LiSong Pro.ttf	Chinese
Apple LiSung Light.dfont	Chinese	MshtakanBold.ttf	Armenian
AppleMyungjo.dfont	Korean	MshtakanBoldOblique.ttf	Armenian
ArialHB.ttf	Hebrew	MshtakanOblique.ttf	Armenian
ArialHBBold.ttf	Hebrew	MshtakanRegular.ttf	Armenian
Ayuthaya.ttf	Thai	Nadeem.ttf	Arabic
Baghdad.ttf	Arabic	NewPeninimMT.ttf	Hebrew
BiauKai.dfont	Chinese	NewPeninimMTBold.ttf	Hebrew
CharcoalCY.dfont	Cyrillic	NewPeninimMTBoldInclined.ttf	Hebrew
Corsiva.ttf	Hebrew	NewPeninimMTInclined.ttf	Hebrew
CorsivaBold.ttf	Hebrew	NISC18030.ttf	Chinese
DecoTypeNaskh.ttf	Arabic	PlantagenetCherokee.ttf	Cherokee
DevanagariMT.ttf	Indic	Raanana.ttf	Hebrew
DevanagariMTBold.ttf	Indic	RaananaBold.ttf	Hebrew
EuphemiaCASBold.ttf	UCAS†	Sathu.ttf	Thai
EuphemiaCASItalic.ttf	UCAS†	Silom.ttf	Thai
EuphemiaCASRegular.ttf	UCAS†	STKaiti.ttf	Chinese
GenevaCY.dfont	Cyrillic	STSong.ttf	Chinese
GujaratiMT.ttf	Indic	Thonburi.ttf	Thai
GujaratiMTBold.ttf	Indic		

Appendix C:
The "Do Not Remove" Font List

Table 25: Do Not Remove These Fonts		
Font	**Location**	**Reason**
From Tiger: Absolutely Necessary		
AquaKanaBold[†] AquaKanaRegular[†] Geneva Helvetica* Keyboard LastResort LucidaGrande Monaco	/System/Library/Fonts	The operating system needs them
Helvetica LT MM Times LT MM	/System/Library/Fonts	Preview uses them for font rendering
From Tiger: Recommended		
Courier Symbol Zapf Dingbats	/System/Library/Fonts	Common Web and cross-platform fonts
Comic Sans Georgia Trebuchet Times New Roman Verdana	/Library/Fonts	
From Adobe		
All fonts in folder	/Library/Application Support/Adobe/PDFL/7.0/Fonts[††]	Acrobat and Acrobat Reader need them
All fonts in folder	/Library/Application Support/Adobe/Fonts/Reqrd/Base	Adobe applications need them
* May be replaced by another version of Helvetica in any Fonts folder the system can access. † May not be essential; anecdotal evidence indicates it is. †† The number in the path may be different		

Appendix D:
Binary and Hexadecimal Numbering

You weren't expecting anything on the third R—'rithmatic—in this book, but Unicode uses hexadecimal references, as do several font utilities, and it helps to know the basics.

The number system we use is base 10. It has 10 different digits (0-9), and each "place" in a multi-digit number represents a power of 10, which increases by one as you move to the left. A digit represents how many of each power of 10 is included in the total. The number 256 is:

Decimal 256

Power	10^2	10^1	10^0
Value	(100)	(10)	(1)
Digit	**2**	**5**	**6**
Totals	200	50	6

The computer is a binary animal, existing in a world of on/off, yes/no circuits and decisions. A binary numbering system has two different digits (0 and 1), and each place in a number represents a power of 2, increasing by one as you move left. Decimal 281 is 100011001:

Decimal 281 = 100011001 binary

Power	2^8	2^7	2^6	2^5	2^4	2^3	2^2	2^1	2^0
Value	(256)	(128)	(64)	(32)	(16)	(8)	(4)	(2)	(1)
Digit	**1**	**0**	**0**	**0**	**1**	**1**	**0**	**0**	**1**
Totals	256	0	0	0	16	8	0	0	1

Because it's so difficult to read binary numbers (by the time you reach 5000, you need a 13-digit string of ones and zeroes), humans who commune deeply with computers use hexadecimal, or hex: base 16. Following the rules for other bases, you use 16 different digits and increase each place by powers of 16. Of course, there aren't 16 different digits, so we substitute the letters A-F for the numbers 10-15.

(We don't need a "digit" for 16 because that's represented by a jump to the next place; our base 10 system tops out at 9.) Decimal 1,090,255 is hex 10A2CF:

Decimal 1,090,255 = 10A2CF hex

Power	16^5	16^4	16^3	16^2	16^1	16^0
Value	(1,048,576)	(65,536)	(4096)	(256)	(16)	(1)
Digit	**1**	**0**	**A (=10)**	**2**	**C (=12)**	**F (=15)**
Totals	1,048,576	0	40,960	512	192	15

As you can see, hex numbering is compact: the seven-digit decimal number is 21 characters in binary but only six places in hex.

Hex numbers are often broken up into groups of four digits for easier reading in computer code, just as commas break up long decimal numbers.

But why hex? Aren't "higher" base systems even more compact when it comes to digits? Yes, but hex has some special advantages in how it relates to the binary base of computers: a double-digit hex number represents that so-basic computer unit, a byte of eight bits (half of which, by the way, is a *nybble* or *nibble*—really!). And, each power of 16 coincides with a power of 2 ($16^1 = 2^4$, $16^2=2^8$, and so on) in an exquisite pattern that warms the cockles of a mathematician's heart. So, hex serves as a sort of compressed, handy dialect of binary.

So, when you're in Character Palette and the help tag shows that the selected character has an ID of 2299 (the upper figure in this picture), the next character is *not* 2300. The next hex number replaces the rightmost 9 in 2299 with the character for 10, which is A; so, the next character ID is 229A.

Appendix E: Keyboard Control on Steroids

System Preference settings give you choices regarding what you can control from your keyboard. Several of the settings involve things that can make font-related things easier:

◆ **Focus on the Font panel:** You have to specifically click on the Font panel to "activate" it before you can use any keyboard controls in it. That is, unless you know that pressing Control-F6 automatically moves the "focus" to a floating palette like the Font panel. Oddly (and annoyingly), it doesn't work as a toggle—using the key combo again doesn't shift the focus back to your application window; use Control-F4 for that. These are the default settings, which can be changed or turned off in the Keyboard Shortcuts tab of the Keyboard & Mouse preference pane.

◆ **Define the scope of the Tab key:** By default, the Tab key moves you to text boxes and lists in palettes and dialogs, but you can include all the controls (buttons, sliders, pop-up menus, and so on) in the tab sequence. Use Control-F7 to toggle between the standard and the full tabbing capability, or toggle it in the Keyboard & Mouse preference pane, at the bottom of the Keyboard Shortcuts tab (**Figure 91**).

This setting changes the behavior of all your dialogs—even Open and Save; this can be a good thing or drive you crazy when you don't want to tab to every little thing. But with Control-F7 acting as an instant toggle, even after the dialog is open, there's no reason not to use it wherever you want.

Figure 91

The manual setting for Tab controls in the Keyboard & Mouse pane.

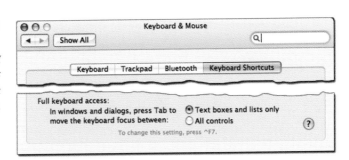

◆ **Change the keyboard commands:** If you want to use something other than Control and a function key to trigger any of these commands, just change the shortcut in the Keyboard Shortcuts tab: click directly on the shortcut of any checked item, and press the new shortcut key combination.

♦ **Watch out for Control-F1:** The list of keyboard controls in the Keyboard Shortcuts tab starts with Turn Full Keyboard Access On Or Off assigned to Control-F1. You might assume that it refers to the "Full keyboard access" area at the bottom of the window (as shown in **Figure 91** on the previous page); that would be reasonable, but wrong.

Turn Full Keyboard Access On Or Off actually refers to the next five items in the list of keyboard controls, starting with moving the focus to the menu bar and ending with moving the focus to the floating window; triggering the first item (with its default Control-F1) toggles the next five items on and off as a group. It has nothing to do with the full keyboard access as described in the window.

♦ **Make it easier on a PowerBook:** On laptops, the function keys are tied to hardware controls, such as brightness and volume. To use the keyboard shortcuts described above, you have to add the fn key to the sequence to override the default hardware control. If you'd like to reverse that—so that it's the hardware controls that need the fn key included—use the Keyboard tab of the Keyboard & Mouse pane, and check Use the F1-F12 Keys to Control Software Features.

Appendix F: Users and Accounts

If you've ignored the whole user account thing up until now and feel practically illiterate when you run into Fonts folder pathnames, or references to setting up a separate account to test your font problems, relax: it's simpler than you think.

Mac OS X is designed as a shared system, serving the needs—and preserving the privacy—of more than one user, whether the users are various employees or a few family members. If you're the sole user, you have to put up with some nonsense that's a result of the shared-Mac approach, with multiple places to store (and misplace) things, folders that seem to have the same names, and the concept of having an account on your Mac—an account with an administrator, who, in all likelihood, is you. You run into the surface issue of this approach every time you install software and you're asked for an administrative password (and doesn't that make you feel important?).

For most practical purposes, you can think of a Mac as starting with a single user account, a setup for a single user. Each user account has an owner, the person who has a password to use it. At least one user account has administrator privileges; the owner of an account with these privileges is allowed to make system-wide changes on the Mac that can affect all the accounts on it—like installing applications or updating system software. The first user account that's set up on your Mac OS X machine automatically has administrator privileges. So, if you're the only user, you have an account with administrator privileges. (You are the boss of you.)

The multi-user mindset of the operating system results in a hierarchy of resources and privileges:

♦ **System stuff:** These are things the Mac needs to keep humming—everything from starting up, to putting a dialog on the screen, to opening an application when you double-click a document.

♦ **Communal stuff:** Things that every user account can access, like applications, which are normally installed only once, in one place, and shared by everyone.

♦ **User stuff:** Things that are private to each user, such as documents (obviously) and environmental things like the Desktop background and preference settings.

If your Macintosh is set up with only one user account, you won't see much difference between the system stuff (which, for the most part you get to ignore), the communal stuff (because you're the commune), and the user stuff. But the operating system still observes the separation of system, commune, and user. If you do share your Mac with a spouse, child, or coworker, it may already have multiple accounts and you might be familiar with the effects of those separations.

How does this relate to fonts? For starters, there's a Fonts folder for the system stuff, another for the communal stuff, and another for the user (for each user on a multiple-account Mac). See? The multiple-Fonts-folders approach makes sense now that it's in context, right? And the fact that there's another Fonts folder if you have Mac OS 9 available on your Mac via the Classic environment... that's easy to absorb. And if you're on a network, there might be a network Fonts folder for everyone to share—no big deal. There: five Fonts folders described in a single paragraph, and you're not even breaking a sweat.

Appendix G: Mac OS X Font Samples

This appendix includes all the Roman and dingbat fonts included with Mac OS X as of the Tiger version (10.4.x). All the sample text is 12 points; apparent differences in the type size are due to the design of each font.

American Typewriter

ABCDEFGHIJKLMNOPQRSTUVWXYZ

abcdefghijklmnopqrstuvwxyz

1234567890

The quick brown fox jumps over the lazy dog.

Andale Mono

ABCDEFGHIJKLMNOPQRSTUVWXYZ

abcdefghijklmnopqrstuvwxyz

1234567890

The five boxing wizards jump quickly.

Apple Chancery

ABCDEFGHIJKLMNOPQRSTUVWXYZ

abcdefghijklmnopqrstuvwxyz

1234567890

Sixty zippers were quickly picked from the woven jute bag.

Apple Symbols

₲ F £ m ₦ Pts Rs ₩ ₪ ₫ € ₭ ₮ ₯ ₰ ℊ ℋ ℌ ℍ ℎ

✳ ♠ ☏ ☺ ☇ ☆ ☎ ☠ ☣ ☤ ☮ ☹ ☺

♠ ♡ ◇ ♣ ☐ ☑ ☒ ☒ ☒ ☒ ☒ ◯ ⊙ ⊖ ● ●

♩ ♪ ♫ ♭ ♮ ♯ ♻ ♲ ♲ ♲ ♲ ♲ ♲ ♲

Arial

ABCDEFGHIJKLMNOPQRSTUVWXYZ

abcdefghijklmnopqrstuvwxyz

1234567890

Five wine experts jokingly quizzed sample Chablis.

Arial Black

ABCDEFGHIJKLMNOPQRSTUVWXYZ

abcdefghijklmnopqrstuvwxyz

1234567890

Jackdaws love my sphinx of black quartz.

Arial Narrow

ABCDEFGHIJKLMNOPQRSTUVWXYZ

abcdefghijklmnopqrstuvwxyz

1234567890

My faxed joke won a pager in the cable TV quiz show.

Arial Rounded Bold

ABCDEFGHIJKLMNOPQRSTUVWXYZ

abcdefghijklmnopqrstuvwxyz

1234567890

A large fawn jumped quickly over white zinc boxes.

Baskerville

ABCDEFGHIJKLMNOPQRSTUVWXYZ

abcdefghijklmnopqrstuvwxyz

1234567890

Viewing quizzical abstracts mixed up hefty jocks.

Big Caslon

ABCDEFGHIJKLMNOPQRSTUVWXYZ

abcdefghijklmnopqrstuvwxyz

1234567890

How razorback jumping frogs can level six piqued gymnasts.

Brush Script

ABCDEFGHIJKLMNOP2RSTUVWXYZ

abcdefghijklmnopqrstuvwxyz

1234567890

We have just quoted on nine dozen boxes of gray lamp wicks.

Chalkboard

ABCDEFGHIJKLMNOPQRSTUVWXYZ

abcdefghijklmnopqrstuvwxyz

1234567890

Jo may equal the fine record by solving six puzzles a week.

Cochin

ABCDEFGHIJKLMNOPQRSTUVWXYZ

abcdefghijklmnopqrstuvwxyz

1234567890

Fred specialized in the job of making very quaint wax toys.

Comic Sans MS

ABCDEFGHIJKLMNOPQRSTUVWXYZ

abcdefghijklmnopqrstuvwxyz

1234567890

Six crazy kings vowed to abolish my quite pitiful jousts.

Copperplate

ABCDEFGHIJKLMNOPQRSTUVWXYZ

ABCDEFGHIJKLMNOPQRSTUVWXYZ

1234567890

PACK MY BOX WITH FIVE DOZEN LIQUOR JUGS.

Courier

ABCDEFGHIJKLMNOPQRSTUVWXYZ

abcdefghijklmnopqrstuvwxyz

1234567890

How quickly daft, jumping zebras vex.

Courier New

ABCDEFGHIJKLMNOPQRSTUVWXYZ

abcdefghijklmnopqrstuvwxyz

1234567890

Sympathizing would fix Quaker objectives.

Didot

ABCDEFGHIJKLMNOPQRSTUVWXYZ

abcdefghijklmnopqrstuvwxyz

1234567890

The jay, pig, fox, zebra and my wolves quack!

Futura

ABCDEFGHIJKLMNOPQRSTUVWXYZ

abcdefghijklmnopqrstuvwxyz

1234567890

Jay visited back home and gazed upon a brown fox and quail.

Geneva

ABCDEFGHIJKLMNOPQRSTUVWXYZ

abcdefghijklmnopqrstuvwxyz

1234567890

Puzzled women bequeath jerks very exotic gifts.

Georgia

ABCDEFGHIJKLMNOPQRSTUVWXYZ

abcdefghijklmnopqrstuvwxyz

1234567890

The exodus of jazzy pigeons is craved by squeamish walkers.

Gill Sans

ABCDEFGHIJKLMNOPQRSTUVWXYZ

abcdefghijklmnopqrstuvwxyz

1234567890

Five or six big jet planes zoomed quickly by the tower.

Helvetica

ABCDEFGHIJKLMNOPQRSTUVWXYZ

abcdefghijklmnopqrstuvwxyz

1234567890

Just keep examining every low bid quoted for zinc etchings.

Helvetica Neue

ABCDEFGHIJKLMNOPQRSTUVWXYZ

abcdefghijklmnopqrstuvwxyz

1234567890

Crazy Fredrick bought many very exquisite opal jewels.

Herculanum

ABCDEFGHIJKLMNOPQRSTUVWXYZ

ABCDEFGHIJKLMNOPQRSTUVWXYZ

1234567890

BRAWNY GODS JUST FLOCKED UP TO QUIZ AND VEX HIM.

Hoefler Text

ABCDEFGHIJKLMNOPQRSTUVWXYZ

abcdefghijklmnopqrstuvwxyz

1234567890

We promptly judged antique ivory buckles for the next prize.

Impact

ABCDEFGHIJKLMNOPQRSTUVWXYZ

abcdefghijklmnopqrstuvwxyz

1234567890

Jeb quickly drove a few extra miles on the glazed pavement.

Lucida Grande

ABCDEFGHIJKLMNOPQRSTUVWXYZ

abcdefghijklmnopqrstuvwxyz

1234567890

My grandfather picks up quartz and valuable onyx jewels.

Marker Felt

ABCDEFGHIJKLMNOPQRSTUVWXYZ

abcdefghijklmnopqrstuvwxyz

1234567890

West quickly gave Bert handsome prizes for six juicy plums.

Monaco

ABCDEFGHIJKLMNOPQRSTUVWXYZ

abcdefghijklmnopqrstuvwxyz

1234567890

Quick wafting zephyrs vex bold Jim.

Optima

ABCDEFGHIJKLMNOPQRSTUVWXYZ

abcdefghijklmnopqrstuvwxyz

1234567890

Harry, jogging quickly, axed zen monks with beef vapor.

Papyrus

ABCDEFGHIJKLMNOPQRSTUVWXYZ

abcdefghijklmnopqrstuvwxyz

1234567890

A quick movement of the enemy will jeopardize six gunboats.

Skia

ABCDEFGHIJKLMNOPQRSTUVWXYZ

abcdefghijklmnopqrstuvwxyz

1234567890

Freight to me sixty dozen quart jars and twelve black pans.

Symbol

ΑΒΧΔΕΦΓΗΙϑΚΛΜΝΟΠΘΡΣΤΥςΩΞΨΖ

αβχδεφγηιφκλμνοπθρστυϖωξψζ

1234567890

Τηε θυιχκ βροων φοξ φυμπσ οϖερ τηε λαζψ δογ.

Times

ABCDEFGHIJKLMNOPQRSTUVWXYZ

abcdefghijklmnopqrstuvwxyz

1234567890

All questions asked by five watch experts amazed the judge.

Times New Roman

ABCDEFGHIJKLMNOPQRSTUVWXYZ

abcdefghijklmnopqrstuvwxyz

1234567890

Grumpy wizards make toxic brew for the evil Queen and Jack.

Trebuchet MS

ABCDEFGHIJKLMNOPQRSTUVWXYZ

abcdefghijklmnopqrstuvwxyz

1234567890

The job of waxing linoleum frequently peeves chintzy kids.

Verdana

ABCDEFGHIJKLMNOPQRSTUVWXYZ

abcdefghijklmnopqrstuvwxyz

1234567890

The vixen jumped quickly on her foe, barking with zeal.

Webdings

Zapf Dingbats

Zapfino

ABCDEFGHIJKLMNOPQRSTUVWXYZ

abcdefghijklmnopqrstuvwxyz

1234567890

Jim just quit and packed extra bags for Liz Owen.

Index

Why would an Index need an introduction? Because I wanted to point out that the letters used for each alphabetic segment come from free fonts. There are thousands of free fonts out there; a few of my favorite free-font sites are listed on page 62.

I've included the name of each of the fonts used in this Index, and provided a sample of its character set with an alphabet of combined upper- and lowercase letters, and numbers. If it seems that there are only uppercase or only lowercase letters for some fonts, it's because some fonts have only one or the other—or only a subtle difference between the two. I've noted where each font was downloaded from, but many free fonts are available on multiple sites. (The actual URLs for the sites are on page 62; in the interest of brevity, the samples identify each site by a simple name in brackets—and where the brackets are missing, the font doesn't have them!)

A *Angelina*   [dafont]
ABCDEFGHIJKlmnopqrstuvwxyz 1234567890

AAT (Apple Advanced Typography), 9
accented letters, 167–171
access order for fonts, 15
accessing
  Adobe fonts in Font Book, 127
  alternate keyboards, 191
  AppleScript scripts, 82–83
  fonts in subfolders, 11
Accounts preference pane
  activating Fast User Switching, 223
  disabling font manager components in, 219
**Additional fonts optionally installed by
  Tiger, 236**
Adobe applications. *See also* **Adobe InDesign**
  font name bracketed in menu, 283
  CMap files requested for Creative Suite, 284
  font folders for, 14
  missing font faces on menus, 284
  Multiple Master fonts and, 7, 148, 289
  precedence of Unicode ID and GID in, 152–154
  troubleshooting font problems, 283–284
Adobe fonts
  accessing from Font Book, 127
  Expert Sets, 155
  precedence of Unicode ID and GID for,
    153–154
Adobe Fonts folder
  about, 14
  archiving, 216
  checking for outdated, 95
  managing fonts in, 94–95
Adobe InDesign
  alphabetization of font lists, 138, 139
  font name bracketed in list, 283
  Multiple Master fonts in, 148
  using Symbol font in, 159–161
Adobefnt.lst, 231
All Caps character style, 157
All Characters view (Character Palette), 177, 178
alphabetization in font menus, 137–139
alternate keyboards
  accessing, 191

  reasons for using, 188–189
  understanding, 189–190
alternate letters and numbers, 155
Apple Advanced Typography (AAT), 9
Apple applications
  accessing AppleScripts, 82–83
  precedence of Unicode ID and GID for Adobe
    fonts in, 153–154
  smoothing PostScript fonts in Classic, 81
Apple Chancery, 157
Apple fonts
  TextEdit's handling of GIDs, 151–152
  Unicode ID and GID precedence in Adobe
    programs, 152–153
Apple Symbols, 157
AppleScript, 82–83
applications
  checking if fonts installed by, 43
  closing before changing fonts, 213
  Fonts folders for, 12–14, 43
  precedence of Unicode ID and GID in Apple,
    153–154
  smoothing PostScript fonts in Classic, 81
application Fonts folders, 12–14, 43
  Adobe, 14
  Microsoft, 14, 95–96
  subfolders in, 13
AquaKanaBold.otf, 15
AquaKanaRegular.otf, 15
Arabic fonts
  incorrect display of, 280
  needed for Safari browsing, 93
  using Tiger versions of, 31, 109
Archive and Install option, 226
archiving
  font backups, 41–42
  fonts and utilities, 215–217
**"Are you sure you want to remove this font?"
  dialog, 88–89**
ASCII standards, 16–17
Asian fonts
  identifying names of, 27, 38
  representing in ASCII, 17
  special input methods for, 165
  typeface references, 147
ATM Light, 81

Independence   dafont

abcdefghijklmnopqrstuv 123456790

JellyBelly   [dafont]

ABCDEFGHIJKlmnopqrstu 123456790

KellyAnnGothic   dafont

ABCDefghijklmnopqrstux 123456790

Quixotte {dafont}

ABCDEFGHIJKlmnopqrstuvw 1234567890

Ransom HighFonts

ABCDEFGHIJklmnopqrstuV 1234567890

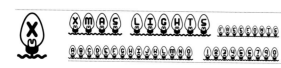

Coupons

Design Tools Monthly

FontAgent Pro

Layers Magazine

MyFonts

PopChar

Small Dog Electronics

Spell Catcher X

DesignTools Monthly™

The Executive Summary of Graphic Design News

It's Your Life

— Please Choose One —
- ○ Don't Make a Living
  - ☐ Read Stack of Magazines
  - ☐ Visit Websites All Day
- ◉ Make a Living
  - ☑ Get Design Tools Monthly

[OK]
[Cancel]

As a graphic design professional, you don't have time to constantly read magazines and visit websites, so we summarize all the important stories for you: industry news, new hardware and software, updates, bug fixes, tips, fonts, useful books and websites, and upcoming events.

By reading **Design Tools Monthly**, you can keep up with all the important changes in our industry — and still get your work done. You'll also enjoy our online Software Closet, which brings you updates, bug fixes, and the best free utilities, plug-ins and fonts.

Subscribers in 41 countries have relied on us since 1992. Here's a no-risk way to see why:

Let Us Send You a
Free Issue!
(and Save $50!)

Visit www.design-tools.com/tcf to receive your free issue.

To receive your $50 discount (for new subscribers only), mention code TCF when subscribing.

Design Tools Monthly™
www.design-tools.com

FontAgent Pro

The new face of font management and repair

FontAgent Pro 3 from Insider Software is the world's most advanced font manager for the Macintosh. With a few clicks, you can repair, optimize and organize your fonts, then build font libraries and cascading sets that you can activate, manage, secure, print, and preview. FontAgent Pro is the only font manager that offers workgroup font sharing with zero configuration and no hassle.

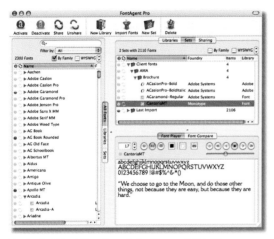

Unrivaled Font Preview, Selection and Printing

FontAgent Pro gives you more ways to view, select and print your fonts. List, sort and search all your fonts easily. Search font names, foundries, custom comments and other metadata with ease. Use FontAgent Pro's unique Font Player™ to "play" a text string through all your fonts automatically so you can choose the right one. Or narrow your selection to a few fonts and view the string side-by-side using Font Compare.™

To purchase FontAgent Pro 3, download a trial copy or get more information, visit Insider today at www.insidersoftware.com or call toll-free 1-866-366-8778 or +1-520-229-1212

www.insidersoftware.com

* Offer expires 12/31/07. Limit of 2 per customer. Call for volume license pricing.

The Industry's Only Workgroup Font Sharing

FontAgent Pro is the only product that lets you share fonts in your workgroup with zero config and no font server. All you do is install FontAgent Pro Workgroup Edition on your Macs and start sharing fonts It's that simple.

Unique Powerful, Cascading Sets

Organize fonts into meaningful, maintainable sets and subsets by client or project. While other font managers limit you to creating sets in one long, unmanageable list, FontAgent Pro gives you the power of cascading sets so you can organize your fonts into more meaningful, easier-to-maintain, client and project hierarchies.

NEW! Secure Fonts and Sets from Changes

FontAgent Pro's unique security enables you to protect fonts, sets and preferences from unauthorized changes. It allows you to password-protect separate configuration settings for each user on a system. Using these new capabilities, admins can implement standard FontAgent Pro configurations, libraries and sets across their organizations.

Unparalleled Font Activation Power

FontAgent Pro activates and deactivates fonts in more ways than any other font manager, saving system resources and simplifying font menus by activating just the fonts you need—in both Mac OS X and Classic. Auto-activate fonts in Mac OS X applications including the Adobe Creative Suite, QuarkXPress and Microsoft Office. And while other font managers limit you to activating entire suitcases or sets, FontAgent Pro lets you activate a library, set, subset, font or even an individual typeface —all with a single click!

Proven Font Repair and Organization

For the last decade, FontAgent has been the industry leader in font integrity validation and organization, so you can depend on FontAgent Pro to automatically optimize and organize your fonts, prevent the addition of duplicate fonts to your library, and improve system performance and reliability.

Connected Font Management Server Solution

Besides being the most reliable font management solution in the industry, FontAgent Pro is now the most connected. With the addition of FontAgent Pro Server, you can ensure font integrity and consistency across your entire workflow, and on every computer in your department or enterprise.

Catch a Rising Starlet!

Baka

Etelka Text

Pendulum

Cilantro

Grilled Cheese

PopChar™

Tired of searching and remembering keyboard combinations for umlauts and other special characters? Want to get the most out of your fonts?

PopChar makes "typing" of unusual characters easy without having to remember keyboard combos.

Whenever you need a special character, click the little "P" in the menu bar to display a table of characters. Select the desired character and it instantly appears in your document.

Save $5

What do you get when you buy from Small Dog Electronics?

service   selection   value   expert advice   small dogs!

Now, $5 off your next web order!

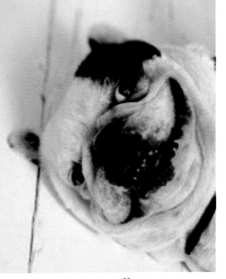

Small Dog Electronics

something to smile about...

It corrects your spelling as you type...
It proofreads everything you write...
It's a dictionary... it's a thesaurus...

...it's like having your favorite English*teacher in a box!

- Interactive spelling and typing correction in virtually all Mac OS X applications
- Includes 9 language dictionaries
- Comprehensive Thesaurus and Dictionary look up
- Extensive text manipulation tools and writing statistics
- Customizable shorthand glossary with autocorrect
- Integrated with the standard Mac OS X Spelling Panel
- Word Completion
- Internet Look Up from online Dictionary Servers
- Available from the Mac OS X Services menu
- Use spoken commands to "drive" interactive checking

*Or other language

SpellCatcher checks spelling and provides thesaurus lookups for many languages.

Save $10.00

Only one use per customer

Good towards full-feature $39.95 version ONLY

Use Coupon Code SCXTIDBITSTC497

rainmakerinc.com

Analyze and Solve Nonspecific Font Problems

(You're using the most recent Tiger update • No recently installed fonts)

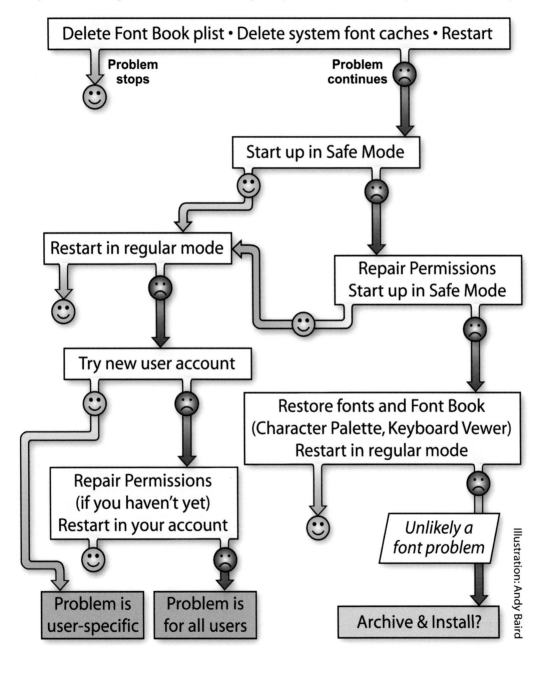

Delete Font Book plist • Delete system font caches • Restart

Problem stops ☺

Problem continues ☹

Start up in Safe Mode

Restart in regular mode

Repair Permissions
Start up in Safe Mode

Try new user account

Restore fonts and Font Book
(Character Palette, Keyboard Vewer)
Restart in regular mode

Repair Permissions
(if you haven't yet)
Restart in your account

Unlikely a font problem

Problem is user-specific

Problem is for all users

Archive & Install?

Illustration: Andy Baird

Faces, MS PGothic. Smile: U+263A, GID 17872; Frown: U+2639, GID 17871

Scissors: Zapf Dingbats U+2703